D1046165

DISCARD

With One Bold Act

"Barbara Garland Polikoff has given us a superb portrait of Jane Addams the person — not just the larger than life reformer, heroine, international figure we know from every textbook. *With One Bold Act* enriches all those other perspectives by starting (as Addams herself did in *Twenty Years at Hull-House*) with a full and probing look at Laura Jane Addams or "Jenny" Addams, the talented determined, meditative, socially-circumscribed girl from Cedarville, Illinois. In a skillfully researched and gripping narrative, calling forth the voices not only of Addams but of scores of people who knew and worked with her, Polikoff shows how Jane Addams and her allies worked their way outward from a late-Victorian world of large families, frequent deaths, crippling ennui, and severe limitations on young women. Most of all, the book shows just how "bold" the act of founding Hull House was, as a personal step and a social challenge. Looking at Addams from this perspective, Polikoff casts light on both her tremendous accomplishments and her various foibles. The curious mixture of rebelliousness and respectability that many have noted in Addams is here clarified by the exploration of a complex personality, brilliant, full of grit, and yet always a bit insecure. This fascinating figure, in some ways precociously mature, but ever-growing throughout her life, emerges vividly from the pages of this splendid book."

Henry C. Binford
Associate Professor of History
Northwestern University

Copyright @ 1999 by Barbara Garland Polikoff.

Printed in the United States of America.

Publisher's Cataloguing-in-Publication Data:

> Polikoff, Barbara Garland
>   With one bold act : the story of Jane Addams /
> Barbara Garland Polikoff. — 1st ed.
>   p. cm
>   Includes bibliographical references and index.
>   LCCN: 99-94785
>   ISBN: 0-9670658-0-1

> 1. Addams, Jane, 1860-1935. 2.Women social
> workers—United States—Biography. 3.Women
> social reformers—United States—Biography. 4.
> Hull House (Chicago, Ill.)—History. I. Title.

> HV40.32.A33P65 1999   361.3'092[B]
>   QB199-337

The great majority of photographs, most of them taken by Wallace Kirkland, are used with permission of the Jane Addams Memorial Library of the University of Illinois at Chicago. All others are from the private collections of Sadie Garland Dreikurs and Barbara Garland Polikoff.

Cover photograph - Dedication of Jane Addams Memorial Park, Chicago, October, 1997 by Barbara Garland Polikoff

> Boswell Books
> 17 E. Monroe, #212
> Chicago, Ill. 60035
> Phone: 312-641-5570
> Fax: 312-641-5454

With One Bold Act

The Story of Jane Addams

($16.95) 9/99 Boswell Books

In loving memory of my "Gypsy Aunt," Sadie Garland Dreikurs, and to the many women, among them Chicagoans Janice Greer, Founder and Director of Sullivan House, Bernardine Dohrn, Director, Juvenile Justice Project, Northwestern University, and Lois Weisberg, Commissioner of Cultural Affairs, City of Chicago, who with unflagging labor and love keep the spirit and vision of Jane Addams alive.

"Talented, aspiring women caught in the shackles of Victorian mores were forced to create an extraordinary life event to liberate themselves from the expectations of traditional society. With one bold act, moving to an impoverished neighborhood and opening the doors of their home to their immigrant neighbors, Jane Addams and Ellen Gates Starr freed themselves from the expectation that they would play out the conventional plots of marriage, motherhood or self-sacrificing maiden aunt. Instead they created the original, vibrant world of the Settlement."

With One Bold Act

Acknowledgements

I am indebted to the University Library, University of Illinois at Chicago, for permission to quote liberally from The Jane Addams Papers, Microfilm Edition, Jane Addams Memorial Library, as well as to camp out for days at a time in the Special Collections reading room. My thanks also to the Swarthmore College Peace Collection, Swarthmore College, and to the Sophia Smith Collection, Smith College, for permission to quote material in their archives. I also wish to thank the devoted volunteers who staff the two room Cedarville Historical Museum for their gracious help.

I am endlessly grateful to Allen F. Davis whose book, *American Heroine, The Life and Legend of Jane Addams*, forged a path that helped me find my way through a veritable mountain of material; to Barbara Sicherman for her book, *Alice Hamilton, A Life in Letters*, which was both enlightening and a pleasure to read; to Mary Ann Bamberger and Pat Bakunas of the Special Collections Library of the University of Illinois at Chicago, who rescued me when I foundered in my research, as did Mary Ann Johnson, Director of the Jane Addams Hull House Museum. James Weber Linn's loving biography of his Aunt Jane gave me the opportunity to eavesdrop on their many private conversations.

Abundant thanks to Alex Elson, Alice Ryerson Hayes, and Adele Simmons for sharing their Hull House memories and personal documents; to my mother, Julia Garland, children, Deborah Eve, Daniel and Joan, sons-in-law, Lyle and Gene, and my dear friends Sandy Brown, Rochelle Distelheim, Julie and Bill Geller, Julie Hall, Jean Mulligan, Irene Patner and Susanne Sklar for their loving encouragement; and most especially to my superb, indefatigable and charming Editor-in-Residence, Alexander Polikoff.

Jane Kohen Winter, proofreader extraordinaire, and Mike Afflerbach, computer wizard, gave unstintingly of their time and expertise.

Contents

Jane Addams, during first years at Hull House

"There was in the earliest undertakings at Hull-House a touch of the artist's enthusiasm when he translates his inner vision through his chosen material into outward form."

With One Bold Act

The Story of Jane Addams

Barbara Garland Polikoff

Boswell Books
Chicago

Sadie Ellis Garland, "Gypsy Aunt," 1934

"Everything of significance that has happened to me stemmed from my association with Jane Addams and Hull House."

An Invitation

As a child I treasured my Sunday visits to Hull House where my aunt and uncle, artists Sadie and Leon Garland, lived in an airy loft reached only by a small wooden bridge that connected their dwelling to the other Settlement buildings. Once across the bridge I would be greeted by my aunt, dark-eyed with lustrous, black hair caught in a bun at the nape of her neck. She often wore long skirts batiked by my Uncle Leon in shades of wine and blue that swirled above her sandals. While Leon painted at his easel, oblivious to us, my aunt and I would pull our chairs close together, facing the large window that overlooked the brown and gray roofs of the city. It was storytime.

I listened mesmerized as my aunt would tell an old Russian fairy tale, or a true story about Jane Addams and the children who lived in the tenements with the sooty gray and brown roofs. My favorite Jane Addams story was about the handsome but poor trapeze artist who could not find a job and was close to starvation. When Miss "Kind Heart" heard how badly he needed work, she appointed him Master Window Washer. So happy was the daring young man to be working again that while hanging aloft or standing on a window sill he would execute amusing and terrifying tricks for the crowd of children gathered on the street below.

A half century passed with its many changes. My aunt, eighty-five years old, long thick hair silver-gray, continued to live above the city — on the 24th floor of a highrise overlooking Lake Michigan. The walls of her rooms were hung with paintings by Leon and her many Hull House colleagues. Sculpture, pottery and metal work were scattered like deep-hued flowers on shelves, desk and table tops.

My visiting day was now Thursday. I taught in a school near her highrise and once a week I would kick off my shoes and stretch out gratefully on the cranberry velvet chaise lounge which had become "my" chair. One fall afternoon, as we watched the play of colors in the twilight sky, I broached the subject I had been thinking about for a long time. Would she tell me her many stories about Jane Addams and Hull House so that I might tape them? Oh, she said, I ramble so much now and lose my train of thought. I assured her that her "ramblings" were a most interesting part of our conversations. And so we embarked on a serene and lovely time for us both — sitting for hours in her livingroom for "storytime," as we had long ago when she was my "Gypsy Aunt" and I her "Sunday daughter."

By the time my aunt died in 1996 at the age of 96 she had passed on to me memories of Jane Addams and Hull House that spanned 24 years. Thanks to that rich legacy, and the mother lode of material in the Jane Addams Memorial Library at the University of Illinois in Chicago, I feel privileged to invite you into the world of Jane Addams and Hull House.

Chapter 1

The Miller's Thumb and the Wagon Wheel

Sadie Ellis had been attending classes at Hull House for five years when she was told that Miss Addams wished to see her. Hardly able to contain her nervousness, she climbed the long stairway to Miss Addams' office. At Sadie's timid knock Jane Addams greeted the 16-year-old warmly, delighted to give the shy girl the news that she and her friend, Blanche Maggioli, had each been awarded a scholarship to the Art Institute of Chicago.

Sadie's art classes had begun by a lucky chance. Blanche was to have her first music lesson at Hull House and had asked Sadie to go along for moral support. Sadie had never been to the Settlement before and was awed by its maze of somber brick buildings and the sheltered courtyard where the play of water in a small stone fountain mesmerized her. Upon entering the music school, Sadie and Blanche were told that the teacher was running late. They decided to pass the time by drawing the bright red geraniums blooming on the waiting room table.

A tall, light-haired woman walked into the room and paused, her attention caught by the girls' drawings. "Why, you girls are artists! You should be in Miss Benedict's class." And Emily Edwards, assistant art teacher, whisked the startled friends to the art studio where Enella Benedict solemnly inscribed their names in the class book.

Walking home with the news of the scholarship, Sadie rehearsed what she would say to her parents if they objected to her going all the way to the Art Institute for classes. If that should happen, she would ask Miss Addams to talk with them. No one, not even her father, would be able to refuse "Miss Kind Heart." Looking back on her life seven decades later, Sadie concluded that everything of importance that had happened to her from that day forward stemmed from her association with Jane Addams and Hull House.

It was just such a child of poor immigrant parents that Jane Addams had hoped Hull House could help when in 1889 she and Ellen Gates Starr had founded the Settlement on Chicago's West Side. As president of the Woman's Peace Party she had been traveling and lecturing in the United States and abroad for the past six months and had been able to spend little time at Hull House. She missed closeness with her neighbors, particularly the young people with whom she felt a special bond.

The year was 1916. Jane Addams, or Miss Addams as she preferred to be called by all but family and intimate friends, was looking particularly tired. She was 56 years old, plagued by chronic back pain, and had never fully recovered from a serious kidney disease. Neither condition, however, prevented her from working ten to twelve hours a day, well over the number she claimed to be inhumane when imposed on factory workers.

Jane Addams was accustomed to both poor health and hard work. She was also accustomed to harsh criticism from the press. Not, however, to the malicious missives hurled at her since she had become a leader in the international peace movement. The very journalists who had once dubbed her Saint Jane, sentimentalizing her work with the poor, now described her as one of the "shrieking sisterhood." Colleagues with whom she had shared her pacifist beliefs had dropped from the fold, urging her to do the same.

Businessmen, longtime supporters of Hull House, were withdrawing vital financial support. Increasingly, she felt out of touch with the people among whom she lived and worked. For Jane Addams, who had always drawn nourishment from being part of her community, such alienation was an open wound.

Perhaps on that afternoon, with the sun laying a shawl of warmth across her shoulders, she had leaned back in her chair and let her mind drift to the time when she had been as young and shy as Sadie Ellis. How different from the childhood of this daughter of Russian immigrants had her own childhood been.

Born on September 6, 1860, in the hamlet of Cedarville, Illinois, Laura Jane Addams had grown up in a two-story house with tall windows, spacious rooms and a kitchen commodious enough to seat ten of her father's millhands for lunch. An avid reader, John Addams had made a second floor parlor of his home available as the Cedarville Union Library. It was there that Jenny, as Laura Jane was then called, would seek out her father for treasured private moments. The living room, holding her stepmother's gleaming piano, was easily as large as a Chicago tenement flat in which an immigrant family of five might live. Gracious old elms shaded the front yard which sloped down to the road, then the main artery between Freeport, Illinois, six miles south of Cedarville, and Madison, Wisconsin.

John Addams had not begun married life as a wealthy man. In July 1844, a 22-year-old worker in his father's gristmill in Sinking Springs, Pennsylvania, he married Sarah Weber, sister-in-law of the owner of the mill in Kriedersville at which he had apprenticed. Sarah, five years older than John, had attended boarding school and came from a family more socially mobile than John's. But she was attracted to the ambitious young man who had read all the books in the village library and exuded a quiet self-confidence.

With small savings enhanced by generous wedding gifts, the young couple started out on a honeymoon dictated more by practical than romantic concerns. Sarah's father, Colonel George Weber, had long thought it would be financially wise to build a mill in "the west." He was to join the newlyweds in New York, on their way to northern Illinois where they hoped to make a home.

John Addams kept a careful daily journal of the trip. The first entry reads: "Myself and Wife left Kreidersville at four a.m. in a two-wheeled conveyance," first for Somerville, New Jersey, and "thence by Railroad, and arrived at the Great City of New York at 11 o'clock P.M., traveling 47 Miles in three hours. Thence, after two days of sightseeing, by boat to Albany — a night trip, 160 miles in nine hours. . ." The young couple, with Colonel Weber whom they met as planned, then continued west, arriving in Chicago, a "city commenced ten years ago and has a population of 8 thousand, nearly every person is engaged in some mercantile business, in my opinion too many for the place."

After three months of exploration Sarah and John decided to settle in the "Alps of Illinois," the lovely rolling country north of Freeport, sparsely settled by a few second-generation pioneers like themselves. John bought a small gristmill on the banks of the Cedar River, a modest stream more aptly called Cedar Creek, where in 1849 a village was incorporated and given the name Cedarville. Colonel Weber built a mill about 30 miles to the southwest.

John and Sarah Addams prospered. They were soon able to build a new mill and barn, and in 1854 a home that came to be known as the finest in the village. Built in the then popular Greek Revival style, it stood on a hill in the verdant valley carved out centuries ago by Cedar Creek. In his Cedarville memoir, an acquaintance of the Addams family recalled the striking garnet red glass in the transom of the front door which gave, especially to a child, a rosy tint to the world outside.

Gentle but resolute, Sarah Addams managed the domestic domain of child-rearing and household care with a mastery comparable to her husband's business skills. She bore nine children but only five lived beyond the age of two: Mary, born in 1845, Martha in 1850, John Weber (called Weber) in 1852, Alice in 1853, and Laura

Jane in 1860. The markers in the Cedarville Cemetery explain why April was a sad month for the Addams family. Georgiana died April 12, 1850, at the age of ten months; Horace, two months old, died, April 15, 1855; and two-year-old George died April 7, 1859.

With the help of a hired girl, Sarah produced the household's candles, soap, rugs, socks and mittens, preserved its vegetables and fruit, and baked its bread. When her husband was away on business trips, Sarah knew enough about the workings of the mill to keep it running.

At age 32, John Addams, by then a founding member of the Republican Party, was elected a state senator, a position he held for the next sixteen years. Farsighted, confident, and not afraid to take risks, he spearheaded the building of a railway across the northern part of Illinois that was eventually consolidated with the Chicago and Northwestern Railroad. Forty-eight years later that railroad would furnish free rides to campers on their way to the Hull House camp in Waukegan, Illinois. In this and many other ways, Jane Addams was to find the fabric of her father's life woven into her own.

On a frigid January day in 1863, 49-year-old Sarah Addams, seven months pregnant with her ninth child, went to the aid of a wagon-maker's wife in labor. Off in another part of the county, the doctor did not arrive as expected and Sarah delivered the baby herself. On her way home, exhausted, Sarah collapsed and her infant was stillborn. A week later she died and was buried beside her stillborn child and her three other deceased children. The village newspaper expressed the sentiments of family and friends: Sarah Addams would "be missed everywhere, at home, in society, in the church, in all places where good is to be done and suffering relieved."

Mary took Sarah Addams' place, a forbidding responsibility for a 17-year-old. Much like her mother, she was intelligent, capable and devoted to the well-being of others. She had the able help of Polly (Mary) Bear, her mother's childhood nurse who had followed the family to Cedarville, and a hired girl from town as well as a handy-man and a woman to do the laundry.

Two-and-a-half-year-old Jenny attached herself to Mary and Martha, but her clear favorite was her father. She yearned to be as much like him as possible, a desire that prompted her to spend hours at the mill, pressing the wheat grains falling from the mill-stones between her thumb and forefinger so she too would have a "miller's thumb." But all her diligence came to nothing and her thumb stubbornly stayed its same boring shape, not marvelously flattened like her father's.

Jenny loved to hear John Addams tell stories about his youth. Looking back on her childhood in her autobiographical book, *Twenty Years at Hull-House*, published in 1910, Jane Addams wrote:

> [With the] sincere tribute of imitation which affection offers to its adored object. . . I was consumed by a wistful desire to apprehend the hardships of my father's earlier life in that far-away time when he had been a miller's apprentice. I knew that he still woke up punctually at three o-clock because for so many years he had taken his turn at the mill in the early morn-ing and if by chance I awoke at the same hour, as curiously enough I often did, I imagined him in the early dawn in my uncle's old mill reading through the entire village library, book after book, beginning with the signers of the Declaration of Independence. Copies of the same books, mostly bound in calfskin, were to be found in the library below, and I coura-geously resolved that I too would read them and try to under-stand life as he did. . . Pope's translation of the 'Iliad,' even fol-lowed by Dryden's 'Virgil,' did not leave behind the residuum of wisdom for which I longed. . .

Eight-year-old Jenny wearied of rising at 3 a.m., began to sleep to a normal hour, and entered the more welcoming world of Louisa May Alcott's *Little Women*, a book she would reread many times. But the fact that at such a young age Jenny actually rose at that dark hour and attempted to read Pope and Dryden must have signaled to her father that his youngest daughter was a most unusual child. Jenny, in turn, centered on John Addams "all that careful imitation which a little girl ordinarily gives to her mother's ways and habits."

In legislative sessions in Springfield, John Addams had become both friend and legal advisor to Abraham Lincoln. It was a special treat for Jenny when her father, in his sober, resonant voice, read from the packet labeled "Mr. Lincoln's letters." The letters always began, "My dear Double-dee'd Addams." (The extra D had been added by an ancestor, Isaac Adams, who wanted to differentiate himself from a cousin with the same name.) In one such letter Lincoln asked his friend, John Addams, how he was going to vote on a matter before the legislature. He trusted that Addams "would vote according to his conscience," and it was "a matter of considerable importance to me to know how that conscience was pointing."

"There were at least two pictures of Lincoln," Jane Addams wrote, "that always hung in my father's room, and one in our old-fashioned upstairs parlor, of Lincoln with little Tad. For one or all of these reasons I always tend to associate Lincoln with the tenderest thoughts of my father." Jenny was four-and-a-half years old when she came home from play one day to find a black band and an American flag fastened to each gate post. She ran up to her father's room to inquire what the flags and bands were for, then stopped, amazed to see her father weeping. "The greatest man in the world has just died," he told her. "Abraham Lincoln."

It was one of Jenny's earliest introductions to that vast, unknown universe lying outside the two white gate posts. Another occurred when she walked into the house and found her father quietly talking to a Negro man. She was told afterwards never to speak to anyone of seeing that man or any other Negro in their home. Many years passed before Jenny was to learn that John Addams was an ardent abolitionist and the Cedarville house had been a stop on the Underground Railroad.

Jenny had had tuberculosis of the spine at a very young age and was left with a slight curvature that caused her to walk somewhat pigeon-toed and hold her head a little to one side. Convinced that she was ugly, she would hang back while walking with her father in Cedarville and Freeport, loathe to have strangers think that such a handsome man had such a homely daughter. She harbored the painful concern that her father might be relieved not to be seen with her.

Emerging from the Freeport Bank one afternoon, John Addams saw Jenny dutifully waiting for him. She later recalled that transforming moment when, "With a playful touch of exaggeration, he lifted his high and shining hat and made me an imposing bow." That public acknowledgment convinced Jenny that her father was not at all ashamed of her. Though she was able to walk by his side with equanimity after that, she never broke free of feeling that she was unattractive. Following the typically self-conscious adolescent years, she paid little attention to dress or hairstyle. Years later Louise Bowen, patroness of Hull House, would purchase a new dress for Jane Addams (preferably gray, black or navy blue) when she wearied of seeing her friend in the same clothes week after week.

In fact, Jenny was a pretty child with dreamy, blue-gray eyes and thick brown hair. Living mostly in a world of adults, and spending a great deal of time with her father, a reserved man with little inclination for seeing the lighter side of life, she tended to be serious and introspective. An early entry in Quaker John Addams' journal attests to his aim to settle in the new land and do honor to God and selves. Guided by an "inner light," John Addams not only resolutely lived by those words but passed their sober message on to young Jenny.

Allying herself "doggedly" to her father, Jenny was drawn into moral concerns at a remarkably early age. At eight years old she had been given a wool cape which she described as "gorgeous beyond anything she had worn before." On Sunday morning, readying herself for Bible class, she put on the cape and went to show it to her father. But instead of being complimented, she was told to take off the new cape and wear the old one. It would keep her just as warm and would not make the other girls feel badly for not having anything nearly so beautiful.

> I complied with the request [Jane Addams later wrote] but I fear without inner consent, and I certainly was quite without the joy of self-sacrifice as I walked soberly through the village street. . . My mind was busy, however, with the old question eternally suggested by the inequalities of the human lot. Only when I neared the church door did I venture to ask what could be done about it.

John Addams conceded that little could be done about equalizing people's material possessions. For that reason, in school or church "where everyone received the same portions," she should not wear an expensive cape that would set her apart from her schoolmates. A stern lesson for an eight-year-old.

Jenny's dreams at that age were disturbingly real, particularly the one she dreamed

> night after night, that everyone in the world was dead except myself, and that upon me rested the responsibility of making a wagon wheel. . . I always stood in the same spot in the blacksmith shop, darkly pondering as to how to begin, and never once did I know how, although I fully realized that the affairs of the world could not be resumed until at least one wheel should be made and something started.

The dream was so real that the next morning would sometimes find Jenny, "standing in the doorway of the village blacksmith shop, anxiously watching the burly, red-shirted figure at work."

"Do you always have to sizzle the iron in water?" she asked.

That's what makes the iron hard, the blacksmith explained. Despairing of ever being able to sizzle iron in water, or go through all the other steps necessary to make a wheel, Jenny would return home, feeling the weight of failure, but telling no one, not even her sister Mary, what was troubling her.

One day, happily accompanying her father to Freeport in the

family buggy, Jenny saw the slums of the city for the first time. Distressed at the poverty of the dwellings and the children playing on garbage heaps, she asked her father "why people lived in such horrid little houses so close together." When he answered that they could afford no better, she replied that when she grew up she would "of course, have a large house, but it would not be built among other large houses but right in the midst of horrid little houses like these."

In the Jane Addams Room of the simple, two-room historical museum in Cedarville, some memorabilia of Jane's childhood are on exhibit — a worn coin purse filled with fossils, her joke and riddle book, and a handkerchief case made for her father. The letters to her sister Alice, at Rockford Female Seminary, written in a painfully cramped script with a liberal spattering of misspelled words (the poor spelling that persisted through adulthood may have been caused by a mild dyslexia), speak of ordinary things:

> It is good skating and has been for a couple of weeks. . . Mr. March preached hear to day but I did not go he preaches so long. . . Mrs. Carey is very sick with the dropsy they do not think she will live. I have got a new water proof it is a great deal nicer than any other ever was. . . They had a crasy man came hear last evening and this morning he wanted to tune and play on our piano. . .

So, we learn with relief there was a little girl here who collected fossils, read riddles, went ice-skating and wrote letters to her sister begging for letters in return. Interwoven among the relentlessly somber moments with which Jane Addams documents her early childhood, there were ordinary days of play and irresponsibility to give some balance to the life of a child who dreamed repeatedly of her duty to make a wagon wheel on which the affairs of the world depended.

Chapter 2

"Once to Be Young"

*J*ohn Addams could hardly have chosen a wife less like Sarah Addams than Anna Haldeman. The aristocratic and attractive widow of a successful Freeport businessman, Anna had been brought up in an intellectual family and was self-confident, used to having her own way, and prone to bad temper when crossed. She was a poised and enthusiastic hostess who left all work to hired help and set the tone of a social evening by choosing the menu, the silver and the flower arrangements with great care. After she moved into the Addams house, known to the family as the Homestead, Anna had a two-story bay window added to the living room and upstairs parlor, a china cabinet built into a corner of the dining room, and an area on the first floor converted to an office for her husband.

To John and Sarah Addams the purchase of a piano would have been an extravagance. To Anna it was a necessity, and her upright piano was ceremoniously placed in the Addams household. Capable of great generosity if she loved and approved, disdain or hostility if she did not, Anna Addams' move into the Addams home six years after Sarah Addams' death brought a sea-change for everyone.

Mary, who may have harbored some resentment toward Anna

for sweeping in and claiming the house her own, soon left to attend Rockford Seminary. However eight-and-a-half-year-old Jenny might have felt about her demanding stepmother, so different than her self-effacing, permissive sister, she was grateful to Anna Addams for bringing her eight-year-old son George into the family. (Anna's other son, Harry, graduate of a European medical school, was working in a physician's office in Freeport.) Bright, adventuresome, and passionately interested in science, an interest he stimulated in Jenny, George drew his new companion out of her solitary, introspective ways into the fascinating world of the Cedarville countryside and succeeded in making her feel she was the equal of any boy. Jenny, well able to keep up with George's expeditions through the Cedarville woods, along the creek and into mysterious, dank caves, proved her hardiness when she and George were playing by the creek and George tried to seize a muskrat under water. The feisty creature clamped its jaws on George's hand instead and Jenny and a neighbor boy freed him by cutting off the muskrat's head with a penknife.

George's rescues of Jenny were more imaginary than real. Calling himself the "Green Knight," he wielded a green wooden sword with which he fought off many a harmless snake, gallantly "saving" Jenny just as she feared all was lost. When Jenny and George weren't off on a "crusade" they spent hours playing at the Addams mill. Courting danger, they would perch on a log as it floated slowly toward the buzzing mill saw and jump off just in time to escape a "sudden and gory death."

In *Twenty Years* Jane Addams recalled those summers with great affection:

> [We] carried on games and crusades which lasted week after week, and even summer after summer, as only free ranging country children can do. . . We had of course our favorite places and trees and birds and flowers. It is hard to reproduce the companionship which children establish with nature, but

certainly it is much too unconscious and intimate to come under the head of aesthetic appreciation or anything of the sort. When we said that the purple wind-flowers — the *anemone patens* — 'looked as if the winds had made them,' we thought much more of the fact that they were wind-born than that they were beautiful: we clapped our hands in sudden joy over the soft radiance of the rainbow, but its enchantment lay in our half belief that a pot of gold was to be found at its farther end.

One summer Jenny and George imitated ancient rituals learned from their reading of Greek mythology. They built an altar on the bank of Cedar Creek before which they solemnly placed captured snakes and one out of every hundred walnuts they had gathered, pouring fresh cider over the walnuts "in tribute." In tribute to what? James Weber Linn, Jane Addams' nephew and first biographer, speculated that it might be a tribute from the two "free-roaming country children" to the goodness of life.

Life *was* good to Jenny then, though her stepmother imposed more rigid rules than Mary ever had. She also had to share with Anna Addams the attentions of her father which, until then, had been focused almost exclusively upon her. But strengthened by her friendship with George, Jenny slowly adjusted to her stepmother's ways. Although George was her clear favorite, Anna Addams treated Jenny as one of her own and in time Jenny grew fond of her.

With her marriage to John Addams, the distinguished Illinois senator, Anna Addams looked forward to leaving Cedarville several times each year for the more sophisticated society of Springfield. But the frenetic round of social events in the capital city, so appealing to Anna, repelled her reticent husband who despised the small talk and political backbiting. Two years after their marriage, John Addams decided not to run for the Senate again. Anna Addams exerted the force of her considerable will to make him change his mind, leading to late-night discussions so strenuous that a guest in the downstairs bedroom recalled being kept awake by them. But in John Addams the self-assured Anna had met a will that firmly asserted itself and remained the dominant force in the Addams household.

Anna Addams did the next best thing. She set about creating in her Cedarville home the cultural atmosphere and sophistication she had hoped to enjoy in Springfield. She presided with grace at formal dinner parties regularly held in the Addams living room. Her guests were local celebrities such as Richard Oglesby, governor of Illinois, and State Representative Lyman Trumbull. Jane Addams' ease in the homes of royalty and heads of state was gained in large part from being included at a young age in many of the formal dinners presided over by her elegant stepmother.

Every evening the family sat down to a table set with a white tablecloth and good china and silver. Often a music or reading hour would follow dinner. Anna would play the guitar and sing a wide repertoire of songs. When Jenny and George were older she introduced them to Shakespeare and would assign each of them parts to read aloud. It was a special pleasure for Jenny when her father took a role in the chosen drama. Sometimes passages from a novel would be read. Anna was an enthusiastic novel reader, a radical passion for a woman at a time when novels were condemned as trivial, if not dangerous. She understood Jenny's great affection for *Little Women* far better than Sarah Addams would have.

One wonders if John Addams foresaw what a change his artistic, gregarious wife would make in his sober, Quaker-quiet household. Anna's imperious ways with servants, her love for high fashion, and the whirl of social activity into which she often plunged the house were significant departures from what John Addams had previously known. Notwithstanding, he seemed to take pride in his handsome, accomplished wife and accepted most of the changes with comparative equanimity.

He was not equanimious, however, about the unexpected and intense romance that developed between his daughter Alice and Harry Haldeman. Nor was Anna. Both parents feared that the two headstrong, temperamental young people were of too explosive a nature to be suited for each other. But Alice and Harry would not be deterred. As the young couple drove away after their wedding, Anna, noticing tears in her husband's eyes, said. "I don't feel a bit more sorry for your Allie than I do for my Harry."

The bride and groom settled in Mitcheville, Iowa, where Harry, in whom brilliance had bred arrogance, began the practice of medicine. Only a few years had passed before he claimed to be the only physician west of the Alleghenies who had set a broken neck for a patient who fully recovered. Alice possessed a keen business sense as well as an acerbic wit, which stood her in good stead in discourse with her husband.

Jenny was only an average student. For one who read so much, she was a surprisingly poor speller and lost all the spelling bees in which she participated. It requires a stretch of the imagination to accept that the same girl who wrote letters to her sisters characterized by crippled handwriting, poor spelling, and a childish reporting of "news," was the Addams daughter who had risen at three in the morning and worked her way through Pope and Dryden. Yet by the time she reached 15, Jenny's writing had become fluent, intelligent and witty. Responding to an invitation from her 16-year-old cousin, Vallie Beck, to visit in Iowa, she wrote:

> I cannot number dancing among my accomplishments and my knowledge of cards is very limited indeed. . . I should be delighted if you could find it convenient to pay us a visit. I could safely promise you picnicking, boating, horseback rides and so forth, but nothing very far out of that line, for you know we are six miles from a lemon. [Six miles was the distance from Cedarville to Freeport and the nearest grocery store.]

At 16 Jenny had grown into a slim young woman who stood five-foot-three. Her brown hair was livened by a hint of gold (at 29 she was described by Alice and Harry's daughter, Marcet, as "that slender, sunny-haired, quick moving lady"), and her face, dominated by extraordinary, large gray-blue eyes, tended to look thoughtful, sometimes sad. In her correspondence with Vallie Beck she exchanged ideas on subjects interesting to most 16-year-olds: friends, school, and the state of their complexions. Writing to Vallie about her nose, which "is simply a piece of flesh, expressing no character whatever," Jenny goes on to say that it "contains eight freckles horrible to relate. I counted them this morning."

In another letter Jenny confides that her summer had passed and she had

> accomplished little in the way of reading or study although I planned to do somewhat of both during the warm weather. I, like Edgar Poe's raven 'sat and perched and nothing more' and found the occupation so delightful that I have continued to sit and do nothing ever since.
>
> The oil of day is fast declining and if I light a torch the mosquitoes will be simply fearful. I therefore close as my last alternative.

By the time she was 16 Jenny knew intimately life's darker side. Chronic and debilitating back pain was a reality which she stoically learned to accept. Her mother had died so early in her childhood that she could not, though she tried, recollect what she looked like. Her beautiful sister, Martha, surrogate mother along with Mary, had died of typhoid when Jenny was six years old.

Indeed, it is likely that every family in Cedarville had lost a child through illness or war. Jenny and George would solemnly whisper the names of the men who had died fighting in the Addams Brigade, named after their Quaker father who had not balked at recruiting men for the Union. When they passed the wind-beaten cabin of the old couple who had lost four sons in the war and the fifth in a gun accident, they became silent and bowed their heads.

So it was, when the Addams family received the sad news that the faithful Polly Bear was dying in the home of her cousin, 16-year-old Jenny was sent as the family's representative. Jenny recalled that wintry day:

> I left the lamp-lit, warm house to be driven four miles through
> a blinding storm which every minute added more snow to the
> already high drifts, with a sense of starting upon a fateful
> errand. An hour after my arrival. . . I was left alone to watch
> with Polly. . . Suddenly the great change came. I heard a feeble
> call of Sarah, my mother's name as the dying eyes were turned
> upon me, followed by a curious breathing, and in place of the
> Polly I knew were the strange, august features, stern and with-
> drawn from the small affairs of life. . . As I was driven home
> in the winter storm, the wind through the trees seemed laden
> with a passing soul and the riddle of life and death pressed
> hard; once to be young, to grow old and to die; everything
> came to that and then a mysterious journey out into the
> unknown. Did she mind faring forth alone?

Jenny realized when the buggy turned up the Addams driveway
that she had forgotten which verse of scripture Polly wanted read at
her funeral. Beset with guilt she confided her "sin" to her father.
"And while he was much too wise," she wrote, "to grow dogmatic
upon the great theme of death, I felt a new fellowship with him
because we had discussed it together."

Following this moment of intimacy, Jenny ran head-on into a
serious disagreement with her father. She had set her hopes on earning a college degree, not a common achievement for women in 1877.
Vassar had been founded in 1861, Smith in 1872 and Wellesley in
1875. Jenny wanted passionately to go to Smith, a degree-granting
institution, but her father was determined that she stay close to
home and attend Rockford Female Seminary as her sisters had.
Though John Addams had encouraged Jenny to read the works of
the world's great thinkers — he had paid his daughter five cents for
each of the lives of Plutarch she read — he did not expect Jenny to
use her intellectual powers to do more than run an efficient household and raise intelligent, God-fearing children. Nor was support to
be expected from her stepmother. In spite of Anna's interest in the
arts and education, she adamantly held to the view that a woman's

place was in the home and ridiculed those who would do away with baby and cradle, aspiring to be statesmen or professors.

Although Jane Addams writes in *Twenty Years at Hull-House* that she had exchanged her gorgeous new cape for the old dull one without "inner consent," she says nothing about her feelings nine years later when her father thwarted her long-held desire to attend Smith College. Had she lived in a time when women felt free to acknowledge their negative feelings, her idealization of John Addams might still have led her to exorcise any trace of resentment toward him. He continued until his death to be the beloved, wise father who "wrapt me in his large Man's doublet, careless if it fit or no."

After a full decade of happy comradeship, Jenny and George were to be separated. As they said their farewells on the eve of George's departure for the school of his choice, Beloit College in Southern Wisconsin, it was not lost on Jenny that as a young man his horizons were unlimited while hers definitely were not.

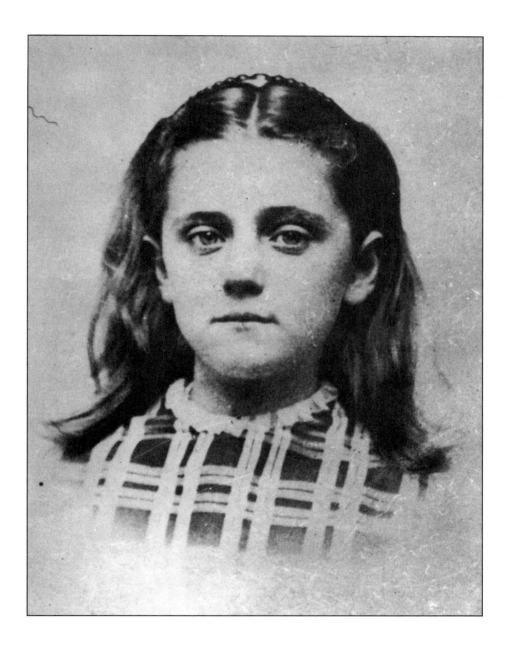

"A child who dreamed repeatedly of her duty to make a wagon wheel on which the affairs of the world depended."
- Jenny at age 8

"It is very important not to pretend to understand what you don't understand... You must always be honest with yourself inside, whatever happens."

- John Addams, to 8-year-old Jenny

"However mopey it might be elsewhere there was intellectual ozone in her vicinity."

- Jane, at Rockford Female Seminary

Anna Haldeman, Jane and George

The Homestead at Cedarville

Chapter 3

"When We Speak We Must Say Something!"

*E*leanor Haworth, a student entering Rockford Female Seminary in September 1877, recalled meeting Jane the first day of school:

> She had very pretty light brown hair, pulled back, and particularly direct, earnest eyes; but she looked as I know I was feeling, very trembly inside. She said her name was Laura Jane Addams and that she had come from Cedarville. . . I have always wondered if I looked as young and worried as Jane did that day.

Jane's timidity quickly disappeared. (She had left the name Jenny in Cedarville with the rest of her childhood possessions.) Her disappointment at not going to Smith College did not keep her from entering enthusiastically into the life of the seminary. Strong will is not always paired with flexibility, but in Jane those two qualities were present to a happy degree.

Jane made friends at Rockford easily, though she possessed a level of reserve that would characterize her throughout her life, perhaps in part a legacy from her reticent father. The students at the seminary were addressed as "Miss" in class and while some balked at the formality, Jane seemed comfortable with it.

The young Rockford woman who became Jane's closest friend was Ellen Gates Starr of Durand, Illinois. Ellen was slight of build, intense, and sharp-witted. Passionately interested in art and religion, she drew Jane into long discussions of theology and Florentine and Greek art. It took no more than a few of these discussions to inspire mutual admiration, each insisting the other was the wiser and better.

When financial concerns required that Ellen leave Rockford after her freshman year to teach school, first in a small town near her home and then in Chicago, Jane wrote her a rather extraordinary letter. She assured Ellen that at the end of her year in Chicago

> you will gain a good deal more than if you had been that time in our noble institution, there is something in being in a big city, in giving something as well as taking all the time, in gaining the ability not to move in ruts, that will give you a self-reliance and education a good deal better than a boarding school will. I think that you have a pretty prosperous look out . . . I am disappointed to think that you are not coming back to Rockford and that our social intercourse is probably over for all time. It is queer though, but a fact that I'm glad when I know some people just so much and then stop — not that I am afraid to go any farther, but there is a sort of fascination to me — you remember them, retain the impressions they leave, go steadily on your way and meet someone else who will sort of finish what they had begun. . . I don't feel exactly that way in regard to your going away but then I don't feel so very bad on the same principle, that two people honestly going ahead are better if they don't meet so much.

Perhaps Ellen realized that Jane's usual sensitivity to her feelings was overwhelmed by her intoxication with ideas. Caught up in a compulsion to clarify and articulate her thinking on all subjects, Jane had advanced her conception of friendship as coolly as if it were a scientific formula. Ellen must have taken comfort in the fact that at the conclusion of the letter Jane abandoned the very principle she had just espoused.

> I know that there is very little time between the 28th of August and the 8th of September. I wish you could take some of it and come and visit me. I would be simply delighted, will meet you in Freeport any day you mention and will take you back just when you think you must go. . . My mother is not at home but I'm sure she would add her invitation to mine.

Throughout her life Jane presented a puzzling paradox to many who sought to know her. Though she tended to be somewhat remote in one-to-one relationships, the poor, the disenfranchised and the despairing instinctively felt her inner warmth and drew close to her as they would to a fire on a frigid day. As in her Rockford days, she was a friendly, enthusiastic member of a group, but tendered few invitations to intimacy.

Fifty young women comprised the student body of the seminary, 17 in Jane's class. The rigorous weekday schedule began at 6:30 a.m. with students making fires in their woodstoves to warm themselves while dressing. Breakfast was then served in the seminary dining room at tables presided over by faculty members. Classes took up most of the day; the customary student load was 15 courses a year with Latin, Greek and German continuing throughout the entire four years. Course offerings included English literature, with a concentration on Shakespeare and the Romantic poets, American literature, Biblical literature, ancient literature, including Chinese, Japanese and Hebraic, mathematics, botany, astronomy, chemistry, geology, philosophy and music. (Jane dropped music after one semester, deploring her lack of musical ability.)

After classes the young scholars were required to exercise by walking briskly on the boardwalk circling the school grounds. Following dinner, again with faculty members at the head of each table, they retired to their rooms for study followed by evening devotions. Jane added a pleasureful dimension to her study of languages by going to a favorite teacher's room for "blessed Sunday morning readings" of the Greek Testament. On occasion she would go to hear her sister Mary's husband, the Reverend John M. Linn, preach in nearby Winnebago, and then, with relief, give up all pretense of seriousness and spend the afternoon delightedly playing with her two small nephews.

On Saturdays a visit from the young men of Beloit College (frequently George was among them) brought welcome respite from this unforgiving schedule. There were chaperoned hayrides and picnics which challenged the more adventuresome or romantic to devise strategies to escape the watchful eyes of the guardian teacher.

Jane excelled in her classes, earning close to an 'A' average. With the goal of a college degree always in mind, she added a number of advanced courses to the standard load so that she would meet the requirements for a Bachelor of Arts degree, not *if* that opportunity arose but *when*. For it would arise; Jane was intent on that.

From an early age Jane had not liked to leave anything half done, even if, her biographer and nephew Weber Linn relates, it was only kicking a stone to school. Once she had launched the stone, she would kick it on its irregular way to the school steps, even if doing so made her late to class. Now, as a young woman, she was fiercely determined to persuade the director of the seminary, Anna Peck Sill, that Rockford should add enough advanced courses to become a degree-granting institution. It would then be on even footing with a male college like Beloit; it did not sit well with Jane that women's colleges had lesser standing than men's.

Anna Peck Sill, founder of the seminary in 1851, was nearly 80 years old, and in the 26 years she had directed the seminary her goal had not altered: to "develop moral and religious character in accordance with right principles. . . that it might send out cultivated Christian women in the various fields of usefulness." The phrase "various fields of usefulness" meant one thing only to Anna Sill — usefulness to God. She measured her success by how many

Rockford students became missionaries.

It was not easy for Jane to withstand the pressure at the seminary to make a lifetime religious commitment. Although she thought of herself as a Christian, her young spirit balked at being tied to "God's work." She had, after all, been brought up by a Hicksite Quaker father who attended all the churches in town but belonged to none, and who had said, when Jenny confessed her inability to understand foreordination (predestination), "it did not matter much whether one understood foreordination or not, but that it was very important not to pretend to understand what you didn't and that you must always be honest with yourself inside, whatever happened." Holding true to that dictum, at least in the privacy of her journal, Jane wrote, "Miss Sills does everything from love of God alone. I do not like that."

As a faculty member of the elite Kirkland School for Girls in Chicago, Ellen had few hours to herself. She often spent them writing to Jane, engaging in arduous explorations of theology and personal belief. Jane struggled with her relationship to the Deity, and felt somewhat envious of the grounding that Ellen's devout belief in God gave her.

"I wish you were here," she wrote to Ellen. (Once the finality of Ellen's absence had registered emotionally, Jane repeatedly begged her friend to visit her.) "Christ doesn't help me in the least. . . Sometimes I can work myself into great admiration for his life, and occasionally catch something of his philosophy, but He doesn't bring me any nearer to the Deity."

"I have been trying an awful experiment," she confided in another letter. "I didn't pray for about three months and was shocked to find I felt no worse for it." In her junior year Jane was able to articulate the difference between Ellen's reaching for religion and her own stumbling quest. "You long for a beautiful faith. . . I only feel that I need religion in a practical sense, that if I fix myself with relations to God and the universe, & so be in perfect harmony with nature and Deity, I could use my faculties and energy so much better and could do almost anything. *Mine* is preeminently selfish and *yours* Ellen is reaching for higher things."

She determined to talk no more about religion: "I find myself growing indignant and sensitive when people speak of it lightly, as if they had no right to, you see, I am not so unsettled as I *resettle* so often, but my creed is ever be sincere and don't fuss." Jane was relieved when Sarah Anderson, a young Rockford English teacher with whom she had become friends, confided, "I do not think that we are put into the world to be religious, we have a certain work to do, and to do that is the main thing."

When she was 28 years old and feeling painfully adrift, Jane would join the Presbyterian Church. Disavowing the dogma, she hoped to satisfy her deep yearning to belong "to an outward symbol of fellowship, some bond of peace, some blessed spot where unity of spirit might claim right of way over all differences." Her longing for a faith that would give her a sense of belonging and community would persist until she was finally able to put it to rest by finding that "certain work" which Sarah Anderson had talked about. Anderson believed with her literary mentor, Thomas Carlyle, that every God-created man is a hero if only he remains true to his creation. To Jane Addams, "remaining true" meant doing one's chosen work.

Certainly John Addams had no desire for his daughter to become a missionary. He viewed the seminary as an institution where Jane could get a basic education in a moral atmosphere, after which she could complete her studies with — mandatory for all educated young women — two years travel abroad. Jane would then, it was hoped, marry a suitable young man and raise a family. John Addams had not taken into account that while guiding his adoring daughter in the paths of morality, and encouraging her knowledge of the classics, he was also imbuing her with his own sense of urgency to do socially useful work. To Jane that work did not mean being a wife and mother in the confines of a household. Her eyes were focused on the somewhat frightening but beckoning world beyond Cedarville and Rockford.

Limited as she was in her worldly experiences, Jane had seen enough to convince her that to compete in a world dominated by men (which she fully expected to do), women had better be armed with knowledge in at least one branch of the physical sciences. In her senior essay she argued that women can only "grow accurate and intelligible by the thorough study of at least one branch of physical science, for only with eyes thus accustomed to the search for truth can she detect all self-deceit and fancy in herself and learn to express herself without dogmatism."

Jane tried in all good faith to climb a variety of branches, including that of the rather esoteric practice of taxidermy. She did reasonably well, she thought, in "stuffing birds," until some unknown trickster sent her a live hawk to kill and prepare. Jane adroitly persuaded a male student to undertake the killing. With substantial help from her taxidermy teacher, she then managed to do a respectable job of "stuffing." Soon after the hawk incident she suggested to George that their customary summer studies should not involve anything as messy as taxidermy, but rather focus on something "clean and accurate like mineralogical chemistry."

Though Jane earned a perfect score in deportment, there was more than a touch of the rebel in her. Recognizing this, her classmates begged her to intercede with Miss Sill whenever they were in trouble. Occasionally Jane instigated the trouble herself. Eleanor Haworth recalled one memorable class on Moral Philosophy:

> Jane insisted on giving the name, Don Quixote, the Spanish pronunciation. We backed her up with laughter at Miss Sill's 'Don Quix-ott.' Miss Sill suspended the whole class for two days, then took us back without comment. At chapel that day Jane took my hymnal and wrote on the fly-leaf:
>
> > Life's a burden, bear it.
> > Life's a duty, dare it.
> > Life's a thorn-crown? Wear it!
> > And spurn to be a coward.

The rigidity and narrowness of life at the seminary began to erode Jane's good spirits. "So much of our time is spent in preparation, so much in routine, and so much in sleep," she wrote in her journal, "we find it difficult to have any experience at all." To add a little spice to their bland life, Jane and four of her classmates embarked on an unusual experiment. They had been fascinated by DeQuincey's book, *Confessions of an Opium Eater*, and decided to induce their own opium dreams to better understand DeQuincey's experience. Jane did not reveal how she and her classmates, secluded in Miss Sill's bastion of religion, secured their small white bag of opium. But secure it they did and solemnly consumed the powder "during an entire long holiday." Alas! Not one of them was transported to a higher realm of consciousness. Quite the opposite. The teacher to whom they confided their disappointment betrayed them by confiscating the DeQuincey book, gave the opium eaters a pill to make them vomit, and ordered the lot of them to family religious services to repent.

After writing for the Rockford Seminary Magazine for three years, Jane became its editor-in-chief. To the distinct displeasure of Anna Sill the tone of the magazine changed. No longer was it a quarterly devoted to the cause of Christian education, but a journal that published poetry and essays on a wide variety of subjects. "We took large themes," Jane wrote, "usually from the Greek because they were the most stirring to the imagination." Her Rockford Magazine essays proved to be seminal: many of those "large themes" centered on concerns and beliefs that she would be involved in, through her writings, speeches, and the legislation she championed, during the rest of her life.

The essay titles she chose did not promise light reading. In "The Element of Hopefulness in Human Nature," she advanced the optimistic thesis that it is the undaunted hopefulness of children that insures the persistence of hope in the human race. Not surprisingly she wrote about Bellerophon and his successful fight with the

Minotaur, contending that "social evils could only be overcome by him who soars above them into idealism, as Bellerophon, mounted on the winged horse, Pegasus, had slain the earthly dragon."

In "One Office of Nature," Jane considered how Goethe's studies of nature brought him in touch with the Divine:

> Probably no man ever came into the pure presence of Nature who was more unworthy to know its secrets than Wolfgang Von Goethe, yet he came in a moment of repentance and kindly Nature received him. . . Goethe bore the curse of his time: He was filled full of its skepticism, hollowness and a thousandfold contradictions, till his heart was like to break; yet it was given to him to change the chaos into creation, and to dispose with ease the distracting variety of claims. He turned away from all the confusion and studied with human eyes the unity and simplicity of nature. It was he who suggested the leading idea of modern botany, that the leaf is the unit of growth, and that every plant is only a transformed leaf. . . In optics again he rejected the artificial theory of seven colors and considered that every color was the miniature of light and darkness in new proportions. He did away with a great deal of the sham learning and cant of the age by teaching modern scientists the high simplicity of Nature. Many of the theories he formed from his discoveries were false, yet even these theories unlocked the narrow ties of the old order, and human nature breathed freer. Goethe was the deliverer of his time: he studied nature throughout his long life, and his last words, while waiting for his eighty-second birthday, were a welcome to the returning spring.

In "Tramps," Jane asserted with an excess of zeal that a man "must give a full equivalent for everything he receives; by disregarding this principle he renders himself abject and mean and merits universal contempt." Notwithstanding her break from life at the Homestead, she had not yet shaken free of her Quaker father's moral judgments.

In her junior year Jane spoke about the progress in women's education which had passed from accomplishments and the art of pleasing, to the development of her intellectual force and her capabilities for direct labor. She wishes not to be a man; nor like a man, but she claims the same right to independent thought and action. . . We. . . are not restless and anxious for things beyond us, we simply claim the highest privileges of our time and avail ourselves of its best opportunities. . . [O]n the other hand we still retain the old ideal of womanhood — the saxon lady whose mission it was to give bread unto her household. So we have planned to be 'Breadgivers' throughout our lives, believing that in labor alone is happiness. . .

As Jane reached the end of her senior year her writing reflected her growing awareness of the extent to which the feminine imagination and intellect had been systematically repressed. Women, she asserted, must develop their intellects and venture into territories held sacred by men. She had personally experienced the strong bias that men, as well as many of her own sex, held against women seeking higher education. A woman was not "built" for such intellectual pursuit; her anatomy was too frail and college attendance would damage her reproductive system, theorized a Harvard Medical College professor. A popular journalist queried, "Must we crowd education on our daughters and for the sake of making them intellectual make them puny, nervous and their whole earthly existence a struggle between life and death?"

As a member of the Rockford Debating Society, Jane argued that the "impervious will of man is at least forced to admit that woman, like himself, possesses an intellect and that she exerts a potent influence in the age in which she lives."

Exerts a potent influence? The young orator, sheltered in the embrace of Rockford Female Seminary, was growing restless and ready to burst the corset strings of Victorian mores. It is not surprising that with such ideas and ambitions, she rejected a marriage proposal from Rollin Salisbury, a bright, hard-working Beloit geology student she had met through George.

George also found himself increasingly attracted to his slim, highly intelligent and articulate 19-year-old stepsister. Jane had always thought of George as her brother and herself as a "loving sister" (the words she used in signing her letters to him), and found his attempts to put their relationship on a romantic level troubling as well as embarrassing. Had she entertained any romantic feelings toward George or Rollin, her firm intent to pursue a career outside the home made marriage impossible. She had only to look at the two dedicated Rockford teachers who were tearfully leaving the seminary to marry.

Classmate Corinne Douglas (who later founded a girls' technical school in Georgia) described Jane as she was reaching the end of her senior year at Rockford:

> I see her as plainly now as though it were but yesterday. The brown hair drawn back, with a decided inclination, never encouraged, to fall apart on the side, the chin raised, the head slightly bent to one side, the face turned at an angle to me as she gave her attention to the speaker. . . We never speculated as to why we liked to go to her room so that it was always crowded when the sacred 'Engaged' sign was not hung out. We just knew there was always something 'doing' where she was, and however mopey it might be elsewhere there was intellectual ozone in her vicinity.

Throughout her four years at Rockford Jane was a faithful correspondent, sending accounts of her days to her family and friends. Her correspondence from Rockford ended with a final letter to her father:

> Our class appointments have been decided, the 2nd honor or salutatorian is Nora Frothingham, the valedictorian is your most humble servant and most loving daughter. Do not think I am puffed up. I too well realize how little it is worth or signifies though my ground of satisfaction is that I hope the home folks will be pleased. . .
> I am engaged just now in antiquarian efforts to dig up

from my brain a deep and mature (?) graduating essay, the result has not been extremely flattering but as there is no haste I calmly wait for an inspiration.

As there are such marked differences in the finances of the class members it seems positively necessary to have our [commencement] gowns alike. I never realized before how paramount a girl's interest in dress is in excess to all others and never in my class Presidency have I made such mighty efforts to keep some kind of peace and order. We have finally worked it down to this, that they shall be white and the entire outfit including gloves, shoes, purse shall come within twenty five dollars. One always finds a great deal in books about the hopes and fears of the last half of the last term of school life. I think I am beginning to realize it. . .

As a freshman Jane had written in her journal: "Always do what you are afraid to do." Three years later she modified her prescription: "To do what you are afraid to do is to guide your life by fear. How much better not to be afraid to do what you believe in doing! Keep one main idea and you will never be lost."

It was that urgency toward action that led her to say, as she and Nora were preparing their commencement speeches, "Nora, when we speak we must say something!"

Jane stood at the podium that day looking — according to yet another male admirer — slight, pale, spirited and charming. She focused her talk on Cassandra and her prophesy that the Greeks would be victorious. "But the brave warriors laughed to scorn the beautiful prophetess and called her mad. The frail girl stood conscious of Truth, but she had no logic to convince the impatient defeated warriors, and no facts to gain their confidence. She could assert and proclaim until at last in sooth she becomes mad." This, Jane proposed, was the tragedy of Cassandra and of most women, "to be right and always to be disbelieved and rejected."

She spoke of women's unique gift of intuition, striking a theme which would run through many of her later speeches, particularly those on the brutality and waste of war. Intuition, she said, endows women with "an accurate perception of Truth and Justice which rests contented in itself and will make no effort to confirm itself, or to organize through existing knowledge."

The special task of women then, is to gain the right to speak and demonstrate that intuition is a pathway to truth. But women must use their other talents as well. "Let her not sit and dreamily watch her child," Jane said. "Let her work her way to a sentient idea that shall sway and ennoble those around her. All that subtle force among women which is now dream fancy, might be changed into creative genius."

She concluded with words which Nora Frothingham said "some of us have remembered and kept as a heritage all through the years":

> We have expressed to each other higher and nobler things than we have probably ever said to any one else, and these years of young life being past, better perhaps than we shall say again. We stand united today in a belief in beauty, genius and courage and that these expressed through truest womanhood can yet transform the world.

A year later Jane was informed that Rockford Female Seminary had become a degree-granting institution and she was invited to attend the 1882 spring graduation at which she would be awarded one of the school's first Bachelor of Arts degrees.

Though weak from an illness that had plagued her all spring, Jane attended the commencement ceremony. Her certificate from the seminary a year earlier had been made out to Laura Jane Addams. Now both she and her school had come of age. Rockford Female Seminary would be officially known as Rockford College, and she was Jane Addams. She never used the name Laura again.

Chapter 4

Rudderless Years

*J*ane and many of her ambitious, forward-looking sister graduates encountered something akin to culture shock when they left Rockford Female Seminary and returned to their families. Their dreams of a life of activity and achievement in the greater world were regarded as inappropriate, even harmful, and were often taken no more seriously by their families than had been their desire to transcend reality into DeQuincey-like ecstasy. Behave, was the message they were given. Put silly dreams behind you and take your proper place in the drawing room and nursery.

"But what shall I do, Papa?" questioned one seminary graduate overcome with ennui upon her return home.

"Do, my dear! Do?" answered her father. "Well, suppose you *do* me a worsted dog on a pair of slippers."

Jane had left Rockford, bent on earning a B.A. degree from Smith in the fall (she had no way of knowing this would become unnecessary), and then going on to medical school. She reasoned that she enjoyed science and as a qualified doctor would be able to work with the poor. Once in Cedarville, however, she felt sapped of energy and purpose. Her spirit and body dragged.

Critical of Jane's intention to pursue a career, Anna Addams did not take well to family members doing other than what she planned for them. Her disapproval of women who sought a professional life made it difficult for Jane not to harbor resentment toward her. Tension, beneath the surface but palpable, began to replace the good will that had prevailed between Jane and her stepmother.

Nor could Jane count on support from her father. In the diary of his trip west as a young husband, John Addams had commented that "upon Canada's shore a feeling of derision crosses one's mind thinking that all this country is subject to the government of a *Woman*, for republicans this will not do." Possibly John Addams had softened his views since that early diary entry, but probably not enough to embrace Jane's plan to attend Smith. As a child Jane had suffered at the merest hint of disapproval from her father. Maturity had not granted her immunity in that regard. After being virtually free of back pain during her college years, she was home only a few weeks before suffering a relapse.

Was it but a month ago that she had confidently called on her Rockford sisters to help transform the world? Her journal from her college years was filled with quotations that dwelt on grand achievement, noble character and fulfillment of one's destiny:

> If the Spring puts forth no blossims [sic] in summer there would be no beauty, in autumn no fruit. So if youth be trifled away without improvement manhood will be contemptible, old age miserable.

> Deeds make habits, habits make character, character makes destiny!

> Never mind trifles in this world, a man must be either an anvil or a hammer.

> For ourselves who perfer [sic] martyrdom to success John Brown is greater than Washington.

But action of grand import was hard to come upon in Cedarville. To make things even more difficult, a tragedy that shook the country took an extra toll on Jane. On July 2, 1881, Julius Guiteau, a mentally disturbed young man and the stepbrother of Jane's closest Cedarville friend, Flora Guiteau, shot President James Garfield in a Washington, D. C. railroad station. Garfield died some weeks later. The senior Guiteau was a cashier in John Addams' Freeport bank and his children, Julius included, had often visited the Addams home.

John Addams had been planning to travel to Wisconsin that summer to explore the possibility of investing in copper mines. Weary of Cedarville's obsession with Julius Guiteau, and thinking that a change of scenery might lift Jane's spirits, he added vacation time to his business trip and invited his wife and daughter to accompany him.

It was rugged country. After a particularly strenuous exploration of a Lake Superior mine, John Addams, not a man to complain, reported feeling sudden, intense stomach pain. Seriously alarmed, Anna Addams and Jane managed to get him to a hospital in Green Bay. Some 36 hours later, John Addams, 59 years old, died of a ruptured appendix.

Mourned by hundreds of neighbors and friends, "the kind gentleman of the district," as one old-timer described him, was buried on August 24, 1881, in a sheltered cemetery close to the Addams home. Nearby was the forest of Norway pine planted with the seed the young bridegroom had brought from Pennsylvania. As the trees had flourished in the new land, so had John Addams. None of the mourners gathered in the cemetery that sunny afternoon could believe that so vital and powerful a man had been struck down so swiftly.

Jane felt severed from her roots. At her feet were her mother's gravestone and the miniature grave markers of her four infant brothers and sisters. The stone marking the grave of her lovely sister, Martha, still looked painfully new. And now, beside her mother's grave, the grave of her father, the upturned earth a wound in the summer grass.

Ten days had passed since her father's funeral before Jane was able to write to Ellen. "I will not write of myself or how purposeless and without ambition I am. Only prepare yourself so you won't be too disappointed in me when you come. The greatest sorrow that can ever come to me has past [sic] and I hope it is only a question of time until I get my moral purposes straightened."

Jane, always her own severest critic, focused her letter on her shameful lack of moral direction and purpose, not on her numbing grief. Her self-esteem, so robust during those years when she generated "intellectual ozone" at Rockford, was all but demolished. Ellen knew her friend well. She wrote back, assuring Jane that she was too much like her father for her moral purpose to have been permanently shaken.

A month later, eager to leave a house where the light no longer shone in her father's study, Jane packed her bags and left for the Women's Medical College of Philadelphia. Anna Addams' eldest son as well as her two brothers were physicians; she agreed that if Jane insisted on a career, medicine was probably the most practical (as well as prestigious) choice.

But Jane found little pleasure in medical studies. Pondering the structure of the nervous system was very different than analyzing a Shakespeare play. Under severe self-pressure to make a career decision, she had either repressed or discounted the fact that, as she later wrote in *Twenty Years*, she had none of the talent for science that George, now a student in biology at Johns Hopkins University, possessed.

> In the long vacations I pressed plants, stuffed birds and pounded rocks in some vague belief that I was approximating the new method, and yet when my stepbrother who was becoming a real scientist, tried to carry me along with him into the merest outskirts of the methods of research, it at once became evident that I had no aptitude and was unable to follow intelligently Darwin's careful observations on the earthworm. I made an heroic effort, although candor compels me to state that I never would have finished if I had not been

pulled and pushed by my really ardent companion, who in addition to a multitude of earthworms and a fine microscope, possessed untiring tact with one of flagging zeal.

Though Jane earned passing grades her first semester, her back pain became so intense that she was forced to leave school and enter the S. Weir Mitchell Hospital of Orthopedic and Nervous Diseases. Dr. Mitchell, while tending wounded soldiers during the Civil War, had witnessed repeatedly how a soldier's stressed mental state could wreak havoc with his body. When he returned to private practice he developed a treatment for women incapacitated by nervous exhaustion — six weeks of complete rest at his hospital, designed among other things to remove patients from over-protective, demanding families. When a patient recovered, which a great number did, Dr. Mitchell's advice was unequivocal — go out into the world, find challenging, useful activity, and ignore family demands that may well have been the cause of your illness in the first place.

Stories, like so many butterflies, hover around individuals as colorful as S. Weir Mitchell, a gifted doctor *and* an author of romance novels. One such story concerned a woman well enough to leave the hospital who stubbornly refused to do so, whereupon the good doctor entered her room and began to unbutton his suit jacket. "Get out of bed by the time I count five or I'll get in there with you," he boomed. The shocked woman vacated the bed with astonishing speed.

No such threat from Dr. Mitchell was needed to get Jane out of bed. Years later, she was to write about college women pulled between family demands and their own desire to accomplish something in the world: "When her health gives way under this strain, as it often does, her physician invariably advises a rest. But to be put to bed and fed on milk is not what she requires. What she needs is simple, health-giving activity, which involves the use of all faculties." Denied this, the young woman "loses something vital out of her life which she is entitled to. She is restricted and unhappy: her elders, meanwhile, are unconscious of the situation, and we have all the elements of a tragedy."

Home again in Cedarville, Jane gave up all thought of returning to the uncongenial demands of medical school. But how was she to follow her own prescription for health-giving activity? Within weeks her back pain returned. Her frustration was so great that when her surgeon brother-in-law volunteered to correct the curvature in her spine, she agreed even though the procedure was new, painful, and gave no assurance of success. Whatever the cost, she had to get on with her life.

Fortunately, the surgery went well and Dr. Haldeman pronounced the operation successful. Much to Jane's distress, however, he prescribed six months of total bedrest. Invited to stay at Alice and Harry's home during the long convalescence, Jane had to muster all her strength to avoid despair at another prolonged convalescence. From her comfortable bedroom in the Haldeman home she wrote to Ellen at the Kirkland School:

> My dear friend,
>
> I remember that all the letters that Dr. Johnson wrote during the year 1783 contain minute accounts of his asthma and the fifty ounces of lost blood. You doubtless retain, as I do, a very dreary impression of these same letters. . .
>
> You see the analogy. . . I steadily resolved during the next six months to write no letters. I was maybe a little ashamed to show to my good friends against what lassitude, and melancholy. . . I am struggling. I have had the kindest care and am emerging with a straight back and a fresh hold on life and endeavor. The first thing I thoroughly undertake will be a course of Homer. I will begin my reformation as Erasmus did his. One of the many results which I hope to find from this long seclusion is that it has brought me back to Books to find more comfort and steadiness than I have discovered in reading for the last two years. . . Alas! my friend that is the saddest result of our lack of intercourse — that I no longer feel sure of what you have read or thought.
>
> My plans for the winter are immature. I probably won't be

strong enough to do much of anything.

In addition to the reading Jane did, she and Alice read Northcote's *Life of Joshua Reynolds* together as well as the biographies of many of Reynolds' bright friends until their enthusiasm was "quenched as in a bog and we stopped in the midst of Cumberland." Jane gravitated toward biography, fascinated by the heroic dimension of human nature. One person of noble mind and right intent could achieve so much!

She passed some of her most pleasant hours reading to her nieces and nephews. James Weber Linn, the most avid of her fans, recalled his "Auntie Jane" reading fairy tales to him as he sat by her bedside. A favorite was the tale of the princess and the frog. "What thou has promised thou must perform!" said the King to his daughter, words that Linn says have echoed in his ears ever since.

When Harry Haldeman at last released Jane from bed he fitted her with a corset of his own design which she was to wear for an entire year. Imprisoned in that cage of steel and whalebone, Jane rode the train back to Cedarville and reported that the corset "pounded and rubbed all the way. I did not have a backache. . . so I guess we can call it a success, although I do hope it will grow more comfortable than it is today." After a few weeks at the Homestead Jane wrote to Alice:

> I want Harry to know the many compliments I get on my improved health and appearance. . . I can do a great many things without getting tired which last summer should have used me up completely and now are a pleasure to undertake. For all of which I shall always feel indebted to you and Harry.

But the Homestead, so long a haven for Jane, now echoed with emptiness. She missed her father dreadfully and at the same time was shamed by the thought of how disappointed he would have been had he seen her in her present state. She attempted to get involved in running the Homestead but did it poorly. And for whom was she running it? She, her stepmother and George, on his occasional visits, were a rather grim trio around the dinner table. Jane's relationship with George had become delicate to negotiate, especially under the watchful eye of Anna Addams, who took few pains to be discreet about her desire for Jane and George to marry.

During these troubled times Jane and Ellen sent tender, heartfelt, sometimes effusive letters to each other.

> My dear friend [Jane wrote], I was very much delighted and comforted to receive your picture. Nothing has pleased me so much for a long time. I have stationed it where I can see you almost any minute I am in the house and the feel of its being there makes a great difference to me.

Ellen responded immediately:

> I received your sweet letter this afternoon, so thoughtful of others and so forgetful of yourself that it was just the sort of reproach to me that I happened to need just now. You make me ashamed that I ever allow myself to fall into a frame of mind to question whether what we get out of existence is worth the trouble it is to exist — as if that were the question at all. My dear, I won't say I admire you for that is a cold word. You have too little vanity to care for admiration but I love you more the longer. . . I know you. . . I will say that I do take it as a strong proof of friendship from you that you write to me in the midst of your troubles and for that reason your letter is a deep pleasure as well as a pain.

Adoring letters such as these were not unusual between close women friends during the 18th and early 19th centuries. The Victorian conception of love between persons of the same sex is difficult to understand by an age immersed in Freud. "Where Victorians saw a beautiful friendship," wrote author Gordon Haight, "the modern reader assumed homosexuality." Who else was there to whom Ellen and Jane could express their deepest feelings than to each other?

In yet another letter Ellen spoke of being "under the weather" and passing some time by rummaging through "the relics of our teens":

> I found your paper on Macbeth and the first half of it seems to me as fine as anything I have ever read on the subject. . . I think you get a good deal tangled up in the last half. . . I also found 'One Office of Nature.' My dear, it is exquisite. I showed it to Miss K. . . She said to me afterward, 'If your friend could write that at nineteen I should think she could write books now.' I said to her, 'If my friend's body had been equal to her mind and if a great many demands on the strength of both hadn't come to her which do not come to most people she would have done a good many remarkable things which the Lord doesn't seem to have intended her to do.'

Jane resisted Ellen's attempt to pacify her for accomplishing nothing. "Failure through ill health is just as culpable and miserable as failure through any other cause. . . I have been idle for two years just because I had not enough vitality to be anything else. . ."

When Jane's distraught sister-in-law, Laura, wrote that Weber had had a mental breakdown, Jane rushed to their home outside Cedarville and soon became the unhappy family's caretaker and business manager. "We have been in the midst of perplexity and a peculiar kind of trouble," she wrote to Ellen. "I have been with my brother Weber almost all the time for this last month. He is now in the hospital for the insane in Elgin and so am relieved from all personal care but we all feel more or less the strain we have been under. I shall stay for some weeks at least with his wife. She needs comfort and help and there is a great deal of business to see to."

Jane also had her own business affairs to manage. She had inherited land as well as stocks and bonds from her father. Although grateful that the legacy would provide her with a modest income for life, she was compelled to spend so much time on financial chores that she confided to Ellen her concern that she "would lose all hold of the softer graces and refinements, but shall always come to you to find them and be cheered up." When life was at last stabilized in Weber's family, Jane, anxious for activity and a change of scene, decided to follow the advice of her Uncle Harry (John Harrison Weber, one of her mother's brothers) and tour Europe. Such a trip had also been part of her father's plan for her following graduation from Rockford.

It was not as total an escape as Jane might have wanted. Anna Addams planned to accompany her, along with Anna's niece and other friends who would be joining them on the way. The intention was to stay abroad for two years, not unusual in the 1880s, when nine days were consumed crossing the Atlantic and many more in traveling from one European country to another. Though still corseted in whalebone and steel, Jane seemed well and happy, according to her Uncle Harry and George Haldeman, both of whom had traveled to Philadelphia to see Anna and Jane off on August 22, 1883.

Pleased to be embarking on the trip, Jane nevertheless felt a vague uneasiness about "spending two years drinking up the culture of the Old World, like any Daisy Miller." (As it turned out, Henry James was a fellow passenger. "I look at [him] most of the time between courses at table," Jane wrote to her sister, "he is very English in appearance, but not especially keen or intellectual.") To Ellen she wrote: "People complain of losing spiritual life when abroad. . . I imagine it will be quite as hard to hold to full earnestness of purpose."

But once on the ship, Jane felt wonderfully free of worry and doubt. She wrote an exuberant letter to Alice:

> We are off and moving away from N.Y. harbor. My last impression of America was the big, beautiful majestic Brooklyn Bridge. I was choked up of course and wept the regulation weep at the last minute, but I am all right now. George and Uncle Harry waved us off. . . I hope you are feeling as cheerful as we do. The salt breeze acts on me like magic and the party are jolly and good natured. Write as often as you can dear.

Chapter 5

The "Scheme"

*I*n her 22 months abroad, Jane was an avid tourist and student. Whatever back pain she suffered did not keep her from making the "grand tour" of Ireland, Scotland, England, France, Holland, Germany, Austria, Italy, Switzerland, Greece, and then back again to London and Paris. She was a prolific writer, keeping notes in her journals and composing detailed letters, eight and ten pages long, to Alice, Mary and Weber. She wrote feverishly, frequently staying up half the night, trying to attain some sense of purpose by carefully documenting what she saw of the great art of Europe, the museums, castles, cathedrals, towns and countrysides, as well as the people whose lives she glimpsed. The paralyzing inertia she had been fighting for two years was replaced with a voracious energy to see and experience everything.

She wrote to Mary about her visit to George Herbert's old church in Winchester, painting an idyllic picture of a building surrounded by trees, set back from a lawn sloping into a branch of the Avon River where Isaac Walton once fished. In contrast to the tranquil Avon scene was the wretchedness of East London, imprinted on her mind so sharply that she was able to describe it in detail 26 years later:

A small party of tourists were taken to the East End by a city missionary to witness the Saturday night sale of decaying vegetables and fruit. . . On Mile End Road, from the top of an omnibus which paused at the end of a dingy street lighted by only occasional flares of gas, we saw two huge masses of ill-clad people clamoring around two huckster's carts. They were bidding their farthings and ha'pennies for a vegetable held up by the auctioneer, which he at last scornfully flung, with a jibe for its cheapness, to the successful bidder. In the momentary pause only one man detached himself from the groups. He had bidden on a cabbage, and when it struck his hand, he instantly sat down on the curb, tore it with his teeth, and hastily devoured it, unwashed and uncooked as it was. . . I have never since been able to see a number of hands held upward, even if they are moving rhythmically in a calisthenics exercise or when they belong to a class of chubby children without a certain revival of this memory, a clutching of the heart reminiscent of the despair and resentment which seized me then.

For the following weeks I went about London almost furtively, afraid to look down narrow streets and alleys lest they disclose again this hideous need and suffering.

As captivated as Jane might have been by the beauty of a country landscape, she could not dispel the cloud that darkened her spirits upon witnessing so much dehumanizing poverty. One of her earliest entries about Blarney Castle in Ireland read: "Owner said to have an income of thirteen thousand pounds a year; ordinary man six shillings a week; could not kiss the Blarney stone, though the castle is very beautiful." Another about Dunloe Pass: ". . . a black valley where the sun does not shine for three months in the year. The poor people have only land enough to raise hay and potatoes. Some of the houses have no windows, and I was told 'they don't need to see in the winters, ma'm, they can sit in the dark.' "

She was particularly sensitive to the quality of women's lives:

We spent last Sunday on the Island of Capri. . . The town and hotels are built up on the saddle and everyone reaches them on donkey back. The donkeys are about as big as good sized rabbits and each has two women to take care of it (and collect the fare-pennies for their trouble). These women carry all the baggage on their heads and even good-sized trunks and are descended from the women who carried all the stones for the villas above, from the sea shore, stone by stone, on their heads. The men are all engaged in corral fishing and go for long cruises, and these black eyed women seem to take care of everything.

In Saxe-Coburg, Germany, Jane was looking out upon the town square from her hotel window when she saw women

crossing and recrossing [the square] in a single file with semicircular heavy wooden tanks fastened upon their backs. They were carrying in this primitive fashion to a remote cooling room these tanks filled with a hot brew incident to one stage of beer making. The women were bent forward, not only under the weight which they were bearing, but because the tanks were so high that it would have been impossible for them to have lifted their heads. Their faces and hands, reddened in the cold morning air, showed clearly the white scars where they had previously been scalded by the hot stuff which splashed if they stumbled ever so little on their way.

Hurrying down to the square, Jane charged the owner of the brewery with treating the women as if they were no better than animals. He glanced at her with "exasperating indifference." She could do nothing but return to the hotel dispirited by the reality that the misery of the poor was accepted as a fact of life. Her moral discomfort, like an incipient headache, grew more intense. She was doing nothing day after day but practicing Italian, German and French, attending concerts, and visiting cathedrals and art museums, all in the cause of acquiring culture.

"There is every temptation while abroad to play the dilettante," she wrote to George, "and many of the people we meet are disappointing on that very account. You doubt whether any good is accomplished in placing yourself as a mere spectator to the rest of the world."

In her letters to George, Jane was affectionate in a sisterly way. "My dear George," she wrote, "May I congratulate you on your birthday and wish you many happy returns of the happy day. I hope that Cedarville is looking as June-like and happy as Canterbury is this morning. . ." There is no record of George's letters in response. One can only speculate as to the complexity of Jane's feelings when George unexpectedly joined her and Anna in Europe for two months in the summer of 1884.

Reflecting in *Twenty Years* on her extended stay in Europe she wrote:

> [The] assumption [is] that the sheltered and educated girl has nothing to do with the bitter poverty and the social maladjustment which is all about her, and which, after all, cannot be concealed. . . [It] breaks through poetry and literature in a burning tide which overwhelms her; it peers at her in the form of the heavy-laden market women and underpaid street laborers, gibing her with a sense of her own uselessness.

After nearly two years abroad, Jane returned to Cedarville more confused and disheartened than when she left. In letters to Ellen she confided that while she might

> not have lost any positive ground, I have constantly lost confidence in myself, and have gained nothing and improved in nothing. . . I was absolutely at sea so far as any moral purpose was concerned, clinging only to the desire to live in a really living world and refusing to be content with a shadowy intellectual or aesthetic reflection of it.

Anna Addams decided to live temporarily in Baltimore in the fall of 1885 to be near George, an unfortunate decision as later events in George's life would prove. Lacking will of her own, and guilt-ridden by any failure to fulfill what was presented as a family obligation, Jane submitted to her stepmother's request to accompany her. It was a frustrating and largely profitless winter. Shying away from Anna's attempts to introduce her to Baltimore society, Jane sought refuge in lectures, and in an almost frantic reading of Goethe, Hawthorne, Tolstoy and George Eliot, though she wrote to Alice that her faculties had been paralyzed since she arrived in Baltimore.

Her account of her visit to a black orphanage revealed that her deep compassion for poor and abandoned people did not always immunize her against the conventional biases of the day. "They take little colored girls and keep them until they are fifteen, training them to be good servants, the children themselves expecting to be that and having an ambition for a good place. I heartily approve." While time spent with her stepmother's society friends left her exhausted and discontented, she felt invigorated by an afternoon spent in a shelter "talking with about sixteen old colored women, who are so interesting I mean to go to see them often."

Family problems as well as her own financial affairs continued to consume Jane's energies upon her return to Cedarville in the summer of 1886. Her brother was again in a mental hospital and after visiting him she went to Harvard, Illinois, for several weeks to help her overburdened and weakened sister Mary. Jane's letters to Alice show how deeply she had grown to love her nieces and nephews: "Stanley. . . suddenly transferred all his affections to me to my great delight. He gains on me every day. The baby sits alone in her high chair and is a vigorous little girl. . . Stanley sleeps with me and is so sweet and charming that it will be harder than ever to leave him."

Although she continued to do some reading, Jane relinquished any attempts at serious study.

> Mary and I read aloud some. . . I am afraid trying to study here would leave me with the same uneasy consciousness that I had not done what I came purposely to do, because I tried to do something else and failed in that. . . I am reading George Eliot's Daniel Deronda, was urged to read it from reading her life and am glad for what it gives me, her books give me more

motive power than any other books I read. . . I have begun to eat voraciously. I weigh 114 pounds, more than I have weighed since I was seventeen.

Jane berated herself for lacking the traditional domestic skills. She was not a good nurse and could not even sew a quilt. "I am afraid," she wrote to her stepmother from Mary's home, "I will never be the typical old maid." She did know how to knit, however, and managed with diligence to produce very credible tiny sweaters for her nieces and nephews. (One of these small garments is on display in the Jane Addams Room of the Cedarville Historical Museum.)

The news from Girard, Kansas, Harry and Alice's new home, compounded Jane's distress. Harry, besieged by restlessness, had given up medicine to become a banker and was having business troubles, while Alice was fighting unaccustomed ill health.

Anna Addams decided once again to follow her son to Baltimore in the fall and again requested that Jane accompany her. Jane had not will enough to refuse. Did Anna secretly hope that the proximity of Jane and George might serve to spark romance in the uncaptured heart of her stepdaughter? Jane was increasingly impatient with her stepmother's ill-concealed agenda. Years later, Weber Linn related a favorite story told by his aunt's friends: While visiting in Connecticut, Jane — now well into her sixties — met a psychic who claimed that if Jane would rest her hands on the table and remain quiet she would be empowered to hear a communication from the dead. Not since her embarrassing failure at Rockford to reach DeQuincey-like nirvana had Jane experimented with the supernatural. But, never having lost her youthful curiosity, she followed the psychic's instructions. A minute passed and then another and then the table began to shake under Jane's fingertips. "That must be my stepmother," she said with amusement. "She is still angry at me for not marrying George!"

Anna expected Jane to serve as her companion on a round of

concerts and museum visits, as well as to pay social calls. Jane again resisted, not always successfully, her stepmother's attempts to introduce her to the Johns Hopkins University society. No doubt the budding scientists found the pale, young woman with the soulful eyes as bewildering as she found them boring. The social evenings always left Jane feeling dispirited, restless, and "much disillusioned with the effect of intellectual pursuits upon moral development." Though she put up a good front in her letters to her sisters and brother, Jane expressed despair in her journal. "I seem," she wrote, "to have reached the nadir of my nervous depression and sense of maladjustment."

One can imagine her state of mind when back at the Homestead, for lack of an alternative, she imposed on herself a demanding study of European art, the only interest she had been able to keep alive since her trip abroad. Finally, her need to do something useful drove her to travel abroad again, but this time with the mission of securing for Rockford College reproductions of great European art. She had just been made a trustee of the College and had presented it with the largest gift it had ever received. She attempted to persuade Alice to accompany her, but after a delay of several weeks Alice replied that she would not be able to go. Jane wrote in response: "I had hoped in a fluttering sort of way that maybe your silence meant you were coming after all." Not wanting to travel alone, Jane invited both Ellen and Sarah Anderson, the Rockford Seminary teacher who had become her friend, to join her, offering to pay half their expenses.

On December 14, 1887, Jane and Sarah sailed for Europe; Ellen was to meet them in Germany. As Jane journeyed to Munich she was "quite impressed with the difference in my age and dignity between this trip and the one before." On the first trip she had been called Mademoiselle or Fraulein. She was now addressed as "Madame with the utmost respect and I felt perfectly at my ease and dignified all the time. . . I am enjoying it all so much better than before."

From Italy she wrote to Alice:

> We have had two days in Florence as restful and happy and sat-
> isfactory as possible. I have gotten much nearer the personali-
> ty and history of the city than I did before, doubtless because
> I am less eager and the absorbing thirst for information, so
> fatal to enjoyment, was allayed during the former sojourn. . .
> We drove to Galileo's tower yesterday afternoon and then
> walked back into the city between the glorious sunset and the
> moonlight. I was quite ready to endorse every extravagant
> thing ever sung or said of the Cathedral as we saw it glowing
> and reflecting the magnificent light. It was at this tower, you
> remember, that Galileo received a visit from Milton and the
> dazzling light was pathetic in its contrast to our thoughts of
> the two men, both persecuted and blind in their last years.

In the envelope of her letter she enclosed a pressed leaf that had
been lying at the base of Galileo's tower.

On the way to Munich Jane stopped to visit the great cathedral
at Ulm. She was fascinated to see, carved in stone, the names of the
Greek philosophers side by side with those of the Hebrew
prophets, and among the disciples and saints was the builder of
pagan temples. She stayed up in her hotel room that night, forget-
ful of time, writing about her hope for humanity which the Ulm
cathedral and its democratic host of stone carvings had finally
enabled her to articulate: that there be a "cathedral of humanity. . .
roomy enough to house a fellowship of purpose. . . beautiful
enough to persuade men to hold fast to the vision of human solidarity." Equality, unity, solidarity. Those words, a legacy from her
father and Abraham Lincoln, rang for Jane that night with the puri-
ty of bird song.

But the long hand of family reached across the ocean to shatter
Jane's hard won equilibrium. In Rome she received a letter from
Alice telling her that Mary's small daughter had died of whooping
cough. Grief-stricken, Jane composed long letters to both her sisters
and brother.

> The time I was abroad before I worried so much about frail lit-
> tle Stanley. . . but Mary [Jr.] was always so strong and sturdy
> and happy that I never dreamed I should not see her again. . .
> I shall always be glad that I was with the dear little girl as much
> as I was last spring and have a distinct picture of her baby-
> hood. It makes me feel very insecure about all of the other
> children.

Yet another piece of information from Alice chilled what had
been Jane's fragile good spirits. George, suffering from an onset of
severe anxiety and depression, had left Johns Hopkins and returned
to the Homestead. Marcet Haldeman, Alice and Harry's only child,
wrote in *Jane Addams As I Knew Her*, a memoir published in 1936,
that George had been in the midst of an intense and stressful period of post-graduate study at Johns Hopkins when his marriage proposal to Jane was rejected. "He was so torn within himself and for
the moment so indifferent to life that he neglected to take the usual
precautions necessary to his work. Brain and body collapsed."
According to Alice, George had walked out of the Homestead,
telling no one that he was leaving, and had been missing for over a
week. The *Freeport Weekly Democrat* carried several articles about his
disappearance, reporting that he "was morbidly sensitive in regard
to the matter of his dependence." Jane wrote to Alice:

> I am dreadfully sorry for George and for his mother too. The
> touch of the melodramatic is so much unlike George that the
> poor fellow must have suffered desperately before he would
> do it. I am not in the least afraid of suicide, he is too good a
> man for that — but he could easily yield to exposure and dis-
> tress and would consider himself justified in that before he
> would do anything he considered dishonorable as stealing for
> rides or food.
>   I fairly weep when I think of his anguish and distress of
> mind. I have seen him depressed. The walking and moving
> about is good for him in a certain way I suppose, if he has
> food enough to endure it on.

While struggling with sorrow over her niece's death and her

stepbrother's illness, Jane succumbed to a severe attack of sciatica. Again she was faced with the hated necessity of complete bedrest. Ellen nursed her for a month, after which Jane insisted that she and Sarah continue on to Naples and Pompeii without her. Ellen resisted but finally, defeated by her friend's determination, acquiesced on the condition that she inform the Addams family of Jane's sickness.

Upon receiving a prompt letter from Weber expressing his brotherly concern, Jane responded:

> Your kind letter cheered me in the midst of my sciatica and remained under my pillow during the monotonous days I spent in bed. . . The kind hearted English rector assured me that half the people in Rome are suffering from rheumatism and neuralgia and that it was the worst winter Italy had for years, so that I haven't even the satisfaction of being unique in my affliction.

Jane was relieved but not heartened to learn that after a week's search by the Freeport sheriff and Harry Haldeman, George was found in ragged clothes and torn shoes walking along the road two and a half miles east of Waterloo, Iowa. When questioned by the sheriff as to the cause of his leaving, George said simply that he had had a little "tiff" with his mother.

Finally well enough to travel, Jane joined Ellen and Sarah in Spain and the three friends did what every tourist in Madrid feels obliged to do — attend a bullfight. Ellen and Sarah were revolted after the killing of one bull, and left the arena. Jane stayed on to witness the slaying of five more bulls. In a letter to her sister-in-law Laura she described the colorful spectacle:

> In the second act, men bewilder the bull with their bright red cloaks and are very graceful and brilliant with a suggestion of danger. The bandilleros who struck the victim with the gaily decorated little swords were apparently in greater danger than the matador himself who did not come in until the bull was so tired out that it was a comparatively easy matter to kill by one clean stroke in its spinal cord. . . The immense audience was

either wild with delight or uproarious with hisses every minute even throwing hats and oranges at the head of our awkward matador. . . I think I would rather not have the children of the family know of the bullfight.

Ellen and Sarah's surprise that she had watched the cruel spectacle for so long caused Jane to ponder her reaction to the brutality played out before her. She concluded that she had been so caught up recalling the great amphitheater in ancient Rome where Christian gladiators gallantly faced martyrdom, that she had not registered the utter cruelty of inciting a bull to anger and then slaughtering it. "The natural and inevitable reaction came," Jane later recalled, "and in deep chagrin I felt myself tried and condemned, not only by the disgusting experience but by the entire moral situation which it revealed."

In the aftermath of her first European trip Jane had "gradually reached the conviction that the first generation of college women had developed too exclusively the power of acquiring knowledge and of merely receiving impressions, that somewhere in the process of being educated they had lost that simple and almost automatic response to the human appeal." Now she unhappily included herself among those "immunized" young women.

"Nothing less than the moral reaction following the experience at a bull-fight had been able to reveal to me that so far from following in the wake of a chariot of philanthropic fire, I had been tied to the tail of the veriest ox-cart of self-seeking." Jane judged herself harshly for having "fallen into the meanest type of self-deception" by accepting the rationalization that all "this travel and study was in preparation for great things to come" — she, who was so determined to see life as it was lived, not as a shadowy reflection!

In *Twenty Years*, Jane wrote:

It is hard to tell when the very simple plan which afterward developed into the Settlement began to form itself in my mind. It may have been even before I went to Europe for the second time, but I gradually became convinced that it would be a good thing to rent a house in a part of the city where many primitive and actual needs are found, in which young women who had been given over too exclusively to study, might restore a balance of activity along traditional lines and learn of life from life itself, where they might try out some of the things they had been taught. . . I do not remember to have mentioned this plan to any one until we reached Madrid in April, 1888.

So it was that the Madrid bullfight became the match that ignited kindling already in place. "I had made up my mind," Jane wrote, "that I would begin to carry out the plan if only by talking about it." Ellen was the person to whom Jane "stumblingly" talked. Intrigued and desiring a change in her own life, Ellen agreed to work with Jane on what the two friends came to call the "scheme." By the time Jane and Ellen left Spain, "the scheme had become convincing and tangible, though hazy in detail."

Jane went on to London (Ellen was obliged to return briefly to Italy) to devote six weeks to studying missions and reading about the growing social reform movement in England. She wrote to Alice that she had become "quite learned about foreign missions and ashamed of my former ignorance. . . I like the mission side of London. . . It is the most interesting side it has." She visited the People's Palace, an institution inspired by Walter Besant's book, *All Sorts and Conditions of Men*, which proposed establishing a place where working class people could come for educational and recreational activities. But the institution that most interested her was Toynbee Hall, the world's first settlement house, named after Arnold Toynbee (uncle of the renowned historian of the same name), a zealous young social reformer who had worked in the Whitechapel district and died at age 31, "extending himself beyond his capacity to help the desperate poor."

Four-year-old Toynbee Hall, headed by its spiritual leader, Canon Barnett, was the home of 15 Oxford graduates who carried out the Canon's belief that to help the poor you must live with them and be available for all manner of daily needs and weekly crises. The fact that Toynbee Hall's workers were university men particularly interested Jane, and she secured an introduction to Canon Barnett to visit the Settlement (so named because the workers settled there) to learn what she could. On the appointed day in June, with the "scheme" alive as fire in her mind, Jane climbed down from the Whitechapel bus, crossed the battered brick yard to "the big house among all the horrid little ones," and knocked on the heavy wooden door of Toynbee Hall.

Chapter 6

"Bien. We Take a House!"

*H*enrietta Barnett, known as the "wife of Toynbee Hall," recognized in Jane Addams a kindred soul. She and Canon Barnett took pains to show their earnest guest the workings of their settlement. If, as a letter to Alice seems to indicate, Jane spent a number of days in Whitechapel, she had time to familiarize herself with Toynbee Hall and observe how Barnett's principles were put into action. Nothing of significance could occur between people, Barnett contended, unless a spirit of friendship existed. To that end he counseled that their Whitechapel neighbors be helped "one by one." In addition, Toynbee Hall's 15 residents became actively engaged in the life of the community, conducting a wide variety of evening classes, aiding teachers in the overcrowded elementary schools, and serving on committees of local charity organizations.

"The most interesting thing I have done in London was a visit to the Toynbee Hall in the East End," Jane wrote to Alice. "It is a community of university men who live there, have their recreating clubs and society all among the poor people yet in the same style they would in their own circle. It is so far from professional 'doing good,' so unaffectedly sincere and so productive of good results in its classes and libraries that it seems perfectly ideal."

Before Jane could move to Chicago, the chosen location for the "scheme," she had to resolve her affairs in Cedarville. The task turned out to be fraught with tension and self-doubt. Jane had to steel herself against her family's claims and skepticism. Alice was able to fathom what Jane was about and lend some measure of support, but Mary regarded Jane's plan with more concern than interest. Anna Addams considered the proposed departure to be little short of betrayal and her two sons were totally unsympathetic: George dismissed the scheme as impractical and urged Jane to stop "frolicking with Liberalism," while Harry scoffed at yet another of Jane's lapses into sentimentality.

In January 1889, after promising Ellen that she would be joining her soon, Jane wrote:

> I was quite sure I would be in Chicago Saturday but simply can't leave Stanley, the little fellow has been threatened with diphtheria and looks like a ghost. I owe so much to Mary in so many tender ways that I feel now as if I ought to stay. I know you disapprove, dear heart, and I appreciate your disapproval, I disapprove myself in a measure, but 'God has made me so' I suppose. Don't scold me, dear. . . Let's love each other through thick and thin and work out a salvation.

It is interesting to speculate what John Addams would have thought about Jane's scheme. It is likely he would have opposed his daughter stepping outside the prescribed domestic role to join men in the larger world. And what a world she would choose — the six teeming miles on Halsted Street between the river and the stockyards. Would Jane, so dependent on her father's approval, have been able to hold to her plan had he lived to oppose it?

Ironically, it may have been John Addams' death that made it possible for Jane to cut herself loose from Cedarville. As it was, without the passionate and unflagging support of Ellen buttressing her against "the family claim," the scheme may well have remained another abandoned dream. ("It is difficult for the family to regard the daughter other than as a family possession," Jane was to write some years later.)

Anna probably managed nothing more than a chilly farewell to her stepdaughter. It is sad to think of what George must have been feeling — whether his dark cloud grew darker still as Jane closed the door of the Homestead behind her. As Jane later confided to Alice, "I can't help worrying about those two." She must have been relieved when later that year her stepmother took into her home a 12-year-old town girl, Mary Fry, whose mother had recently died. Mary became devoted to her mistress and lived at the Homestead until Anna died at age 91. In turn, Anna was generous to her young caretaker and eventually paid for Mary's tuition to Shimer College as well as Mary's brother's tuition to medical school.

Ellen had found for their base of operations an apartment on Washington Street. Chicago had just built an opulent opera house and plans were underway to erect the largest office building in the country, as well as a stately public library ornamented with intricate mosaic and Tiffany glass. But like a child grown to adolescence too quickly, Chicago was in many ways untamed, crude and brutal. Businessmen competed with each other by lowering wages and prices. Employees were thought of as no more than cogs in the manufacturing wheel, and it was a rare employer who concerned himself with working conditions. While grand stores were built along Michigan Avenue (one displayed overcoats in its window with the advertisement, "Every millionaire owns one"), just a few blocks away foul, crowded tenements housed immigrants who could barely afford the cheapest of outer clothing.

Lincoln Steffens, veteran muckraker, described Chicago as "first in violence, deepest in dirt, loud, lawless, unlovely, ill smelling, criminally wide open, commercially brazen, socially thoughtless and raw," — certainly not a place hospitable to the poor and uprooted. Fleeing famine in Ireland, military service in Germany, persecution in Russia, the immigrants poured into Chicago dreaming of making a life of security and dignity. Instead, they found jobs that paid subsistence wages, dangerous working conditions, gloomy tenement flats and streets flowing with disease-ridden water.

Jane and Ellen plunged eagerly into the task of securing support for the scheme. The years of enforced bed rest and dreary, useless activity still fresh in her mind, Jane had been deadly serious when she wrote to Ellen that the Settlement could be their salvation. She set a demanding schedule for herself, sometimes attending three meetings of prospective supporters during the day and another in the evening. Starting with the contacts Ellen had made while teaching at the Kirkland School, Jane and Ellen visited missions, churches and social clubs, met with businessmen, academics, clergymen and women from the many philanthropic clubs — anyone who might be helpful or sympathetic to their cause.

Jane wrote weekly letters to her sisters and brother to keep them informed of her progress. Her letters often numbered a dozen handwritten pages, and she would ask that the recipient send it on to another member of the family. On February 12, 1889, soon after she arrived in Chicago, Jane wrote to Mary:

My Dear Mary,
    Your kind letter came Saturday morning at the same time with one from Weber and one from Alice. I sat down to read them and made myself late for an appointment with the Clybourne Ave. Mission but they so filled my heart with happiness and good will that it was well worth being late. So many things keep happening and the plan is rolling at such a cheerful pace, as Ellen says, that it is hard to keep you all informed . . . In the first place Mrs. Beveridge has been exceedingly kind to me and I will always feel indebted to her. Moreover she believes in the scheme. She came to lunch with me on Thursday and in the afternoon we called together first on Mrs. Sears whom I had met the day before at the Industrial Arts Society and who is quite determined to have me elected a member of the "Woman's Club" to vivify them as she says and then we met an appointment Mrs. Beveridge had made for me with Mr. Swift, the Swift of the Armour Mission. . .
    I met the entire board of the Armour Mission. . . A Mr. Pond waxed enthusiastic. . . he assured me that I had voiced

something hundreds of young people in the city were trying to express and that he would send us three young ladies at once who possessed both money and a knowledge of Herbert Spencer's 'Sociology' but who were dying from inaction and restlessness.

Jane and Ellen were most impressed by the range of work undertaken by the Armour Mission. It ran a kindergarten, a nursery, a kitchen garden and a great variety of educational classes. The Armour missionaries encouraged the two women to locate their settlement nearby so that each might benefit from the other's work, but one of their staunchest supporters opposed settling near the Armour Mission. "There was plenty going on around there," he said, "and there are places in the city that need it like the devil." Jane and Ellen had no intention of collaborating with Armour, fearing that their fledgling effort might get swallowed up by that large institution.

In addition to her letter writing, Jane recorded in her journal many details of her daily activities.

February 19
    I was almost immediately requested to begin [at The Woman's Club] and talked about fifteen minutes as well as I could. Some of the ladies cried — surprises never cease, Ellen says.

February 26
    This morning I had an appointment with the minister of Moody's Church. He is young and eager although forty years old perhaps, I think he is younger. . . in spirit than either of us. He has a dream of a 'working man's' church beside which our plan must seem paltry. . . but his sympathy never failed and he made all sorts of rash promises.

March 13
    I have a rather disheartening impression that it is much more than a week since I wrote but I have been looking up different 'slums' and usually when I come back am too tired to do

anything. I'm getting just a little bit tired of talking about it [the scheme] and should prefer beginning. We discover so many similar undertakings. . . but we still think we have a distinct idea of our own.

April 1

Our reception Saturday was much dampened by the storm. It was blowing and raging as hard as possible at eight-o-clock. Almost no one came from the south side, about twenty out of the fifty put in an appearance and we are quite sure they are interested. More than half of them were men so that our. . . fear of founding a house for single women and widows is being allayed.

We have seen Professor Swing who had promised us 'money or moral support' as we need, whatever that might mean. I have five or six invitations to speak to different missionary societies on E. London missions. I have accepted four of them because it is a good opportunity of meeting various benevolent people. . .

I have just come from the Maurice Porter Memorial Hospital on Fullerton Ave. It is a beautiful house built for fifteen sick or poor children. I made arrangements there for a little Italian boy nine years old. He has been blind since two. . . It (the hospital) is full now but has had vacancies all spring because no one has applied. It is a curious instance of the need of communication between the benevolent people at one end of the city and the poverty at the other.

If the promises are half fulfilled we will have no trouble on the money side. The Smith College movement in New York is languishing for lack of volunteers, they raised the sum of money they asked for within the first two weeks. When we are once started and need money I think that there will be no difficulty. At present of course we have no use for it nor authority to collect it.

In this succession of meetings Jane projected sincerity and force of will as she spoke about her belief that securing a "mere foothold of a house, easily accessible, hospitable, tolerant in spirit in a poor neighborhood would be in itself a serviceable thing, a place where the dependence of classes on each other would be reciprocal."

From the outset Ellen deliberately informed people that Jane was the leader in implementing the scheme. Jane fought Ellen's insistence on placing herself in a secondary role, but with little success. Ellen chose to support their efforts by supporting Jane. She accompanied her to meetings, receptions, dinners, but spoke only under duress. Most importantly, she gave freely the admiration and love on which Jane seemed to depend. Perhaps it was the toll taken by eight years of confusion and pain, but Jane, strong and purposeful as she was, needed Ellen's approval and admiration, not to soothe a hungry vanity, but rather to subdue the demons of self-doubt that she could never entirely banish.

A wealthy member of the influential Chicago Woman's Club described meeting Jane:

> I remember very well when Miss Addams first brought her plan to our club. I was hurrying from one committee to another, when someone came to walk beside me and began to talk. I paid very little attention until I caught the words: 'A place for invalid girls to go and help the poor.'
> Now the idea of invalid girls helping the poor! I turned in my astonishment to face a frail, sensitive girl. She looked anything but the reforming, extremist type.
> 'Suppose we sit down and talk about it,' I said, and we did. You know she had a physiological, psychological theory on that subject which I still believe is true.

That theory was articulated in a paper Jane was to present some years later. "This paper," she wrote, "is the result of reflections forced upon the writer by the struggles and misgivings she has often witnessed when the 'grown-up' daughter attempts to carry out plans concerning which her parents are unsympathetic or indifferent." The parents had sent the daughter to college where "her individuality was recognized quite apart from family or society claims and she received the sort of training which was deemed successful for developing a man's individuality and freeing his powers for independent action." But following graduation the daughter's attempts to take independent action, to "resist gracing the fireside. . . and adding luster to that social circle which her parents selected for her," are resented, often deemed selfish.

The unfortunate result is that the young woman abandons her dreams and ambitions and quietly submits but at great human cost. "She either hides her hurt," Jane wrote, "and splendid reserves of enthusiasm and capacity go to waste or her zeal and emotions are turned inward and the result is an unhappy woman whose vitality is sapped by vain regrets and desires." And, Jane might have added, is a likely candidate for Dr. Mitchell's clinic for nervous disorders.

Her openness to everything that might help move the scheme forward took Jane to some exotic places. Ellen's dry wit was at work when she wrote to her sister: "Jane thirsts very much for the Anarchists. She is going to hunt up their Sunday School." Which is exactly what Jane did. Ellen decided to let her friend take on the anarchists herself. Jane recalled the afternoon:

> On Sunday afternoon I visited one of the Anarchist Sunday Schools. I had gotten a letter of introduction to a Mr. Stauber, one of the leading anarchists. . . I found a gentlemanly looking man at the head of a prosperous hardware store. He looked as if he was bearing the burdens of all humanity, a thin and spiritual face. He was pleased that I wanted to see the Sunday School, said that Americans never came except the reporters of the capitalist newspapers and they always exaggerated. . . I found about two hundred children assembled in a hall back of a saloon with some young men trying to teach free thought without any religion or politics, the entire affair was very innocent. I was treated with great politeness and may take a class. It seems to me an opportunity to do a great deal of good — it was all in German.

"The scheme is progressing at an astonishing pace," Jane wrote to Mary. "Our heads are not in the least turned by our first flush of success and we realize the slough of despond may be near."

In their search for a place to settle, Jane and Ellen combed likely neighborhoods with the help of school officials, missionary workers and middle-aged "newspaper reporters noticeably older than one ordinarily associates with that profession. . . Perhaps," she mused, "I was only sent out with the older ones on what they must all have considered a quixotic mission."

Jane and Ellen were also guided by a young architect, Allen Pond, with whom they walked miles of unpaved streets, fighting the embarrassment of seeming to be tourists out "slumming." When Jane visited an Italian neighborhood she felt as if she were back in the slums of Rome and Naples. The parents and children spoke nothing but Italian and dressed like Italian peasants. They were more crowded than she had imagined people ever were in America. Four families of seven or eight each lived in one room for which, in constant fear of being ejected, they paid eleven dollars a month.

Finally, after five months of active searching, Jane and Ellen found what they were looking for on Halsted Street: "a fine old house standing well back from the street, surrounded on three sides by a broad piazza which was supported by wooden pillars of exceptionally pure Corinthian design and proportion." The elegant home had been built in 1856 by real estate magnate Charles Hull as a country retreat. Jane described Halsted Street and the surrounding neighborhood:

> Halsted Street is thirty-two miles long, and one of the great thoroughfares of Chicago. Polk Street crosses it midway between the stockyards to the south and the ship-building yards on the north branch of the Chicago River. For the six miles between these two industries the street is lined with shops of butchers and grocers. . . and pretentious establishments for the sale of ready-made clothing. . . Hull House once stood in the suburbs, but the city has steadily grown up around it and its site now has corners on three or four foreign colonies. Between Halsted Street and the river live about ten thousand Italians. . . to the south on Twelfth Street are many Germans and side streets are given over almost entirely to

Polish and Russian Jews. Still farther south, these Jewish colonies merge into a huge Bohemian colony. . . [To] the northwest are many Canadian Americans, and to the north are Irish and first generation Americans. The streets are inexpressibly dirty, the number of schools inadequate, the street lighting bad, the paving miserable and altogether lacking in the alleys and smaller streets, and the stables foul beyond description. Hundreds of houses are unconnected with the street sewer. . . Many houses have no water supply save the faucet in the back yard, there are no fire escapes, the garbage and ashes are placed in wooden boxes which are fastened to the street pavements. . . The houses are for the most part wooden, originally built for one family and are now occupied by several. . . The ward contains 255 saloons. . . this allows one saloon to every twenty-eight voters. . . There are seven churches and two missions in the ward. . . all of these are small and somewhat struggling, save the large Catholic Church connected with the Jesuit College on the south boundary of the ward.

At the time Hull built his hideaway mansion, there had been little between Halsted and Lake Michigan but prairie grasses and sand. Hull's brick home had escaped the 1871 Chicago fire. It was in dire need of repair and had as its immediate neighbors a disreputable looking liquor store and a dingy funeral parlor. Neither of these daunted Jane and Ellen who were more elated over the Corinthian columns and spacious piazza than they were disturbed by cracked plaster and obsolete plumbing.

Upon his death Charles Hull had left the house to his cousin and business associate, Helen Culver. Fortunately, Culver was sympathetic to Jane and Ellen's scheme and rented them both the second floor of the house and a former first floor drawing room, adjacent to the office and storeroom of a furniture company. In the spring of the following year, Culver was to make a generous gift to the young women which Ellen reported to her sister. "Now comes the great item of news. Miss Culver has given us the house rent free for four years, amounting to $2,880 and we have decided to call the house Hull House. Connect these two facts in any delicate way your refined imagination suggests."

"The fine old house responded kindly to repairs," Jane reported to Alice. On September 18, 1889, Jane and Ellen moved into their
new home with housekeeper, Mary Keyser, who had once worked
for Jane's sister Mary and her family. "Bien. We take a house, i.e.
Jane takes it and furnishes it prettily," Ellen exulted, in a letter to her
sister. She added:

> She [Jane] had a good deal of furniture and she intends to
> spend several hundred dollars on some more and of course we
> shall put all our pictures and 'stuff into it.'

To her family Jane wrote:

> [T]he silver and the quilt came yesterday and were put
> immediately into the side board. . . I haven't time to
> describe the other rooms now; they are all as distin-
> guished. This is by far the prettiest house I have lived
> in. . . No young matron ever placed her own things in
> her own house with more pleasure.

Louise Bowen observed, "Miss Addams is really a home lover
and delighted in the arrangement of a room. Whenever she was disturbed or depressed she would move the furniture in all the
rooms. . . It was quite customary to hear the residents of Hull
House say, 'Miss Addams is low in her mind today. She is rehanging
pictures.' "

Jane and Ellen agreed with Canon Barnett that "the establishment of the settlement is the work of those who believe that the
gifts of modern times are good; that culture is gain not loss; that
cleanliness is better than dirt, beauty better than ugliness, knowledge better than ignorance," and set out to make Hull House a
haven of beauty and culture. "A social settlement," she said in a
speech she gave three years later when her ideas had been tested,
"casts nothing aside which the cultivated man regards as good and
suggestive of participation in the best life of the past. . . The one

test which the Settlement is bound to respect is that its particular amount of luxury shall tend to 'free' the social expression of its neighbors, and not cumber that expression."

Jane and Ellen filled the house with fine, old mahogany furniture, some of which belonged to Jane, good china, fine linens and art. Covering the walls of Hull House with reproductions of fine paintings "fell into the hands of Miss Starr. . . She not only feeds her own mind and finds her highest enjoyment in Art, but believes that 'every soul has a right to be thus fed and comforted. . . without art the hungry individual soul will have passed unsolaced and unfed.' "

In his studies of human development the eminent psychiatrist Erik Erikson concluded that many gifted men, Henry James and George Bernard Shaw among them, spent the years between ages 20 and 30 uncertain of what they wanted to do, accomplishing little, and unhappy with themselves. Yet that "moratorium," Erikson contended, was not wasted, but was a needed gestation period in which the young men, unaware as they were, were preparing for their chosen work. If, wrote scholar and feminist, Carolyn G. Heilbrun in *Writing a Woman's Life*, Erikson had included women in his study (which, like most male doctors, he neglected to do), he would have been likely to say the same thing about them.

Certainly Jane Addams' development bore out Erikson's paradigm. The years from age 21 to 29, which she looked upon as an ignoble waste, were crucial to her intellectual and emotional development. The days spent in European museums and concert halls and her perceptions about the people whose culture seeded their country's arts, convinced her that art, whether painting, dance, music, drama or writing, was an absolute necessity in humanizing life. Thus the first building Jane Addams added to Hull House two years after its founding was not the sorely needed nursery, classroom, or clinic, but an art gallery. And the burdensome hours she spent managing complicated family financial affairs had forced her to become an astute businesswoman, skills that proved vital to the solvency of Hull House.

"There's power in me and will to dominate," Jane wrote to Mary while in the throes of her efforts to win support for the scheme. "In many ways I need mankind's respect. It seems to me almost impossible to constantly repress inherited powers and tendencies and constantly try to exercise another set." After so many years of crumbling self-esteem, Jane was able to acknowledge her own power to influence and lead, and felt herself, at last, more worthy of the father whom she so admired.

Excited and a bit overwhelmed that first night in their new home, Jane forgot to close the door that opened onto Polk Street. In the morning she saw that no one had taken advantage of the open door. Predisposed as she was to seeing immigrants in the best possible light, she felt it was a "fine illustration of the honesty and kindliness of our neighbors."

If their neighbors were honest and kindly, they were also puzzled as to why these two educated, well-dressed young women would choose to live in the dirt and squalor immigrants dreamed of escaping. Some, to Jane and Ellen's amusement, were convinced that they were missionaries bent on conversion. Although they had managed to settle into a house among the poor, Jane and Ellen had yet to win their neighbors' trust.

"People have been so good to us," Jane wrote to Anna. "I received a check for $100 from a lady whom I had never seen. If we don't succeed after all our help, we will deserve to fail." But Jane was determined not to fail. This was one more stone she was going to kick all the way to the finish line.

Chapter 7

"Nurse the Sick and Mind the Children"

*T*alented, aspiring women caught in the shackles of Victorian mores were forced to create an extraordinary life event to liberate themselves from the expectations of traditional society. This, says Carolyn Heilbrun in *Writing a Woman's Life*, is precisely what novelist George Eliot did. By her scandalous decision to live with the married author and critic, George Henry Lewes, she escaped intrusive social demands and the compulsion to motherhood, at the same time gaining a life partner.

With one bold act, moving to an impoverished neighborhood and opening the doors of their home to their immigrant neighbors, Jane Addams and Ellen Gates Starr freed themselves from the expectation that they would play out the conventional plots of marriage, motherhood or self-sacrificing maiden aunt. Instead they created the original, vibrant world of the Settlement.

Though she broke new ground, Jane Addams did not rebel against current morality as George Eliot did. True, she had left home and family, but she was acting within the traditional woman's role of nurturer. Though she would be called a radical and a revolutionary, she was neither. She considered herself a middle-of-the-roader, working for reform within the system. She believed passionately in the perfectibility of humankind and that, if given a chance, Lincolnian democracy would work. The solidity of her beliefs and her natural gentleness and empathy lent her an aura of serenity that drew her Hull House neighbors to her. She need not have worried about being accepted; when an oasis is near, the thirsty find it.

As Henry Steele Commager wrote in his introduction to the first edition of *Twenty Years at Hull-House*, "There was nothing dramatic about the opening of Hull-House yet it was an historic event. For here was the beginning of what was to be one of the great social movements in modern America — the Settlement House movement."

Jane and Ellen decided to give themselves a month of quiet before they opened the doors of Hull House to their "audience." The time passed quickly as they worked alongside the dedicated Mary Keyser in a thorough cleaning of the floors, walls, windows and cabinets. When the three women were satisfied that the house was ready for guests, Jane and Ellen set aside one Saturday afternoon and evening for their grand opening so they would not feel obliged to "receive" every afternoon. It turned out to be a wise strategy. The two hostesses, aided by Mary Keyser, were overwhelmed with people curious to meet the "good ladies" and partake of tea and pastries.

Jane had no set plan for what she and Ellen would do on a day-to-day basis. Like an author who discovers what her book is about as she writes it, Jane discovered what Hull House was about by opening its doors and inviting her neighbors in. This lack of planned program was deliberate. Following Toynbee Hall's model, she wanted Hull House to be flexible and able to respond to neighbors' needs as they arose. As Ellen wrote to her sister:

> There are at least a half dozen girls in the city who will be glad to come and stay awhile and learn to know the people and understand them and their ways of life; to give out of their culture and leisure and over-indulgence and to receive the culture

that comes of self-denial and poverty and failure which these people have always known. There is to be no organization and no institution about it. The world is overstocked with institutions and organizations.

Recalling how she had enjoyed the reading hour with her stepmother and George, Jane's first formal act as co-mistress of the house was to send the Italian women of the neighborhood an invitation to a reading by Ellen, in Italian, of George Eliot's *Romola*, in which the novel's heroine, Romola, after a loss of religious faith, goes to the aid of plague-stricken villagers. Describing the beginnings of what came to be called the Women's Reading Club, Jane wrote:

> The Italian women followed the wonderful tale with unflagging interest. The weekly reading was held in our little upstairs dining room. Two members of the club came to dinner each week, not only that they might be received as guests, but that they might help us wash the dishes afterward and so make the table ready for the stacks of Florentine photographs.

Early the next year Jane had further evidence that a reading hour could captivate a following when she met a member of the Boy's Club as he flung himself out of the House during a reading "in the rage by which an emotional boy hopes to keep from shedding tears." Brushing by her he said gruffly, "There's no use coming here anymore. Prince Roland is dead!"

Fond of proclaiming herself Hull House's first resident, an elderly woman who had lived for some years at the Utopian community of Brook Farm and again sought to live where "idealism ran high," gave five consecutive readings from Hawthorne's works, interspersing the tales with personal recollections. "We thus," wrote Jane, "found the type of class which through all the years has remained the most popular — a combination of a social atmosphere with serious study." Later a branch of the Chicago Public Library was established in Hull House making books easily available.

The weekly flow of Jane's letters to her sisters documents the rich harvest reaped from her efforts to spread the word about the Settlement. People began to volunteer help from the first day the door of Hull House opened.

> Miss Trowbridge comes every night. She has a club of little girls. . . Miss Forstall has undertaken a 'Home Library Association' every Friday afternoon. . . We have two boys clubs every Thursday in the dining room. I have 20. They are about 16. They work at Fields' as walkers, errand boys shipping parcels. They are all anxious to come and are respectful. My little ragamuffins downstairs are harder to manage. Miss Starr has help for tonight. Mr. Smiley comes with his violin. . . Mr. French gave an illustrated lecture to 50 young people and parents.

Many of the immigrants who attended the ever-expanding program of classes, lectures, concerts and social evenings at Hull House were men and women who sought relief from the never ending struggle to put bread on their tables and roofs over their heads. Some had been well educated in their mother country and hungered for connections to music, books, art and theater. It was not unusual for an engineer to be reduced to washing floors or a musician to driving an ice wagon. For them Hull House became a genuine refuge. But optimistic as Jane and Ellen were, never in their headiest dreams had they imagined that the one-year-old Greek Club would perform Sophocles' *Ajax* in ancient Greek before a full house.

One of the most ambitious and active groups formed by young neighborhood men was the impressively named Hellenic League for the Molding of Young Men, devoted to the "educational, physical and spiritual development of young Greek men." The League sponsored scholarships and lectures and held athletic and social events. Jane was so interested in the League's work and gave so much attention to its members that the young men thought of her as their "patroness of arts and ideals." One aspiring poet regularly sought her detailed comments on his poetry. When he eventually published his *Sonnets of an Immigrant*, Jane wrote the foreword. Recalling his years at Hull House another young Greek immigrant wrote:

> We would walk into Hull House as though we walked into our own house. . . There was absolute freedom to enjoy the House . . . and the nurturing warmth that animated everything. . . the soft words and sentences of the women of the House, the only soft and kind words we immigrant boys heard in those days. . . Miss Addams was our mother and protector, the immigrant boy's best friend and the only one who understood us.

As Emily Dickinson possessed a gift for words, Edison for invention and Gershwin for music, so Jane Addams possessed the gift for relating to people nonjudgmentally, whatever their age, circumstances or background. Those who sought her counsel, however degraded they might be in their own eyes, felt strengthened by her belief in them. Although she was in her thirties and the men and women who turned to her for help were often twice her age, neither she nor they seemed conscious of the difference.

From the time Hull House opened, Jane was addressed as Miss Addams except by family and a few longtime friends. Was it the quality that a journalist identified as "spirituality" that set her off from others and led colleagues, among them the young university professor John Dewey, to call her Miss Addams? ("I positively feel my callers peering into my face to detect spirituality," she confided to Ellen.) Trying to pin down that special aura emanated by Jane, Ellen wrote to her sister, "It is as if she simply diffused something that came from within herself. . . and I suppose that is exactly what she does do." Indeed, Jane Addams had lived in Hull House for only a short time before some of the neighbors began referring to her as Saint Jane or Miss Kind Heart. (From this point forward we will call her J.A. as did her dear friend, Julia Lathrop.)

As J.A. had hoped, once the neighbors knew and trusted them, it was the neighbors themselves who prescribed the services Hull House would render. Within weeks of opening the Settlement, J.A. and Starr found themselves working to secure support for deserted women, insurance for bewildered widows, damages for injured (machine) operators, furniture from the clutches of the installment store. Most heart-rending was the need of working mothers for childcare. Desperate women either left their infants and toddlers with an already overworked neighbor or locked them in their tenement apartments, sometimes with dire results. Just that year, three children, left alone in the Hull House neighborhood, had been crippled. One had fallen from a third story window, one had been burned, and another, tied for safekeeping to the leg of a chair, suffered a deformed spine.

In the torpid heat of summer the tenement children could not bear being locked up so the mothers were forced to let them play outdoors. A number of these small, hungry, unwashed children wandered into Hull House. (The door was always unlocked and in summer, left ajar.) Finding it blessedly cool, they stayed; soon their brothers and sisters joined them.

Jenny Dow, a lively, affectionate woman from a wealthy Chicago family, miraculously — or so it seemed — appeared at Hull House just as J.A. was trying to find a way to care for this colony of children. Their numbers were increasing as more working mothers began dropping them off at Hull House, confident that the "good ladies" would look after them. Dow volunteered to start a kindergarten and shepherded her charges into the dining room where she brought in supplies so that they could draw, play with toys, and listen to stories. At noon she had to hurry them out so that the room could be cleared for the girls sewing club. The children were given lunch and then, as related by J.A., they "noisily enjoyed the hospitality of our bedrooms under the so-called care of any resident who volunteered to keep an eye on them. . . Hull House was thus committed to a day nursery."

Within three weeks 24 children were registered in Dow's kindergarten, with a waiting list of 70. As a Hull House kindergartner recalled:

> I remember the red brick House well. My mother used to press 3 pennies in my hand and send my sister and me two blocks to the House where we were showered, cleaned and sent to an open air room to dry off. Later we spent our 3 pennies for a bowl of lentil soup, a bologna sandwich and a glass of milk.

Fortunately, Dow had the patience and compassion to deal with the outdated habits of some of the immigrant women. Italian mothers, accustomed to dressing their children in layers of clothes, sent them to Hull House overdressed, even on warm days. When Dow explained that it would be healthier if the children were more lightly dressed, the mothers listened intently, but only a few could shake the customs of a lifetime and Dow had to peel off sweater after sweater from a perspiring child.

One day Dow noticed a five-year-old girl in a "horrid state of intoxication" from breakfasting on wine-soaked bread. Dow went to the child's home to talk to the mother who listened carefully and then triumphantly offered her a small dark glass of whiskey. "See," the woman said, "I have brought you the American drink." Dow left defeated, sure that the woman now thought that American children breakfasted on whiskey.

Just as the sight of the starving man gnawing the rotten cabbage in the East End had imprinted itself on J.A.'s memory, so did the misery of many of the working mothers in the neighborhood. On one occasion a woman was sitting in the nursery, paralyzed by grief. Her frail son had died from a head injury after a freak fall while she was at work.

"Is there anything I can do to help you?" J.A. asked.

"If you could give me my wages for tomorrow," the woman responded, "I would not go to work in the factory. I would like to stay at home all day and hold the baby. He was always asking me to hold him and I never had the time."

That same month, emerging at eleven o' clock from a long meeting in the Board of Education building, J.A. saw a neighbor woman on her knees scrubbing the marble tiling. "As she straightened up to meet me," J.A. wrote, "she seemed so wet from her feet up to her chin that I hastily inquired the cause. Her reply was that she left home at five o' clock every night and had no opportunity for six hours to nurse her baby. Her mother's milk mingled with the very water with which she scrubbed the floors until she should return at midnight, heated and exhausted, to feed her screaming child with what remained within her breasts."

Later she would write:

> With all the efforts made by modern society to nurture and educate the young how stupid it is to permit the mothers of young children to spend themselves in the coarser work of the world! . . . The long hours of factory labor necessary for earning the support of a child leave no time for the tender care and caressing which may enrich the life of the most piteous baby. It is curiously inconsistent that with the emphasis this generation has placed upon the mother and upon the prolongation of infancy, we constantly allow the waste of this most precious material.

What should a humane, sensible society do — subsidize the impoverished woman so that she could stay at home and raise her children or require that she leave them in the care of others so she might work to support them? J.A. deemed it a "wretched delusion" to think a mother could both support and nurture a child. In her early years of living among the poor, J.A. exposed problems that she was able to do little to solve in her day and are still being debated in ours.

Understanding intuitively the immigrant's mute loneliness for his/her native land, J.A. initiated Italian, German, Greek and Polish evenings complete with ethnic food, music, dancing and occasionally, a short lecture on a topic that might be of interest. Eager to induce his often apathetic or suspicious countrymen and women to attend Hull House's first Italian night, resident A. Mastro Valerio, editor of the newspaper, *L'Italia*, sent out 228 printed invitations from "Le Signorine Jane Addams and Ellen Starr." Starr described the evening:

> The room was packed and people were in the halls. . . There were a great many children, babies even and some of the women wore bright kerchiefs on their heads. The rich and vulgar Italians are taking to coming, sporting diamond crosses. We put them on the back seats and peasants to the front. One of the ladies of the diamond cross recited a patriotic poem with great spirit. . . It was quite spiritual and some of the people were quite moved. I was awfully glad things went off so well. Poor Mr. V. had toiled so and was so nervous.

In the early years of the Settlement, J.A. was called upon to perform the humblest services, "to wash the newborn babies, and to prepare the dead for burial, to nurse the sick, and mind the children." One evening the Hull House door was flung open to admit a frantic young girl who reported that a woman in her tenement was "having a baby all by herself. She's hollering something fierce. My mother says it's disgracing the whole house it is." J.A. learned that none of the neighbors would help the young woman because her baby was illegitimate; they feared contamination from her sin.

After telephoning a doctor J.A. asked Julia Lathrop, an early Hull House resident, to accompany her to the woman's flat. By the time the physician arrived, the two amateur midwives had delivered the baby, a little boy whom the grateful mother named Julius, after Julia Lathrop.

As the exhausted women made their way back to Hull House J.A., unnerved by her abrupt initiation into midwifery, said to Lathrop, "Doing things that we know nothing about, like rushing into midwifery, may be carrying things too far," to which Lathrop responded, "If we have to begin to hew down to the line of our ignorance, for heaven's sake, don't let us begin at the humanitarian end. To refuse to respond to a poor girl in the throes of childbirth would be a disgrace to us forevermore. If Hull House doesn't have its roots in human kindness it is no good at all."

J.A. must have agreed. According to Weber Linn, "she would go anywhere, quite alone, if she were summoned, at three-o-clock in the morning just as if she were a doctor. She had doubts all her life, but no fears."

One night J.A. woke to find a man in her room. She sat up in bed as calmly as if in church, and asked the man what he needed so badly that he had to steal. "Something to eat," was his reply. J.A. directed him to take the money he needed from her purse, and to come back at nine the next morning at which time she would see about finding him a job. The man returned and following a lead J.A. gave him, was at work in a printing plant the next day. He soon paid back the money she had lent him.

Such quick reform was not typical. J. A. could do little to reduce wife-beating, a favorite pastime for drunk husbands, but offer the battered wife refuge. Hull House became a haven for women fleeing brutal husbands and prostitutes seeking a way to end a life on the street.

"In the crisis of many lives, Hull House was an asylum," wrote respected literary critic and biographer Francis Hackett, a onetime resident of Hull House. "I recall late one night I went down to answer the door at Hull House. I shall not forget the crouching woman in the swathing shadows below. She had run away from a house of prostitution. In the quietness the woman knew she was safe."

And so the door of Hull House would open countless times during the day and, in emergency, at night. In the first year, 9,000 people crossed its threshold; no one was turned away. J.A. placed a desk and chair in the front reception room and talked with as many people seeking help as she possibly could. In later years she placed a rocking chair in the room which immediately became known as "Miss Addams' chair." No one else would sit in it.

One of the many invitations to visit Hull House went to Mary Kenney, a worker in a book bindery and an active trade unionist. Kenney wrote in her journal:

> One day, while I was working at my trade, I received a letter from Miss Jane Addams. She invited me to Hull House for dinner. She said she wanted me to meet some people from England who were interested in the labor movement. I had never heard of Miss Addams or Hull House. I had no idea who she was. I had been a member of a working girls' club and I was much disgusted with the talk of the group. . . I left the group to give my time to work for a trade organization. I decided that I would not accept the invitation to Hull House. No club people for me!

But Kenney's mother persuaded her daughter to accept the invitation. On the appointed evening Kenney walked into the reception room and was entranced by the fine old furniture, the fresh flowers on the mantel, the sweep of the curving staircase. "If the Union could only meet here!" she fantasized.

> By my manner Miss Addams must have known that I wasn't very friendly. She asked me questions about our Trade Union. . . 'Is there anything I can do to help your organization?' she asked. . . I couldn't believe I heard right! I answered, 'There are many things we need. We're meeting over a saloon on Clark Street and it's a dirty and noisy place, but we can't afford anything better.'
>
> She said, 'You can meet here!' When I saw that there was someone who cared enough to help us and to help us in our own way, it was like having a new world opened up. Miss Addams not only had our [Union] circulars delivered, but paid for them. She asked us how we wanted to have them worded. . . She climbed stairs, high and narrow. There were signs, Keep Out. That didn't stop her. She managed to see the workers at their noon hour and invited them to classes and meetings at Hull House. Later, she asked me to come to Hull House to live. Knowing Hull-House and what it stood for, I called it heaven.

Kenney moved into a room on the second floor and paid the modest room and board that J.A. and Starr had established. Residents were expected to volunteer at least two hours service a week to the neighborhood, which could be anything from teaching English to diapering babies. Potential residents were required to live at the House for a six-month trial period. If they then wanted to remain and the resident council (the governing body of the House) considered them desirable, they became permanent residents with a commitment to live at the Settlement for at least two years.

The number of residents gradually increased from 15 in the 1890s to close to 70 by 1929, with men living in the Men's Building and women living in the old mansion and the Women's Building. There were also apartments for married couples, a few of whom had children, and a separate residential building for working women, named The Jane Club by its residents. J.A. took pride in the fact that it was the women themselves who originated the idea for the cooperatively run home, which they administered with notable harmony.

The Coffee Shop, modeled after an inviting old English inn, with dark wooden panelling and a raftered ceiling, was open to the public and became the favorite breakfast spot for residents. In the evening they gathered for a communal dinner in the elegant dining room lit by Spanish wrought iron chandeliers, with J.A. sitting at the head of one of three long tables. Conversation was often lively and stimulating, embracing subjects related to current events, the arts, and neighborhood happenings. Sometimes however, when the more colorful and opinionated of the residents tangled with each other, conversation would turn argumentative. Dr. Rachel Yarros, who ran a birth control clinic, and her husband, Victor, a newspaperman and partner of Clarence Darrow, both speaking Russian, would sometimes get embroiled in arguments so heated that J.A. repeatedly had to request the vociferous couple to kindly finish their discussion in the privacy of their apartment.

J.A., who relished both hearing and telling a good story, liked to relate her favorite story about the irrepressible Victor, an ardent amateur musician. One evening, attending a concert at Orchestra Hall with score in hand, he took to waving his arms as he "conducted" along with the esteemed maestro, Theodore Thomas. Suddenly Thomas stopped the music, turned to the audience and addressed the reddened face in the tenth row. "Either you conduct the orchestra, Victor, or I, but we both can't do it."

Dr. Alice Hamilton, a professor of medicine at Northwestern University when she took up residency at Hull House in 1897, expressed her relief on learning that Yarros would not be at dinner on a particular night. "One needs good bracing December weather to make one feel up to Mr. Yarros," she wrote in a letter to her sister, "and in Springtime one longs for a little more vagueness and gets cross when a person decides to settle all questions at once."

Francis Hackett described some of the residents who gathered at dinner:

> Miss Benedict in her effacing dress, like a Holbein print. Fraulein [Hannig], big-boned and almost Mongolian looking, with occasional positive utterance, Mrs. Britton, ample and active, her eyes quickly responsive and soft; articulate, very. Mr. Britton with a Raphaelic smile, big and brown, like a St. Bernard, Mr. George Hooker, steel rimmed glasses, hair a little untidy, crammed with statistics on municipal ownership. . . Frank Hazenplug, almost unbearably aesthetic. . . Miss Nancrede [director of Hull House Theater], devotee of Henry James, skilled in vanishing from the successes she contrived, Von Borosini, the Austrian, native as the dawn, kindly and rambling, vague as the mist, Carl Linden the Swede who talked in a slow growl and brought with him the outdoor feeling, the unsentimentalism, the strong color that he put in his paintings, Miss Alice Hamilton, clear as an etching, liberally intelligent, discerning with a voice of such fine music that could only be matched by the candor of her eyes, Norah Hamilton, shy, sidelong, original, a Bronte. . .[I]n that strange haven of clear humanitarian faith I discovered what I suppose I had been seeking — the knowledge that America had a soul.

As Hull House gained in reputation, many illustrious guests joined the dinner group, among them Carl Sandburg, Vachel Lindsay, William Butler Yeats, Frank Lloyd Wright, W.E.B. DuBois, and from abroad, Prince Kropotkin (the Russian anarchist who lived at Hull House for several months at J.A.'s invitation), Alymer Maude, the disciple and translator of Tolstoy, John Galsworthy, Lord Robert Cecil, prime minister of England, and leading English economists Beatrice and Sidney Webb (always anxious to make guests feel at home, J.A. accepted the cigarette Beatrice Webb offered her, the first and last cigarette she ever smoked). Gertrude Stein, in Chicago to collaborate on a project with composer Virgil Thomson, wore a black velvet vest and pants — unheard-of apparel for a woman at that time. She entertained the diners by reciting, "Pigeons in the grass, Alas, Alas." Henry Demarest Lloyd pronounced dinners at Hull House more stimulating than any held in the best clubs in town.

Beatrice Webb with the dry-ice humor of the British, disagreed.

> First an uncomfortable dinner, a large party served, higglede-piggedly. Then a stream of persons, labour, municipal, philanthropic, university, all those queer, well-intentioned or cranky individuals, who habitually centre around all settlements! Every individual among them must needs be introduced to us (a diabolical custom from which we have suffered greatly in America). . . Other days of our stay at Hull House are so associated in my memory with the dull heat of the slum, the unappetizing food of the restaurant, the restless movement of residents from room to room, the rides over impossible streets littered with unspeakable garbage, that they seem like one long bad dream lightened now and again by Miss Addams' charming grey eyes and gentle voice and graphic power of expression. We were so completely done up that we settled 'to cut' the other cities we had hoped to investigate. . .

The weekly residents' meetings took place after dinner with J.A. leading discussions that addressed everything from the choice of new wallpaper (no one wanted to change *anything* in the treasured dining room) to whether space should be provided for a birth control clinic. If a subject were discussed for an interminably long time with no decision on the horizon, J.A. would unapologetically abandon any pretense of Lincolnian democracy and announce, "Ladies and Gentlemen, since you have been unable to come to a decision, I am forced to make the decision for you." More often than not, the residents were relieved to have the matter decided.

University of Chicago professor and educator John Dewey, after serving on the board of Hull House for several years, observed amiably that the board carried on discussion after discussion but in the end always did what Jane Addams wanted. J.A. seemed innocently unaware, however, that she was so often the decision maker. When she was in her 70s and suffering from serious health problems, a resident asked her if she had thought to make provision for a successor. She replied, "I don't rule Hull House when I'm alive. Why would I want to rule it from the grave?"

One evening J.A., who enjoyed writing poetry but was not particularly adept at it, proposed that the residents skip business affairs (attendance was low) and instead improvise poems. The suggestion was not received with enthusiasm. Volunteering to start the improvisation off, J.A. recited a four-line verse:

> My eyes are blue
> My eyes are blue
> I say it twice
> 'Cause there are two.

The remainder of the improvisations remain unknown.

When the residents numbered 20, J.A. wrote:

> Diversified in belief and in the ardor of the inner life as any like number in a similar group. . . an effort was made to come together on Sunday evenings for a household service, hoping thus to express our moral unity in spite of the fact that we represented many creeds. But although all of us reverently knelt

when the High Church resident read the evening service and bowed our heads when the evangelical resident led in prayer after his chapter and although we sat respectfully through the twilight when a resident read her favorite passages from Plato and another from Abt Vogler, we concluded at the end of the winter that this was not religious fellowship and that we did not care for another reading club.

The residents gave up the Sunday service, accepting, as J.A. interpreted it, that it was quite as necessary to come together on the basis of the deed and common aim within the household as it was in the neighborhood itself.

For several years J.A. tried in vain to persuade George and Anna Haldeman to visit Hull House. To George she wrote, "I have always hoped that you would see the house and what we are trying to do and represent to the neighborhood. It is not to stem the poverty nor to give merely social pleasures but to fortify people who need fortitude. . . with the best that we can procure for them." She went on to tell him about the helpful and warm relationships that were being formed between Hull House workers and their neighbors: "People so diverse in circumstances yet really alike in feeling, it is this opportunity given to both classes. . . that we care most for."

"Miss Starr's mother is visiting us this weekend," J.A. wrote to Anna Addams. "She is so delighted with the house and our enjoyment of it that I am sure if you came you would have something of the same feeling. We were so amused this morning by her wistful look when she said she wished this beautiful old house were in a better neighborhood without reflecting that if it were we would not be in it."

"In spite of poignant experiences," J.A. wrote in *Twenty Years*, "or perhaps because of them, the memory of the first years at Hull House is more or less blurred with fatigue, for we could, of course, become accustomed only gradually to the unending activity and to the confusion of a house constantly filling and refilling with groups of people. . . All one's habits of living had to be readjusted. . . To thus renounce 'the luxury of personal preference' was, however, a mere trifle compared to our perplexity over the problems of an industrial neighborhood situated in an unorganized city."

Early one morning, J.A. heard a knock at the door and opened it to find two very cold people. One of them, Florence Kelley, recalled that first meeting with Jane Addams:

> One snowy morning between Christmas 1891 and New Year's 1892, I arrived at Hull House, Chicago a little before breakfast time and found there Henry Standing Bear, a Kickapoo Indian, waiting for the door to be opened.
> It was Miss Addams who opened it holding on her left arm a singularly unattractive, fat, pudgy baby belonging to the cook who was behind with breakfast. Miss Addams was a little hindered in her movements by a super-energetic kindergarten child, left by its mother while she went to a sweatshop for a bundle of cloaks to be finished.
> We were welcomed as though we had been invited. We stayed, Henry Standing Bear as helper to the engineer several months, when he returned to his tribe, and I, as a resident seven happy, active years. . . I cannot remember ever again seeing Miss Addams holding a baby, but the first picture of her gently keeping the little Italian girl back from charging into the snow, closing the door against the blast of wintry wind off Lake Michigan and tranquilly welcoming these newcomers, is as clear today as it was at that moment.

As Jane Addams and Ellen Gates Starr had hoped, educated, dedicated women were drawn to Hull House in its early years: Julia Lathrop, Florence Kelley, Alice Hamilton, Louise Bowen. A remarkable group, they not only enriched life at Hull House but pioneered reforms that dramatically improved the quality of life for children, working people, the elderly, and the mentally disabled. Perhaps not since the founding fathers, who by lucky happenstance were all born about the same time and in the same place, had such a group of individuals pooled its genius for the good of its country.

And, as J.A. had predicted, the women of Hull House were happier than they had been in years.

The Charles Hull house as first seen by Jane Addams and Ellen Gates Starr.

Alleys were the neighborhood "playgrounds".

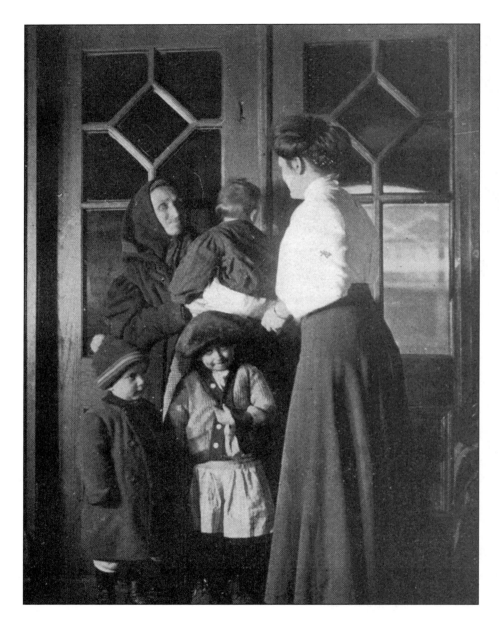

Hull House neighbors being greeted by a Hull House resident.
During the first year 9,000 people passed through Hull House doors.

Immigrant mothers and children in the Hull House neighborhood.

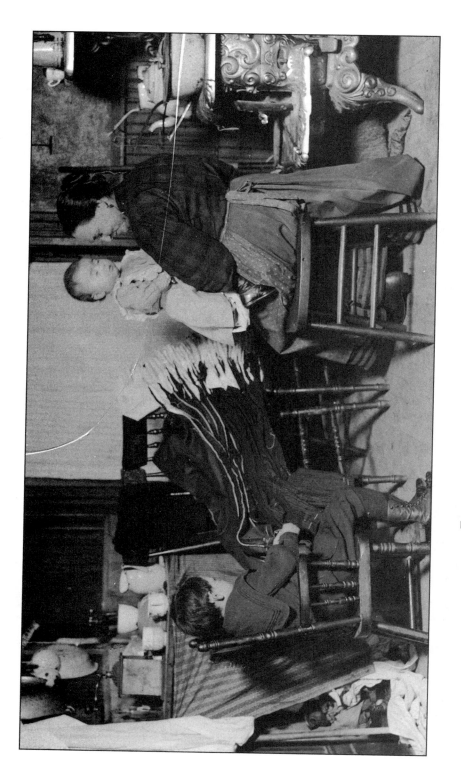

Tenement family with completed "sweat work".

Washing clothes to be hung on tenement roof to dry.

Street Market

Hull House, Halsted Street, 1910

OPENING OF

HULL=HOUSE

PLAY GROUND

Polk Street, Near Halsted

Saturday, May 1st, 1897,

AT 3 O'CLOCK, P. M.

"The air is warm, the skies are clear,
Birds and blossoms all are here,
Come old and young with spirits gay,
To welcome back the charming May."

MUSIC BY THE BRASS BAND

...Kindergarten Games---May Pole Dance...

ALL KINDS OF RACES

Children in party attire celebrate opening of Hull House playground.

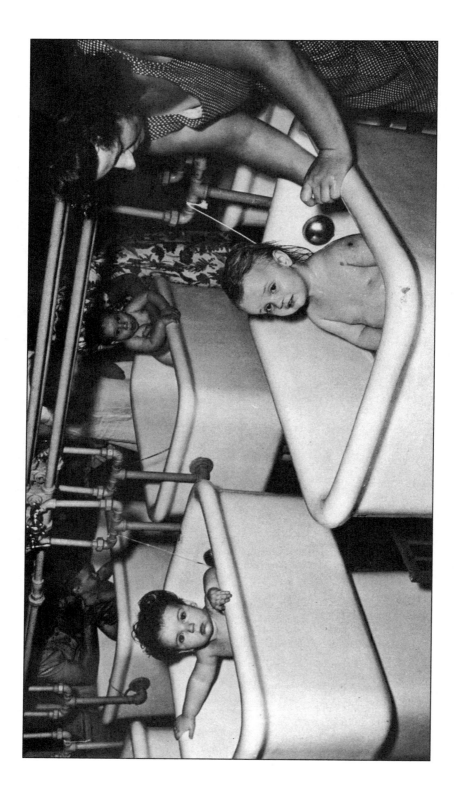

Bath time in Dr. Alice Hamilton's Hull House well-baby clinic.

Chapter 8

"The Pure Milk of the Word"

*J*ane Addams and Julia Lathrop were in the Hull House nursery when a friend of Lathrop's walked in carrying a parrot in a gilded cage. "The bird is a gift to the children," the woman said. "He'll be no threat to the tiny innocents. He knows not one single swear word."

Her dark eyes alight, Julia Lathrop assured her friend that the lack in the parrot's education would be "rectified by the children in the nursery." Then, quickly, as if in defense of the children, she tossed off a quatrain from George Herbert:

> Children pick up words
> As pigeons pick up peas
> And scatter them again
> As God may please.

Julia Lathrop's ability to see the comic side of life was an effective antidote to J.A.'s tendency to be over-serious. Twenty-five years later in her memoir, *My Friend Julia Lathrop*, J.A. reported that "the parrot lived a long and blameless life in our nursery. I am happy to say that he never learned to swear, perhaps because he failed to make use of his opportunities."

Born two years apart in adjoining Illinois counties, beloved daughters of powerful men, Lathrop and J.A. were both raised in gracious homes amidst comfort and culture. Both were encouraged to continue their educations at Rockford Female Seminary, but there the similarity ended. Lathrop's father, happy to see his daughter's dawning independence, supported her desire to transfer to Vassar after her freshman year. Mrs. Lathrop was active in the suffrage movement and her daughter had grown up with the model of a strong woman willing to do battle for what she believed.

Following graduation Lathrop assisted her father in his law office, doing much of his writing and secretarial work. Hungry for more intellectually challenging activity, she earned a law degree but passing the bar examination did not mean that a woman could find a position as a lawyer; the law was a male domain from which women were automatically excluded. Determined to do useful and satisfying work, Lathrop gravitated to Hull House and became one of its earliest residents. Intellectually compatible, J.A. and Lathrop enjoyed a lifelong friendship. At the time of her death, J.A. was working on the memoir devoted to her friend.

When Lathrop sought J.A.'s advice as to what she could do at Hull House, J.A. gave her usual response. "Look around. See what the neighborhood needs. Then decide what you can do best and do it. If it doesn't work, try something else. You'll find your way."

While Lathrop was "looking around" she observed the many elderly Greek men who languished, bored and lonely, in their dreary tenements. She invited them to Hull House at 4 o'clock on Sunday afternoons to read and discuss the works of Plato. Only a few men climbed the stairs to the Hull House piazza on the first Sunday afternoon, but news soon spread and the Plato Club's discussions became one of the staples of the Hull House program, often not ending until 10 p.m. As described by J.A.,

> the discussions ranged far and wide, almost confounding John Dewey himself, then a young professor in the University of Chicago who occasionally led the club. The membership was composed largely of elderly men who had read philosophy of

sorts all their lives and had made up their minds regarding the purposes of the universe. One member who always disagreed with the class leader 'on principle,' as he proudly stated, was once betrayed into a speech which sounded as if he and Plato and Julia Lathrop were at last on common ground. When the latter expressed her pleasure to Mr. Dodge that he agreed with her he stuttered in his excitement, 'I agree with you, Miss Lathrop, not at all, not at all — it is you who agree with me!' To lessen his discomfiture as the club members expressed amusement, Lathrop commented that it was of course important to know who had shifted his point of view — it might have been she or it might have been Mr. Dodge, but she was quite sure that it was not Plato.

Lathrop's "looking" also led her to the Chicago Relief Agency which, by contrast with the Plato Club, was inexpressibly grim. To determine whether families qualified for relief, Lathrop climbed steep tenement stairs or descended into damp basements in the ten-block area surrounding Hull House. She described the immigrants as they waited to receive their food and fuel allotments from the agency:

> It was a solid pressing crowd of hundreds of shabby men and shawled or hooded women standing hour after hour with market baskets high above their heads, held in check by policemen. . . A woman was crushed — in one instance killed, and an ambulance called to take her away. . .
>
> When once the applicant penetrates the office, he is in the great dingy waiting room of the Cook County Agency. [H]e is called on by the visitor upon whose report fuel already has been granted, the allowance of food and one bar of soap carried home in the basket, the coal being sent later from the contractor.

When a smallpox epidemic swept through the tenements making families even more desperate for help, Lathrop, risking exposure to the disease, continued to deliver bags of emergency coal and food to stricken families. On one occasion Lathrop, joined by

Florence Kelley, by then the chief factory inspector in Illinois, discovered that thousands of pieces of contaminated "sweat work" — garments taken from factories and worked on at home — had been sewn by ill women and then sold to the public. Lathrop and Kelley went to court to have the practice stopped and emerged victorious. The presiding judge wrote of the incident:

> I saw these two women do what the health department of the great city of Chicago could not do. The authorities were afraid not only of personal contagion but of damage suits if they destroyed the infected garments. . . As a result of a joint attack by Miss Julia Lathrop and Mrs. Florence Kelley they were induced to act and they destroyed thousands of dollars worth of clothing. Working together, these women saved hundreds, perhaps thousands of lives.

The following year the governor of Illinois, John Peter Altgeld, appointed Lathrop to the State Board of Charities, a non-paying job which she held for seventeen years. She visited county hospitals, poorhouses, mental institutions and the children's detention home in an effort to better the quality of care inmates received. In her memoir of her friend J.A. reflected:

> One likes to think of her going the rounds of those dreary places, talking to the inmates and uncovering intolerable conditions which had always been taken for granted just because no one made it his business to do anything about them. One likes to think of the revelation she must have been to some of the stodgy officials who shuddered at the idea of any change. One wonders, for instance, what they thought of her when to test out a newfangled fire escape in an institution harboring helpless women and girls, she tucked her skirts around her ankles and slid down from an upper floor, to see if the thing really would work and not scare to death the fleeing inmates.

In the summer of 1892 J.A.was asked to speak at the School of Applied Ethics in Plymouth, Massachusetts, on the general theme of philanthropy and social progress. When J.A. and Starr had founded Hull House they were at the cutting edge of a growing settlement movement in the United States. Unknown to them, in 1885 a young American, Stanton Coit, after working at Toynbee Hall for three months, had returned to the United States and established the Neighborhood Guild on the Lower East Side of New York. It closed when Coit returned to England, but two years later, at the very time the doors of Hull House were being opened, seven university women moved into a battered New York tenement and began College Settlement. By 1891 there were six settlements in the United States, a number that grew to one hundred by the end of the century.

In *Twenty Years* J.A. described the Plymouth conference:

> There were Miss Vida Scudder and Miss Helena Dudley from the College Settlement Association. . . , Miss Julia Lathrop and myself from Hull House. Some of us had numbered our years as far as thirty, and we all carefully avoided the extravagance of statement which characterizes youth, and yet I doubt if anywhere on the continent that summer could have been found a group of people more genuinely interested in social development or more sincerely convinced that they had found a clue by which the conditions in crowded cities might be understood and the agencies for social betterment developed.

The meeting was held on a golden afternoon on the shores of a pond a few miles from Plymouth. The lecturers included a Columbia University professor who talked about the emerging science of sociology, the term "sociology" having been coined only that year at The University of Chicago. J.A. presented two papers, *The Subjective Necessity for Social Settlements,* and *The Objective Value of a Social Settlement.* (She was later to apologize for the ponderous titles.) Her years with the Rockford Debating Society stood her in good stead. Her voice was soft but clear, its lack of strength more than compensated for by her ability to make each member of the audience feel that he or she was being spoken to directly.

After three years of living the settlement life, J.A. had clarified and refined her ideas. Writing the two papers forced her to articulate them. In *The Objective Value* she divided the activities of Hull House into four areas. "They are not formally or consciously thus divided," she explained, "but broadly separate according to the receptivity of the neighbors. They might be designated as the social, educational, and humanitarian; I have added civic — if indeed a settlement of women can be said to perform civic duties." (She would have said that Kelley, Lathrop, Bowen and Hamilton *were* performing their civic duties; she was not yet willing to claim that she was.)

J.A. observed that Hull House found the first generation of immigrants easier to work with than the second or third because the first generation still retained a connection to its ancestory and native culture. A number of Bohemians and Italians still celebrated their holidays, wore traditional holiday clothes and shared festivities with cousins; the Germans still "sang a great deal in the tender minor of German folksong or in the rousing spirit of the Rhine."

Hull House sought to strengthen that connection to counteract the alienation and rootlessness immigrants felt in their new country. Initiated by A. Mastro Valerio, it held an Italian Night every Saturday evening. Entire families of Italian neighbors were served Italian food and encouraged to share their heritage of songs and dances. Similar evenings were organized for Jews and Germans. "Perhaps the greatest value of the Settlement to them because of their superior education," J.A. said, "was in placing large and pleasant rooms with musical facilities at their disposal, and reviving their almost forgotten enthusiasms."

The sons and daughters of the immigrants, however, rejected anything having to do with European life, yet lacked the resources to adopt American customs and amenities. Unanchored, and spiritually homeless, they were vulnerable to the lure of drugs, alcohol and crime.

J.A. concluded by saying that while Hull House had strong philanthropic tendencies it is unfair to apply the word philanthropic to Hull House as a whole. . . Working people live in the same streets with those in need of charity, but they themselves, so long as they have health and good wages, require none of it. As one of their number has said, they require only that their aspirations be recognized and stimulated, and the means of attaining them put at their disposal. Hull House makes a constant effort to secure these means for its neighbors, but to call that effort philanthropy is to use the word unfairly and to underestimate the duties of good citizenship.

In *Subjective Necessity* J.A. emphasized the need for the settlement to provide an outlet for privileged and educated young people who

feel a fatal want of harmony between their theory and their lives, a lack of co-ordination between thought and action. . . Well-meaning parents set their daughters up to feel this disharmony by teaching them from babyhood to young adulthood to be self-forgetting and self-sacrificing, deliberately exposing them to the misery in the world by accompanying them to lectures on famines in India and China, on the poor in Siberia and the East End. But when the daughter graduated from college and attempted to do work to alleviate the suffering of the 'submerged tenth' the family claim is strenuously asserted; she is told that her efforts are 'unjustified and ill-advised.'

The settlement attempts to make up for this societal ignorance by providing educated young women an outlet for action. J.A. continued:

We conscientiously followed the gift of the ballot upon the gift of freedom to the Negro, but we are quite unmoved by the fact that he lives among us in practical social ostracism. We hasten to give the franchise to the immigrant from a sense of justice, from a tradition that he ought to have it while we club him with epithets deriding his past life or present occupation and feel no duty to invite him to our house.

The Hull House workers, among them educated and cultivated

young women, strove to remedy the ostracism and neglect of minorities and the poor, simultaneously implementing the ideals of a social democracy while satisfying their own need for intellectual challenge and emotional fulfillment.

At the conclusion of the conference J.A. commented that she was "naturally very proud of my colleague, Julia Lathrop, who was so able in conference and in debate and whose quick wit did much to dilute the moral intensity which at times threatened to engulf us. . . We were all careful that week-end to avoid saying that we had found a life's work, but as the years would show, everyone in that summer group remained dedicated to the settlement movement."

As they left the tranquil Plymouth retreat, Lathrop persuaded J.A. to stop in New York at the editorial office of the Forum magazine to try to get her papers published. She "urged that the idea they were trying to embody at Hull House should be put before the country while settlements were still young so as not to confuse the public with half-achievements and partial failures." J.A. reluctantly agreed but once at the publisher's office she lost heart and wanted to leave.

"Don't cave in," Lathrop admonished. "This is our chance to give the public the pure milk of the word."

Fortunately the Forum editor, Walter Hines Page, accepted both papers and the jubilant friends returned to Hull House, later to receive a generous check. The papers were printed in a book, *Philanthropy and Social Progress*, a collection of writings that grew out of the Plymouth conference. J.A.'s essays were praised and did much to launch her as a writer and national authority on the settlement movement.

She had also begun work on another publication, *Hull-House Maps and Papers*, which, from a modest beginning, grew into a five-year project. Beginning in 1890, a group of Hull House residents surveyed an area within a third of a square mile around Hull House, block by block, house by house, documenting with multi-colored maps the inhabitants' nationality and income. The study revealed that the average weekly income of a workingman was $5 or less. Italians, for example, were generally employed on railroads where they worked twenty to thirty weeks a year for an average wage of $1.25 a day. That meant a yearly income of $150 to $225 with which to feed, shelter and clothe a family.

The scope of *Hull-House Maps and Papers* expanded with the contribution of an article, "Wage Earning Children," by Florence Kelley and Alzina Stevens. Focusing on the nearby Italian colony they revealed that boys as young as eight years old, working as news-boys and bootblacks, left their homes at 2:30 in the morning to get the first editions of the newspapers, and after a morning selling papers, bootblacked the shoes of the passing crowd until evening. For all this work they earned pennies, did not go to school and were growing up illiterate and in poor health. Other essays by Hull House residents dealt with studies of the Chicago ghetto, Cook County Charities, and the Bohemian and Italian colonies. Ellen Gates Starr wrote on art and labor, J.A. on the settlement and the labor move-ment.

Published in 1895, *Hull-House Maps and Papers* was the first semi-scientific study of an American immigrant community. (By 1900 an astounding 80% of Chicago's population were immigrants.) It helped establish Hull House as a center of social studies research and J.A. as one of the main thinkers in the emerging field of soci-ology. "I find I am considered quite the grandmother of American settlements," she had written to Alice as early as 1893. She was then 33 years old.

The investigative work and writing done by Hull House resi-dents interested several University of Chicago faculty members, particularly John Dewey, who believed a reciprocal relationship between reformers and social scientists was vital to the life of both institutions. After a visit to Hull House he wrote to J.A., "Every day I stayed there only added to my conviction that you had taken the right way. I am confident that twenty-five years from now the forces now turned in on themselves. . . will be finding outlet very largely through channels you have opened up. . ." Dewey became a good friend of Hull House and was one of its first trustees when it was incorporated as Hull House Association in 1895.

In addition to J.A.'s demanding Hull House activities, her responsibilities to her unfortunate family increased. Her sister Mary was ill with tuberculosis in Pennoyer Sanitarium in Kenosha, leaving four children at home with a husband unable to care for them. J.A. was so concerned about the frail youngest child, Stanley, that she brought him to Hull House to live with her, thus adding a constant worry as well as pleasure to her life. She also kept in close touch with Mary's older children, loaned money to the eldest, John, watched over the education of James Weber at the University of Chicago, and attempted to help Esther, expelled from Rockford College, keep her college and romantic life on track. She paid most of her sister's medical bills, and settled her brother-in-law's estate.

Much to J.A.'s bewilderment and distress, Alice was critical of the way she handled their sister's estate. In *American Heroine, Life and Legend of Jane Addams*, Allen F. Davis suggests that Alice's criticism of Jane was due in part to her jealousy over her younger sister's growing fame. "What is on your mind and why are your letters so reproachful?" J.A. asked after receiving a particularly harsh letter from Alice. "I cannot imagine why you say that you fear that the children and finances are cutting you off from your natural sister."

J.A did not allow Alice's disapproval to staunch her flow of affectionate letters: "I do wish you would write me oftener. I get very anxious sometimes. I wake up in the night with a great longing for you." Alice did continue her regular summer visits to Hull House with her daughter, Marcet (who became good friends with Florence Kelley's daughter, Margaret), and joined J.A. and friends for their customary Hull House Thanksgiving.

Matters had also worsened at Cedarville. George Haldeman secluded himself in his room, seeing no one but Mary Fry and his mother. Anna Addams would never know when he might disappear from the Homestead, to return after an absence of many days, looking, Mary Fry reported, thin and pale as a ghost. In despair over her brilliant son's decline, Anna had become more outspoken about blaming J.A. for George's depression. Indeed, so strained had the relationship between the two women become that when J.A. visited Cedarville she stayed at her brother and sister-in-law's home instead of at the Homestead.

In spite of her private sorrows, chronic back pain and twelve-hour workdays, J.A. managed to be a prolific and dedicated writer. Though she was able to speak articulately, even eloquently, without preparation, she labored over her writing, revising and then revising again. One summer both she and Marcet, who had become a free-lance journalist, retreated to Bar Harbor to write. Marcet watched with fascination as her aunt cut the first draft of her essay into fragments, then spread the fragments on the dining room table and proceeded to fit the various pieces together, all the while reciting the text under her breath.

J.A.'s first book was quilted together in this way, with new material written to hold the separate parts in place. When she submitted a portion of the book to an editor he decided that there were "great possibilities in Miss Addams." Published under the title of *Democracy and Social Ethics*, it was admired by one critic for its "masculinity of mental grasp and surefootedness" (qualities apparently not to be regarded as feminine), and demeaned by another for its sentimentality and "puerile optimism." It sold fairly well and did much to increase J.A.'s stature as a respected thinker.

Though J.A. ultimately wrote over five hundred published articles and eleven books, she felt it a failure that she had not managed to write more. Nonetheless, as one book followed another the demand for her as a lecturer grew, especially at the universities of Chicago and Wisconsin. To many of the students attending her lectures, some of whom became interns at the Settlement, she was thought of not as the saint, but as the sage of Hull House.

Chapter 9

Losing Battles

*F*lorence Kelley, described by Weber Linn as "the finest rough and tumble fighter for the good life for others that Hull House ever knew," was not about to let J.A. settle into the role of sedate grandmother. In the Chicago of the l890s industrial progress too often depended on the exploitation of the poor. There were crucial battles to be fought and Kelley was determined to pull J.A. away from her desk and into the trenches.

In her autobiography Kelley revealed that her father spoke to her when she was very young about serious, adult matters which left a lasting impression. The duty of his generation, he had said to his precocious eight-year-old, was to build up great industries in America so that more wealth could be produced for the whole people. "The duty of your generation will be to see that the product is distributed justly. The same generation cannot do both."

Though it would be hard to find two people more dissimilar in manner and style than J.A. and Kelley (who was born one year earlier than J.A. in September 1859), in important ways their lives ran on parallel tracks. Kelley's family, like the Addams family, suffered the loss of beloved children. Kelley wrote:

I was the third of eight children, all fine, healthy boys and girls. . . five of whom died from infections now considered preventable. After the death in 1859 of my elder sister Elizabeth, age two years, entries in the family Bible followed with pitiful frequency. There were, all told, five in twelve years, Marian, aged 11 months, Josephine, 7 months, Caroline, 4 months and Anna, six years.

Both daughters adored and were influenced by egalitarian fathers who served in legislatures for many years and had an association with Lincoln. Congressman Kelley, reelected 14 consecutive times to the House of Representatives, had been the representative from Pennsylvania on the committee that notified Lincoln of his nomination. Florence Kelley, like J.A., endeavored to emulate her distinguished father. At the age of ten, wholly on her own, she began to read through his extensive library, "starting at the ceiling at the southwest corner of the study and continuing the process every time we were at home. . ."

But unlike J.A., Kelley had no formal schooling. Her mother, understandably apprehensive, kept her last surviving daughter home from school where she might pick up an illness. Notwithstanding, Kelley was admitted to Cornell University in 1876 at the age of 16 as one of its first women students. She recalled:

Entering college was for me an almost sacramental experience. Two long years I lived for it, since that lonely morning when I found, . . . in my father's wastebasket, Cornell's offer of equal intellectual opportunity for women. . . and forwith begged Father to let me prepare.

A friend described Kelley as a woman who "blended knowledge of facts, wit, satire, burning indignation, prophetic denunciation — all poured out at white heat varying from flute-like to deep organ tones." She was also, as a Hull House resident recalled, "kind, generous, and a born story-teller who we would wait for, no matter how late she returned from work, so we could gather 'round, cups of steaming cocoa in hand, to hear her relate the happenings of her day. And no day for Florence was without stories to tell."

Openly suspicious of those eager to deify J.A., Kelley exclaimed upon the departure of an effusive J.A. admirer, "Do you know what I would do if that woman calls you a saint again? I'd show her my teeth and if that didn't convince her, I would bite her!" As author Christopher Lasch observed, praising J.A.'s goodness was a way to avoid answering the hard questions she posed, one of which was the question Kelley was persistently asking, namely, Is industrialization compatible with humanity?

Though her education was interrupted by a crushing three-year illness, Kelley completed her course work and was one of the first women to graduate from Cornell. Imagine her fury when she was denied entry into the all-male University of Pennsylvania School of Law. She had little trouble, however, gaining admission to the University of Zurich where she studied law, became fluent in French and German, translated one of Friedrich Engels' books into English, and acquired a husband — a Russian Jewish doctor with whom she joined the Socialist Party. The alliance with the Party lasted; the alliance with the doctor did not. Convinced that their tumultuous marriage was unsalvageable, she brought her three children to Illinois, divorced her husband, and reclaimed the name Kelley.

All that she had heard about Hull House led Kelley to believe that it would afford her a base from which to do community work. J.A. helped her settle her children in suburban Winnetka with J.A.'s friends, the liberal Tribune journalist Henry Demarest Lloyd and his wife, Jesse Bross, daughter of the former lieutenant governor of Illinois. With her children safely nested and close enough to visit on weekends, Kelley set out to help remedy the inequalities in the city that enabled Marshall Field to spend $75,000 on a birthday party for his 17-year-old son while an immigrant mother boiled sewing spools in water to flavor "soup" for her children.

Kelley's first endeavor met with failure. She established a women's employment agency in a corner room of Hull House formerly inhabited by a morgue, but soon had to close down because of the unavailability of jobs. Kelley's next foray into community work would start her on a lifelong crusade against the institution of the sweatshop: she was appointed an inspector for a federal study of urban slums with responsibility for the square mile around Hull House.

Strong and energetic as Kelley was, getting around the Hull House neighborhood during winter was still a challenge. Mounds of coal-blackened snow walled in the streets, and horse-drawn vehicles were often stalled by the collapse of an overburdened, starving animal. Badly injured horses would be shot and hoisted to the top of the black mounds, not to be removed until the snow melted.

Tenement dwellers Kelley visited fared little better than the overworked horses. The shops and factories in which they labored were often located over foul-smelling stables or in ill-lighted, unventilated rooms below street level. After a 14-hour work day, an immigrant father made his exhausted way home to a dinner of watery soup and potatoes and fell into bed, only to rise the next morning to start the deadly regime once again.

A Yiddish song expressing the misery of factory life was translated into English and performed with fervor by the Hull House choir.

> The roaring of the wheels has filled my ears
> The clashing and clamor shut me in
> Myself, my soul, in chaos disappears
> I cannot feel or think among the din. . .

Another choir favorite, "A Working Girl's Song," was written by Harriet Monroe, founder of *Poetry Magazine*, and put to music by music director Eleanor Smith:

> Sisters of the whirling wheel
>   Are we all day;
> Builders of a house of steel
>   On time's highway.

139 0467

> Giving bravely hour by hour
> All we have of youth and power. . .
>
> Green are the fields in May-time
> Grant us our love-time, play-time
> Short is the day and dear. . .

Particularly sensitive to the lot of the young because of her own family's losses, Kelley was outraged by the army of very young children doing "sweat" work. It was not unusual to see a 4-year-old collapsed in sleep on a littered tenement floor, cotton basting threads still clutched in his hand. As many as two hundred girls, 4 to 12 years old, worked at crowded tables in a caramel factory, wrapping and packing in a room filled with steam erupting from the boiling candy. For several weeks before the Christmas rush the girls worked from seven o' clock in the morning to nine o'clock at night, with 20 minutes for lunch and no supper, a six-day work week of 82 hours. In the tobacco trade, children were poisoned by nicotine, in frame factories their fingers became stiff or paralyzed from contact with chemicals, and in textile factories they developed curvature of the spine as they bent over their machines. In one neighborhood machine shop, for lack of a machine guard costing no more than a few dollars, three boys were injured, one whom died of his wounds.

What could be done to prevent these horrors? Kelley and Lathrop supplied J.A. with an answer — enact a law prohibiting children under 15 from working, and limiting the work time of women and older children to eight hours a day.

Kelley loved a good fight; J.A., who strongly favored negotiation, did not. Nevertheless, with the zeal of a seasoned activist, she joined her two friends in their campaign for a humane labor law and traveled to Springfield to lobby Illinois legislators. Back in Chicago, she spoke on the proposed law almost every night for three months to trade unions, charitable foundations, churches and social groups.

In June 1893, the Illinois Factory Act was passed. Though it had some loopholes, the three campaigners were elated. Governor

Altgeld added to their high spirits by appointing Kelley chief factory inspector for Illinois, the first woman ever to hold the job. As two of her 12 assistants, Kelley hired Hull House residents, the indefatigable Mary Kenney, and Alzina Stevens, who as a child had lost two fingers in a textile mill.

The victory was short-lived. Hull House was located in the 19th ward, home to "50,000 souls, seven churches, two missions, ten parochial schools, no public schools and 255 saloons." The ward was presided over by ward boss Johnny "Da Pow" Powers, King of the Boodlers and proud of it. Boodle (graft) was as routine to Powers as daily bread. Mayor Carter Harrison once described Powers and his fellow council members as "a low-browed, dull-witted, base-minded gang of plug-uglies with no outstanding characteristic other than an unquenchable lust for money." Powers managed on an alderman's salary of three dollars a week to own an expensive home, two saloons, and several gambling emporiums. He was not about to force businessmen contributing to his coffers to observe the Factory Act.

Even though the 19th ward suffered the highest death rate in the city, partly because of sweatshops and factories that employed nine- and ten-year-olds, the Factory Act went unenforced under Powers' regime. Kelley's first attempt to have a penalty imposed upon the employer of an 11-year-old boy who had lost the use of his right arm was ominously unsuccessful. The district attorney to whom Kelley had taken the case listened disdainfully. "You bring me this evidence this week against some little two-by-six cheap picture frame maker," he said, "and how do I know you won't bring me a suit against Marshall Field next week?" Kelley left the district attorney's office and registered in Northwestern University Law School. In 1894, she earned a law degree which enabled her to practice in Illinois.

J.A. visited the stark tenements trying to persuade parents to send their children to school instead of to the factories. But her words rang hollow in the face of a family's irrefutable need for sons and daughters to be wage-earners. Attempting to solve the problems of the poor was like playing with Russian dolls. You opened the first doll only to find another inside, and another inside that. Unlike the dolls, however, the problems of the poor did not get smaller.

Two years after its enactment the Illinois Supreme Court struck down the eight-hour provision of the Factory Act as unconstitutional. Disheartened but determined, J.A., Lathrop and Kelley continued to fight for the eight hour day. But not until 1912, during Woodrow Wilson's presidency, did they have the satisfaction of seeing such legislation finally adopted.

J.A.'s advocacy of the Factory Act hardly endeared her to Chicago businessmen. Believing it their right to set their employees' working hours, they called J.A. a meddling Socialist and Hull House a nest of radicals. If J.A. were a radical, her defenders said, it was a radicalism of tolerance. She refused to censor those who wished to speak at Hull House, whether they were Socialists, single taxers, atheists, union organizers, evangelists or anarchists.

Wealthy, conservative donors to Hull House began to withhold their contributions to the Settlement. The zealous Miss Addams had gone too far. Members of the Fortnightly, a club of society women who had supported J.A.'s work, suddenly turned cool. "The public mind. . . falls into the old medieval confusion," J.A. wrote. "[He] who feeds or shelters a heretic is upon *prima facie* a heretic himself." As Muriel Beadle, chronicler of the club's history, wrote:

> Everyone agreed that it was praiseworthy for Miss Addams and her young ladies in residence to establish day nurseries and hold English language classes for immigrants. But the Hull House women began to step on sensitive toes when they helped to cut off the supply of child labor, agitated for improvements in tenement housing and intervened in strikes. In this role they were 'radicals'. . .

J.A. became even more controversial when she moved beyond

arguing for an eight hour day to advocacy of a worker's right to organize and bargain. In an article for *Hull-House Maps and Papers* she asserted:

> [If] the settlement is convinced that in industrial affairs lack of organization tends to the helplessness of the isolated worker, and is a menace to the entire community, then it is bound to pledge itself to industrial organization. And at this point the settlement enters into what is technically known as the labor movement.

With worthy intentions, George Pullman of the Pullman Company had built what he deemed a model company town on a tract of 3,000 acres. He called the town "Pullman" and equipped it with brick homes, an arcade and bank, a post office and stores, a theater, library and hotel. (No saloons were permitted.) Providing workers with ideal working conditions, he believed, would make them happier and more productive.

But in Pullman's self-styled dream of a worker's Utopia, productivity, not happiness, was the priority. Five days after the 1893 World's Colombian Exposition ended, the stock market crashed and hard-hit railroad companies began to cancel orders for the expensive Pullman sleeping cars. Pullman responded by cutting both the hours and the wages of his workers, while refusing to lower their rents. Although utility bills and food left many employees with no cash for anything else, Pullman insisted that there was no connection between the wages he paid and the rent he charged. He fired the men who tried to negotiate with him, and evicted them from their homes the next day. He also fired those employees who took part in a boycott of Pullman cars called by the newly organized American Railway Union, led by the young Eugene Debs (who, however, had advised against the boycott).

The Pullman stike of 1894 stalled the country's entire rail system. J.A. was one of a six-member arbitration committee convened to settle the strike. The committee repeatedly urged Pullman to negotiate to end the deadlock, but he adamantly refused. J.A. visited the town of Pullman, and after satisfying herself that the workers' grievances were justified, went to the company offices in yet one more attempt to persuade Pullman to negotiate. She was brushed off without a hearing. Wasn't it a known fact that J.A. was a unionist, maybe even an anarchist, most certainly a Socialist?

While J.A. balked at being called a unionist or anarchist, being identified as a Socialist didn't bother her. On one of her visits to Hull House, her niece, Marcet, by then a confirmed Socialist, asked J.A. whether, in these changing times, she was changing into a Socialist. Marcet recorded their ensuing conversation in her memoir of her aunt:

> 'I am much more nearly one than I used to be,' was her reply. She explained that she believed in many socialistic measures and was friendly to the principle of collectivism, but could not condone the whole Socialist program. . . She objected especially to the Socialist emphasis on the class struggle, arguing that sharp, fixed class lines did not exist in America as in Europe. . . She added as an afterthought she didn't like 'labels' anyway.
>
> 'Why, Aunt Jane,' I exclaimed banteringly, 'you're plastered all over with them.'
>
> As we both swiftly reviewed in our minds some of these different labels — social worker, feminist, suffragist, pacifist — Aunt Jane's eyes shone with appreciation at the accuracy of the thrust. I suggested that she just wasn't ready for the Socialist label. She smiled, and we left it at that.

The Pullman strike dragged on month after month, bringing in its wake violence and mass looting. Pressured to end the stalemate, President Cleveland called in federal troops, but that only worsened the situation. Debs was arrested on a charge of stopping the mail, and Kelley and Alzina Stevens organized a mass meeting to raise money for his defense. J.A. avoided the meeting, retreated to her desk and wrote a paper, "The Modern Tragedy," later to be changed to "A Modern Lear," first delivered as a speech to one of her earliest supporting organizations, the Chicago Women's Club.

There is a parallel, she contended, between George Pullman and King Lear. Just as Lear felt betrayed by the ingratitude of his youngest daughter, Pullman was bitterly disappointed over what seemed the ingratitude of his employees. Both men had fallen in love with being the good "king" and had lost touch with the human feelings of those they ruled. "It is so easy," J.A. wrote, "for the good and powerful to think that they can rise by. . . pursuing their own ideals, leaving those ideals unconnected with the consent of their fellowmen." It was crucial for a leader to learn what people wanted and "then help provide the channels in which the growing moral force of their lives will flow. . . Is it too much to hope," she asked, "that some of us will carefully consider this modern tragedy. . . and be spared useless industrial tragedies in the uncertain future which lies ahead?"

J.A. was anxious to publish "A Modern Lear," but it was rejected by nine different editors. "Our schedules are crowded," "not enough space," "not right for us" were the editors' stock words to avoid saying that they found her essay too controversial or were loathe to publish criticism of Pullman. When Henry Demarest Lloyd asked if J.A. would send him a copy of the essay she replied:

> I am quite ashamed of this poor copy - but I am pleased and proud that you want to read it. Will you kindly return it when you have read it? In doing that you will be following the example of most of the illustrious magazines in the country.

The essay was finally published in 1912 in *Survey,* the principal journal of social work. By that time there was no longer any risk involved.

The Pullman strike turned out to be a disaster for the workers. Those who had been active participants had to leave Pullman because they could find no work there. New employees were forced to sign a contract prohibiting them from ever joining a union. After months without work, some former employees drifted back to the community and took their old jobs at reduced wages. It was a dismal end to a painful struggle.

J.A. recalled that terrible summer in *The Second Twenty Years at Hull-House:*

> Chicago was filled with federal troops sent there by the President of the United States. . . I walked the wearisome way from Hull-House to Lincoln Park — for no cars were running regularly at that moment of sympathetic strikes — in order to look at and gain magnanimous counsel, if I might, from the marvelous St. Gaudens statue which had been but recently placed at the entrance to the park. Some of Lincoln's immortal words were cut into the stone at his feet, and never did a distracted town more sorely need the healing of 'with charity toward all' than did Chicago at that moment.

Chicago needed to heal, and so did J.A. During the worst of the crisis, her beloved sister Mary died.

Ellen Gates Starr

"One must always remember the hungry individual soul which without art will have passed unsolaced and unfed, followed by other souls who lack the impulse his should have given."

Julia Lathrop

"Ignorant or not, we have to do what we can in any emergency.
If Hull House doesn't have its roots in human kindness it is no good
at all."

Alice Hamilton, M.D.

"Life in a settlement does several things to you... Among others it teaches you that education and culture have little to do with real wisdom, the wisdom that comes from life experience."

Mary Rozet Smith

"I have been having another rough time with my conscience about my wealth. I wonder how it would be to escape from the 'conviction of sin' for about ten minutes."

Florence Kelley

"To hasten the day when all good things of society shall be the goods of all the children of men and our petty philanthropy of today superfluous – this is the true work for the elevation of the race, the true philanthropy."

Louise Bowen

"Although the people I met at Hull House lived a life far removed
from the kind I led, yet after all we are all cast in the same mold, all
with the same feelings, the same emotions, the same sense of right
or wrong, but alas, not with the same opportunities."

Jane Addams, with 11-year-old nephew Stanley

"Nothing is more certain than that each generation longs for a reassurance as to the value and charm of life, and is secretly afraid lest it lose its sense of the youth of the earth."

The Residents' Dining Hall, about 1930.
Jane Addams at end of middle table, Sadie Ellis Garland at end of back table.

Typical living quarters of Hull House resident.

Reception room at Hull House, intake desk in foreground.

Chapter 10

The Warm Circle

*W*hen last visiting Mary at the Pennoyer Sanitarium, J.A. had noted the blush of color in her sister's cheeks and dared to hope that she was regaining her health. But Mary's rosy complexion turned out to be the last blaze before the fire died. Not yet 34 years old, J.A. had already endured the deaths of her mother, father, 16-year-old sister, a four-month-old nephew, a two-year-old niece, and her dearly loved family nurse, as well as the severe mental illnesses of her brother and stepbrother. To that long list was now added the sister who had been mother to her after her own mother's death and the closest link to her father. With Mary's death, the death of John Addams was in some measure repeated. In a letter to Alice, J.A. confessed to a grief so deep as to be almost unbearable.

What sustained J.A. then, and later, were her close, long-lived friendships with some of the extraordinary women who gravitated to Hull House. In addition to Ellen Gates Starr, Julia Lathrop and Florence Kelley, there were Mary Rozet Smith, Louise Bowen and Alice Hamilton.

Mary Rozet Smith, daughter of a wealthy Chicago manufacturer, lived with her mother and father in an elegant mansion on Walton Street. She attended the Kirkland School for Girls, and instead of college chose to travel abroad with her parents. Twenty years old, "tall, shy, fair and eager," she sought to fill the void in her life with something worthwhile. A casual invitation to visit Hull House from her friend, Jenny Dow, one year after the Settlement was founded, set her on the road she would follow the rest of her life.

Hull House was the perfect place for Smith, who had no special talent centering her strong energy and generous spirit. She took on any and all duties, from putting out mailings and making the arrangements for J.A.'s many trips, to assisting in the nursery and leading a Hull House Girls Club. Obliged to live at home because of her parents' poor health, she was nonetheless accepted as a Hull House resident and shared many dinner hours with the talkative company that gathered around the dining room tables every evening.

Smith's commitment to Hull House led her to finance musician Eleanor Smith in establishing the Hull House Music School in 1892. Soon known as the most progressive and professional music center in the city, the school boasted Benny Goodman as one of its most illustrious early students as well as a number of young musicians who went on to play in the country's major orchestras. In 1895 Smith persuaded her father to build the Hull House Children's Building, a spacious nursery and children's center with a wide porch for outdoor play (where the clean-spoken parrot reigned supreme). She also became a Hull House trustee and frequently covered a financial deficit for the Settlement as it struggled for solvency in an economically battered city.

J.A. was grateful to Smith for her financial help, but felt concerned that their relationship might be buried beneath monetary transactions. This concern, as well as the ten-year difference in age between them, disappeared as the two grew to be intimate friends. Though Weber Linn and most others characterized Mary Rozet Smith as possessing "serenity, quick insight, warmth, and a heart at leisure from itself," her letters disclose an inner strife that she may have revealed only to her friend and mentor:

I have been having another bad time with my conscience about my 'wealth' and I've been in the depths of gloom until yesterday when the sight and sound of you cheered me. I do not feel any more righteous now, but a good less stony and not wanting the earth to swallow me as much as I did. I wonder how it would feel to escape from the 'conviction of sin' for about ten minutes. I do hope that dying does that for one. I seem to be lapsing into melancholy, but I'm really hilariously cheerful — comparatively speaking — and full of gratitude to you and overflowing with affection.

The nourishment of Smith's steady and undemanding devotion contributed significantly to J.A.'s ability to continually renew her will and energy for work that too often yielded little but defeat and exhaustion. Theirs was an emotional attachment, partaking little of the intellectual give-and-take J.A. enjoyed with Starr, Lathrop and Kelley. Complex as J.A. was, she found the generous, loving nature of Smith restful in a way that Starr's driving intensity could never be. And Smith received respite from her plagued conscience by aiding the woman who was working to improve the quality of the immigrants' burdened lives. Her friendship with J.A. was such that she was able to give her friend what Marcet called a "tender tonic of criticism" that J.A. accepted from no one else. According to Marcet, "Mary Rozet had a genius for sweetly reminding Jane Addams of small, yet on their level, needful things, and for helping keep in their true proportion concerns and feelings that might easily have been overlooked."

In 1904 the two friends bought a cottage a mile away from Louise Bowen's summer home in Hull's Cove, a small fishing village near Bar Harbor, Maine. The time J.A. spent there had "a healing domesticity" that helped her weather the stresses of her life. She and Smith took great joy "in watching from the porch of the house a beautiful sunset in the west, while at the same time they could look out the other way at a great red moon rising out of the waves of the sea." Years later when they were forced to give up the cottage because of J.A.'s. poor health, they were brokenhearted. "They decided," Bowen recalled, "to make as many people happy as they could by giving away everything it contained. I remember well. . . their neighbors to whom the lovely things went — the laundress, the poultry man, the vegetable man, the milk man. Truck after truck backed up to their door and took away furniture and beautiful things that they had accumulated from all parts of the world."

When it became obvious that Robert Wood, director of South End House on Chicago's South Side, was attracted to Mary Smith, J.A. cautioned her friend not to be "an iceberg nor a tombstone when the siege begins." But Smith showed interest in nothing but her life at Hull House. In characterizing J.A.'s relationship with Smith, Weber Linn wrote, "The friendship of Mary Smith soon became and always remained the highest and clearest note in the music of Jane Addams' life."

In her memoir, *Growing Up in the City,* Louise Bowen wrote:

> I had heard Jane Addams speak at a meeting concerning the great strike at the Pullman Company. I remembered she likened Mr. Pullman to King Lear, and she seemed so fair and dispassionate in setting forth the reason. . . that I was much impressed. . . Soon after I went over to Hull House to visit a friend, and. . . I remember giving some money to be used for the poor. . .

Bowen's donation was the first in a long line of contributions to Hull House, including the money to build Bowen Hall. Without the financial support of Mary Rozet Smith and Louise Bowen, it is doubtful whether Jane Addams could have kept Hull House alive.

Louise DeKoven was raised in a family of great wealth, and was told what to think and how to behave by a rigid father and a religious and conventional mother. Her happiest days as a young girl were spent on her grandfather's farm where she was free of the restrictions imposed on her at home on Walton Street. (The farm was later sold and transformed into the busy intersection of Wabash and Adams in downtown Chicago. Weber Linn commented that the meager $50,000 paid for the farm would barely buy a piece of land large enough for a cow to lie down on.) She had been an honor student at the Dearborn Seminary in 1875, and one of twelve girls chosen to read their senior essays at the graduation ceremony. Her father, considering it unwomanly to speak publicly to an audience of both men and women, enlisted one of Louise's male cousins to read her essay for her.

Bowen's memoir, *Open Windows*, described the typical education of the young society woman of the day:

> I was made to practice one hour a day at the piano, and after several years of study was able to play *Coming Thru the Rye* and *Nearer My God to Thee*. I also took lessons in making wax flowers. . . [My] fancy work consisted of hemming sheets and wash cloths. By the time I made my entry into society I was ignorant in everything and accomplished in nothing.

Though Louise DeKoven's childhood was insulated from the harshness and suffering of the world, she was made aware by her parents that she would inherit great wealth and must learn to spend it for the good of others as well as for herself. After she had married the successful lawyer, Joseph Bowen (with whom she "fell in love at first sight"), and the oldest of their four children was of school age, Bowen determined not to follow the path of the rich and indulged. Regal but not haughty, self-confident and strong-willed, she was unusually open to lifestyles drastically different from her own. When she showed an interest in working at Hull House, J.A. urged her to join the newly formed Hull House Women's Club so that she might help the immigrant women talk through their problems and make motions properly. Bowen enrolled in a course on parliamentary procedure, joined the club and became its secretary.

Six months later she was asked to serve as president. "I'll accept only under one condition," she told her sister club members. "That you all quit chewing gum. It makes me nervous when I look down and see everyone's mouth moving in a different rhythm." An anti-gum chewing motion was promptly made and passed unanimously.

Bowen described a Women's Club meeting:

> I can see the crowded room now, filled with tired women, a few of them with shawls over their heads, some of them with babies in their arms or clinging to their skirts. There was always a good deal of noise, the women were restless, the air was heavy and stuffy but no one wanted a window opened. On the front row sat the eldest members of the club, most of them wore black bonnets with ribbons tied under their chins. They had an invariable habit of going to sleep and when I was speaking and saw them begin to nod it always acted as a tonic because I brightened up and tried to be so entertaining or star-tling in my remarks that they would come to with a jerk, and the test of my speaking was could I keep that front bench looking intelligent and awake?

When Bowen first joined the Hull House Women's Club she purposely wore her simplest clothes and was driven to the meetings in a nondescript buggy. But she found

> the women wanted good clothes; they liked to have me drive up in a motor and to see it standing in front of the club house on Polk Street. I always told my friends that I had to keep up a certain number of social activities in order to get my name in the papers to please the Club. Many a time they would say, 'We saw your name in the paper as being at the opera.' . . . 'We were glad to know our club president was at a ball.'

Working with the Club meant a great deal to Bowen.

> Not even in church did I ever get the inspiration or the desire for service so much as when I was presiding at a meeting of the club and sat on the platform and looked down on the faces of 800 or 900 women gathered together, all intensely earnest and all most anxious perhaps to put over some project in

which they were interested. The club proved a liberal education for me.

In her book, *The Fortnightly of Chicago*, Muriel Beadle wrote:

> In 1918, Mrs. Joseph T. Bowen became an honorary member of The Fortnightly. That astounding woman was then fifty-nine years old, yet she had almost as much productive activity ahead of her as was already on her record. After Lucy Flower had brought the Juvenile Court into being, Louise Bowen had made it work. . . Then she carried on as President of the Juvenile Protective Association. . . She was one of the founders of the Visiting Nurse Association and President of the Woman's Board of Passavant Hospital. . . But her greatest enthusiasm was Hull House.

Bowen recalled her husband's reaction, upon hearing her address a Hull House audience:

> I was speaking one evening at a meeting at Hull House on 'Courage.' My husband had accompanied me, and I could see him sitting behind a woman with a large hat. In my speech I said I was happy to say that I had become a suffragist. . . I well remember my husband's face. It said as clearly as if he had said it straight to me. 'What is Louise going to do next?'

Bowen and J.A. spent a great deal of time traveling together on speaking tours advocating suffrage. In *Open Windows*, Bowen wrote:

> We had many causes in common and so had good times together, often going off on speaking tours for two or three days. I well remember the first time we went away together. . . She pleased me greatly by saying, 'Would you take a room with me because I don't like to be alone very much?'. . . [We] were sometimes heckled, [but] she was always ready with a reply. . . On one occasion, at Carnegie Hall in New York. . . Miss Addams had been kept until last since she was the most important speaker. She was a little provoked at this, as she was very tired, and when the presiding officer called upon her, about

11:30, to give her address, she got up quietly and said, 'It is so late that I will just say that my address is 800 South Halsted Street, Chicago.' There was a roar from the audience and she was applauded so many times that she had to say a few words.

In 1895, when there seemed to be no alternative but to add a Board of Directors to Hull House, a measure J.A. had resisted as long as she could, Bowen became its treasurer, a position she was to hold until after Jane Addams' death. As president of the Juvenile Protective Agency, in 1913 she wrote the first study of the life of blacks in Chicago "in an attempt to ascertain the causes which would account for a greater amount of delinquency among colored boys and for the public opinion which so carelessly places the virtue of a colored girl in jeopardy." It proved to be a significant piece of work and, though Bowen did not suggest social equality as a solution to the race problem, for its day it presented an unusually thoughtful analysis.

Defying social expectations for women of her wealth and status, Bowen was a staunch foot soldier out in the streets, investigating, campaigning, speaking, lobbying, never balking at the nitty-gritty work that is the life-stuff of the true reformer.

Dr. Alice Hamilton was appointed Professor of Pathology at the Women's Medical School of Northwestern University in 1897 when she was a mere 26 years old. It was a phenomenal feat at a time when universities rarely admitted women to medical school and even more rarely, if at all, hired them as faculty. (Eager to do further study in pathology and bacteriology, Hamilton was rejected by Johns Hopkins, which did not permit women in its doctoral programs.) One might suppose that Hamilton, accomplishing so much in the face of persistent and demoralizing opposition, was armed with impervious self-confidence. The opposite was true. Throughout her amazing life she was haunted by self-doubt. Responding to a letter from her sister Agnes she wrote:

Talk about making me feel better; it [your letter] made me feel unutterably blue. It simply showed me what a beautiful high idea you have of my work and what a low one I have of myself. For I don't think of it as a mission of healing at all. In the first place I don't feel as if I were healing. When a surgical case heals up, or a typhoid goes home well I feel as the backers of the victorious man in a prize-fight feel. They have been watching the fight and helping and encouraging their champion. . . but he has done the fighting not they. . . I simply have placed myself in a position that will show if there is [something special in me] or not and day by day I am finding out there isn't. And some day you will find it out too, only I hope I die first.

Self-doubt did not keep Hamilton from speaking her mind. With her special brand of dry humor she had protested when, as an overworked intern, she was required to fill prescriptions: "So besides all the other methods of killing, I am to have the chance of poisoning my patients too!"

Hamilton's desire to help the poor led her to Hull House. A few days after she became a resident she confided to her sister, Edith (a classical scholar, renowned for her book, *The Greek Way*), that she was reduced to school-girl timidity by Jane Addams whom she revered.

Mrs. Kelley I find approachable and I can enjoy talking to her very much but Miss Addams still rattles me, indeed more so all the time and I am at my very worst with her. I am really rather school-girly in my relations with her; it is a remnant of youth which surprises me. I know when she comes into the room. I have pangs of idiotic jealousy toward the residents whom she is intimate with.

Dismayed at the infant mortality rate in the neighborhood, Hamilton established a well-baby clinic in the basement of the old mansion. On Tuesday and Thursday mornings the clinic provided baths for the infants in 12 small bathtubs installed in the gymnasium shower room, a measure Hamilton instituted to prevent infections in children who might not otherwise feel a drop of water for weeks at a time.

Hamilton attempted to surmount the Italian mothers' deep-rooted aversion to putting their babies in water by first rubbing the infant with olive oil. The stratagem did not always work; nor did Hamilton's suggestion that the babies' diet be restricted to milk until their teeth came in. "I gave him the breast and plenty of milk," an Italian mother explained, "but he cried all the time. The next day I was making soup and gave him some and he was fine. The next day I was making cupcakes and when one got cool I gave it to him and he was just fine. From then on I just gave him what we all eat and he's happy and fat." After another mother assured Hamilton that her baby was healthy on a diet of fried eggs and vegetable soup, she gave up advocating a milk diet.

Within a year of coming to Hull House, Hamilton became so involved in running the clinic, supervising evening lectures and giving lectures herself, while at the same time feeling dissatisfied with the progress of her own medical work, that she considered moving from Hull House. She wrote to her sister Edith:

> Miss Addams seemed so genuinely distressed at the thought of my going away. She said that I must stay and do nothing at all, that she was sure that it would be better for me in a place where I was happy and had people I liked around me instead of in a lonely boarding house. Well, there is no need for me to tell you that I am going back. [Hamilton had been visiting friends for several days.] I simply must, you know. But as for doing nothing, one might as well resolve to go to a small pox hospital and not catch small-pox.

For Hamilton, earning her M.D. had just been an entry into the valley of indecision. Barbara Sicherman, editor of *Alice Hamilton, A Life in Letters*, says of Hamilton: "Her. . . struggles to find satisfying work. . . persisted for a decade. Intense doubt about her own abilities and goals, combined with exceptionally high standards and a deep need to prove herself, made her best efforts seem inadequate."

Ironically, *because* of its distractions, it was at Hull House that Hamilton, treating babies ill with lead poisoning and typhoid and observing mothers and fathers stricken with the same ailments, found her life's work. There was no better place to study the connection between disease and environment than the factories and tenements of a settlement neighborhood. Hamilton's pioneering research led to an appointment to the Illinois Commission on Occupational Diseases. In her work on lead poisoning she tracked down dispensary and union death records and persuaded workers to cooperate. In her work on poisonous dusts, "she interviewed workers in saloons, climbed dangerous catwalks, and descended deep into mine shafts. She also slept in unlocked mining shacks, and once was mistaken for a prostitute." Her thorough (and highly adventurous) studies, the first of their kind, proved without doubt which Illinois industries used lead and their resulting and shockingly high mortality rates.

Hamilton's work was so exceptional that Harvard offered her an assistant professorship in industrial medicine although no women had yet been admitted into its medical school. Asked how she felt about the appointment, Hamilton responded, "I am not the first woman who ought to have been called to Harvard." She soon became the most eloquent voice advocating better health conditions for American workers. Addressing a graduation class, Hamilton's words were reminiscent of J.A.'s Rockford graduation speech:

> To acquire the joy of work is to have a certain assurance of satisfaction in life, because it grows with use. It is not dependent on other people and even when it tires it does not leave one with the sense of futility that follows pleasure for its own sake.

J.A. was a frustrating patient who usually ignored her doctor's advice. On occasion, however, she would listen to Alice Hamilton, who had quickly overcome her initial shyness to become J.A.'s dear friend and self-appointed medical caretaker. One sweltering August evening, Hamilton persuaded J.A. to leave her desk for a tandem bike ride along the lakeshore. "We leave the 19th Ward steaming, choking and melting," Hamilton wrote to Edith, "and in fifteen minutes we are on the lakeshore spinning along with the air fresh in our faces and the lake before us and the moon just coming up."

Many of J.A.'s most contented hours after the death of Mary Smith were spent visiting Alice Hamilton's country house in Hadlyme, Connecticut. Hamilton had remodeled a wing of the old house expressly for J.A.'s comfort. In a letter to her sister at a time when J.A. was at Hadlyme suffering the effects of a heart attack, Hamilton wrote: "I am leading the disorganized, unplanned life that one leads in a house of sickness. People come and go and I see them or not, and I do very little but it is as if a rope tied me to that sickroom and I am restless if I am not near it."

In later life Hamilton's concern for the mental and physical health of poor women and their children made her a committed advocate of birth control. When she received several letters from clergymen objecting to her endorsement of the book, *Birth Control, Its Use and Misuse,* she responded:

> May I explain first that my interest in birth control has come from my contact with poor people. . . I lived for more than twenty years in Hull House, Chicago and came in intimate contact with poor women, Italian and Irish chiefly. With them there was no question of self-indulgence; it was a pretty desperate struggle to keep up some standard of family life and not to exploit the older children too ruthlessly. . . My only interest in the birth control movement has been the spread of information among poor women for I think that for them it is an urgent necessity to learn ways of preventing pregnancy aside from abstinence. . . I quite agree that the ideal is not to restrict the number of children in a family but to make it possible to have large families without economic disaster, but I fear I shall not live to see such a well-ordered social system so I must work for a system in which family size can be controlled without disaster to the marriage.

Hamilton predicted that she would live to 100. In fact, she lived to 101, dying in 1970, 36 years after the death of J.A. She remained active in the causes she believed in until her death. At an age when most people are glad to retire to their homes and hobbies, Hamilton earned a place in the FBI files for her radical stand on civil liberty issues and fervent opposition to the Vietnam War. The ever-vigilant FBI still kept watch over her so-called subversive activities when she was in her late nineties. All those who cherished her wished that she had lived but three months longer. She would then have been able to celebrate the passage of the Occupational Safety and Health Act, which gave the federal government power to enforce healthier conditions in America's workplaces over which Hamilton had stood watch for so long.

Where did Ellen Gates Starr fit into the growing network of friends who surrounded J.A.? Devoted companions setting out on a bold journey of discovery, the two young women had developed different lifestyles once Hull House was established. Starr was more private than J.A. Though thoroughly involved in the running of Hull House that first year, she retreated from any public notice. As Mary Smith became an increasingly important part of J.A.'s life, the relationship between J.A. and Starr shifted to a less primary place in both their lives. Starr acknowledged this when she wrote to J.A. after browsing through some old letters: "I can see by the way you overrate me in these letters that it was inevitable that I should disappoint you. I think I have always, at any rate for a great many years, been thankful that Mary came to supply what you needed. At all events I thank God that I never was envious of her in any vulgar or ignoble way."

There is a temptation to read between the lines of this rather enigmatic letter. A sense of loss is hinted at — Starr seemed sure that she had disappointed J.A., but there is no clue as to how. She began to spend more and more time with her aunt, Alzina Starr, a prominent and devout Roman Catholic.

Like her English mentors, John Ruskin and William Morris, Starr mourned the increasing loss of handicrafts as industrialization took its toll. To help preserve the art of fine bookbinding she had left Hull House to study in London for 15 months with a master bookbinder. She then returned to the Settlement to set up a book bindery and earn her living selling handmade books. She was able to give lessons to only a limited number of people, for the Hull House bindery was small and she was a very exacting teacher. Her passion cooled when she faced the reality that she was making a product that only the rich could afford.

Increasingly, Starr felt the need to do something more concrete than teach. She began directing the intensity of purpose she had lavished on art to campaigning for better working conditions for women. Shedding her shyness like an obsolete skin, she helped organize strikes, picketed against unfair employers, and on more than one occasion was arrested for her "radical" activities. Though small in stature, Starr's presence on a picket line was usually noticed. She would approach a policeman placing a striker under arrest and say, with considerable refinement, "As an American citizen, I protest against the arrest of this person, who is doing nothing against the law." In one of Starr's court appearances, a policeman testified that she was a rabble-rouser and had yelled at him, "Leave them girls be!" She was released when her lawyer pointed out that Miss Starr would never speak so ungrammatically.

Increasingly impatient with Hull House's principle of tolerance for all points of view, Starr was critical of Jane Addams' propensity for seeing two sides to every question. "If the devil himself came walking down Halsted Street," she said to her friend, "you would compliment him on the curve of his tail!" Starr joined the Socialist Party and in 1916, there being no other Socialist candidate, ran unsuccessfully for alderman in the 19th ward.

Unlike Lathrop, Kelley, Smith and Hamilton, Ellen Gates Starr was not generally liked by the other Hull House residents. Her intensity and abrasive wit could be intimidating. "Mr. Deknatel [a mild-mannered businessman] confided to me," Alice Hamilton wrote to Edith, "that he dreads her [Starr's] coming to dinner and he believes that he will move down to our end of the table. I am so glad I'm safely there already." Like many gifted persons who tend toward zealotry, Starr attracted a small but very loyal following, mainly among her Socialist friends.

By 1920 she had left Hull House, though she continued to spend an occasional morning or afternoon there. Her long quest for religious identity ended when she converted to Roman Catholicism and moved to a convent. As a result of a spinal operation, she suffered a paralysis of her legs which condemned her to a wheelchair. With religion her great comfort, she spent her last years in the convent observing religious practice and reading and writing. Although she remained in touch with J.A. throughout her life, the different paths the two friends traveled created a distance between them that they may have denied but could not bridge.

When writing *American Heroine*, Allen F. Davis had asked Alice Hamilton, then 87 years old, whether there had been a sexual side to J.A.'s relationships with Ellen Gates Starr or Mary Rozet Smith. Hamilton had smiled, responding that it was evidence of how much times had changed that Davis should feel free to ask her that question. She went on to say that though there well may have been some unacknowledged sexuality in many of the close relationships among women in that first generation of college graduates, that was not important. What *was* important was that the women gave to each other the strong emotional support they needed to do their chosen work.

When the author of this biography asked Sadie Garland Dreikurs (formerly Sadie Ellis) the same question, she answered:

> It's become a national sport to figure out who is or is not homosexual. It's bad enough to do that with our contemporaries but to go back in history is risky and usually irresponsible. Women had very close relationships then. My Hull House friend Blanche Maggioli and I, in our teens, vowed that we

would never marry and would devote our lives to art and to each other. Over the many years I knew and lived with Jane Addams in Hull House, there was never the faintest suggestion that she and Mary Rozet Smith were anything but compatible and devoted friends.

Ellen Gates Starr, Julia Lathrop, Florence Kelley, Mary Rozet Smith, Louise Bowen and Alice Hamilton — all life-time friends who helped J.A. maintain, in the face of monumental personal losses, the strong momentum of her life.

Young chef in Hull House cooking class for boys.

Dance class in Bowen Hall.

Violin lesson with volunteer teacher from the Chicago Symphony Orchestra.

Two Hull House firsts: the first public gymnasium in Chicago in 1893 and the first women's basketball team in the city.

A Saturday dance class in Bowen Hall. Clubs of several age groups met each week for folk dancing and socializing.

A typewriting class. The Indian Room artifacts were aquired by Jane Addams on a trip to the Southwest.

Jesus Gonzalez working in Hull House pottery studio.

Jesus Gonzalez, oil painting by Sadie Ellis Garland.

Hull House lithograph by Leon Garland, 1930.

Street Market, woodcut by Bill Jacobs, member of Saturday Painters.

Weaver demonstrating her art in labor museum.

An evening of singing with the Friendly Club, the only Hull House club of adults and children.

The Children's Hour

Behind the scenes at Hull House Theater.

Chapter 11

Tending the Flame

*W*illiam Kent, publicly criticized by Florence Kelley for being the slumlord of an inherited cluster of disreputable tenements adjacent to Hull House, was willing to give the buildings to the House rent-free on condition they be converted into model tenements. J.A. declined the offer, suggesting instead that the blighted buildings be torn down. What, Kent asked, would she have him do with the vacant land?

J.A. had a ready answer. Walking down traffic-clogged, muddy Halsted Street she had been haunted by the contrast between her carefree play with George in the Cedarville woods and the street games of neighborhood children, constantly interrupted by the flow of peddlers' carts, buggies and occasional runaway horses.

"Make it into a playground," she responded. Kent was not prepared for such an answer. Indeed, he was not prepared for J.A. Seemingly mild-mannered, she nevertheless did not mince words. The blight could be turned into a boon, she said, by creating a safe, clean, public playground. It would ease the burden of working mothers forced to lock their children into tenement apartments to keep them safe.

Did J.A. tell Kent the story of a neighborhood woman's 5-year-old son Goosie, so called because his rumpled hair sprouted small feathers from the brush factory where his mother worked? The mother, hanging clothes to dry on her tenement roof, had no safe place for Goosie to play, so she involved him in the "game" of handing her the clothespins. A sudden high wind blew the frail child off the roof and into the alley below, where the horrified mother ran down to find him crumpled on a pile of frozen refuse, his neck broken.

Kent took a few days to agree to what J.A. had proposed. Thanking him for his generosity, J.A. suggested that it would be helpful if he continued to pay the taxes on the land. Still another request from this insatiable woman! Reluctantly, Kent agreed.

On sunny May Day in 1893, Chicago's first public playground opened. Drab Polk Street sprang to life as families dressed in holiday garb thronged to join the celebration. Hull House musicians performed exuberantly and girls in butterfly-colored dresses danced around a be-ribboned maypole. The older boys played ball under the watchful eye of a city-assigned policeman whose duties included acting as umpire and coach. A Hull House kindergarten teacher supervised the youngest children's play, freeing relieved mothers to attend to the necessities of the day.

Some 85 years later, the authors of a sociological study of Chicago's slums charged that the much-praised public playground was built at the expense of tenants evicted from Kent's buildings who were then without shelter. Had those evicted been families with children, it is probable that J.A. would have crowded them into Hull House temporarily, or found other housing as she had done countless times with the suddenly homeless. (Ellen Gates Starr, had she been alive to respond to the sociologists' charge, might have said that it was outside the Hull House sphere of activity to find replacement brothels for "ladies of the night.")

The question persists to this day: Should a proposed public action to benefit the many be abandoned because of the cost to the few? One hundred years after Kent's tenements gave way to a playground, tenants of Chicago's crime-infested, deteriorated public housing high-rises opposed the demolition of their buildings even though they had been promised higher quality replacement housing. Some, because of past betrayals, did not trust the housing authority to build the new housing; others felt so vulnerable that they feared moving into unfamiliar neighborhoods. Hull House resident Edith Abbott, working with J.A. and Graham Taylor for housing reform in 1908, reported that Italian peasants, evicted from foul tenements and offered improved housing in a West Side Italian neighborhood, "looked upon the trip one mile west and across the river as a journey to a far country and felt harshly dealt with because they were forced to leave."

However uncomfortable it was, J.A. had to live with the reality that to help the poor one often had to fight the poor. She wrote: "The mere consistent enforcement of existing laws and efforts for their [the tenement dwellers'] advance often placed Hull House, at least temporarily, into strained relations with its neighbors."

As a founder of the National Playground Association, J.A. traveled the speaker's circuit advocating playgrounds nationwide. "The modern city," she said in speech and print, "gathering together multitudes of eager young creatures as a labor supply for the countless factories and workshops, must give those young people a place and a time for recreation."

The establishment of the Hull House playground had profound significance for J.A. She had studied numerous books on child behavior (she was always reading one book while finishing another); most significant were the works of Friedrich Froebel, founder of the German kindergarten movement. Froebel was the first to conceptualize a child, not as an undeveloped adult, but as a complete being who required his or her own season — childhood — to develop into a fulfilled and productive person.

Froebel confirmed what J.A. had learned from painful experience: children robbed of childhood were likely to become dull, sullen men and women working mindless jobs, or criminals for whom the adventure of crime became the only way to break out of the bleakness of their lives. *The Spirit of Youth and the City Streets*, published in 1909, was of all J.A.'s books the closest to her heart. It addressed, head on, the city's failure to provide healthy, enticing recreational opportunities for its restless, bored, frustrated young people.

> The classical city promoted play with careful solicitude, building the theater and stadium as it built the market place and the temple. . . [Only] in the modern city have men concluded that it is no longer necessary for the municipality to provide for the insatiable desire for play. . . and this at the very moment when the city has become distinctly industrial.

"The stupid experiment of organizing work and failing to organize recreation had brought on a fine revenge," J.A. wrote. The love of pleasure in the young would not be denied, and when it found expression in a variety of sordid pursuits, the city acted as if it had no obligation in the matter and left it to businessmen of dubious morals to provide public recreation. The result was "saloons that seduced young men into alcoholism, dance halls where pimps plied their nefarious trade, entrapping 13- and 14-year-old girls, and the penny theaters that exploited the desire of the young for excitement and exoticism."

Was the behavior of the young influenced by the violence, crime and sexual exploits continually acted out on the screens of the tawdry penny theaters? J.A. had experienced the effects of such movies while attempting to help three street boys, 9, 11 and 13, who had witnessed a stage-coach holdup and murder at a penny theater and then planned a similar exploit.

> They made their headquarters in a barn and saved enough money to buy a revolver, adopting as their watchword the phrase Dead Men Tell No Tales. One spring morning the conspirators, their faces covered with black cloth masks, lay in ambush for the milkman. Fortunately, as the lariat was thrown the horse shied, and although the shot was fired, the milkman's

life was saved.

A neighborhood shopkeeper complained to J.A. that unless he provided his four daughters with money for the five-cent theaters every evening they would steal it from his till, and he feared that they might be driven to procure it in even more illicit ways. Because his entire family life had been disrupted he gloomily asserted that "this cheap show had ruined his 'ome and was the curse of America."

Substitute television for penny theater and J.A.'s voice blends with parents and educators who, in April 1998, were attempting to understand what caused two Arkansas boys, 11 and 13, to carefully plan and execute an ambush of students and teachers, killing five with rifle fire and wounding many more.

Criticized by some for being too much the Victorian lady, J.A. was nevertheless the first of the sociologists to write about the power of the sexual drive in the physically maturing boy and girl.

> At the very outset we must bear in mind that the senses of youth are singularly acute and ready to respond to every vivid appeal. We know that nature herself has sharpened the senses for her own purposes, and is deliberately establishing a connection between them and the newly awakened susceptibility of sex. . . Many young people go to the theater, and what they hear there, flimsy and poor as it often is, easily becomes their actual moral guide.

The job of the settlement house, the school, the church, above all the city, J.A. contended, was to provide appealing alternatives to the sexual lure of the saloon, the dance hall and the penny theater. The alternative settled on by Hull House in its earliest months of existence was that of the arts. As J.A. put it:

> Here the arts are taken seriously. . . [T]here is the music school where music flourishes not as a craft, but as an art. . . I should like to quote a brief passage from Derepa's Study of Cesar Franck because it expresses what seems to me the supreme

quality which. . . must be the heart of any effective system of education. 'To live, to come out of ourselves, to leave the egotism aside by loving something very superior. . . in which we continue to believe, no matter what name we give to it — here is the very basic essence of a true system such as Plato recommended to the worshippers of the celestial Venus. . .'

John Dewey's behavorial studies demonstrated that children made themselves at home in their imaginations and lived in their created worlds for weeks at a time. This did not surprise J.A., who retained vivid memories of her childhood games with George in Cedarville. She wrote:

> Because this fresh imaginative life with its instinct for play is in a sense the mission of art itself we have found at Hull House that our educational efforts tend constantly toward a training for artistic expression: in a music school, a school of dramatics, classes in rhythm and dancing and the school of the plastic and graphic arts. In the last which we call the Hull House Art School the children are given great freedom in the use of color and clay and other media through which they may express those images which are perpetually welling up from some inner fountain, and which suggest not only their secret aspirations, but curiously enough, something of their historic background.

Hull House music students were "taught to compose and to reduce to order the musical suggestions which may come to them." Those suggestions were sometimes folk songs that had never been committed to paper. J.A. was in the audience when children performed a song about a Russian man who grew bored digging a deep post hole until he struck a stratum of red sand which reminded him of his red-haired sweetheart. "All goes merrily as the song lifts into a joyous melody," J.A. said. "I recall again the almost hilarious enjoyment of the adult audience to whom it was sung by the children who had revived it."

Qualified teachers, several of whom played with the Chicago

Symphony Orchestra, made it possible for J.A. to achieve the goal of providing high quality instruction so that at least a few young people might master an instrument. "It is only through a careful technique," she said, "that artistic ability can express itself and be preserved."

Hoping that theater might captivate even the most seasoned of street children, J.A. and Starr had begun a drama program within a year of opening Hull House. Their hope was well founded. The theater appeared to be the one agency which freed restless adolescents from that "destructive isolation of those who drag themselves up to maturity by themselves." J.A. and Starr were amazed at the long hours of rehearsal young thespians devoted voluntarily to learning difficult lines from Shakespeare, Moliere and Galsworthy — often the same young people who had trouble sitting quietly for five minutes in school.

J.A. herself was drawn to the excitement of the theater and would leave tasks undone to help backstage — securing a king's crown to a young actor's head or anchoring a halo to the black hair of a Christmas angel. In time the Hull House Theater, under the direction of professionally trained residents, drew interest city-wide and made several tours abroad. Imagine the excitement of the young actors and actresses, most of whom had never been out of their own small neighborhood, as the great ocean liner carried them to Europe.

Both John Galsworthy and William Butler Yeats journeyed to Chicago to view performances of one of their plays. Yeats made a lasting contribution not only to the Hull House Theater but to American theater in general by inspiring the theater's director to free the stage from its slavery to expensive and elaborate sets. Hull House Theater, with its ever expanding repertoire and the increasing professionalism of its actors and actresses, is credited with fueling the national "Little Theater" movement, with Chicago, then and now, its most active center.

J.A. was keenly disapointed when a young, talented boy or girl was forced to give up music, art or drama lessons to work full time for the family's survival. One sorrowful year six promising students (of a total of 15) who had been required to abandon their lessons when reaching the legal working age, developed tuberculosis due to the double strain of long work hours and bad air. Alice Hamilton wrote to her sister:

> The belief so dear to American life, that opportunities are open to all, that the exceptional child can rise to the highest position in his community if he will, may be true in politics, in business, even in the learned professions, but certainly not in the arts. One of the saddest things in the lot of the poor is the crushing down of artistic talent. . . when the promising artist, Italian, Mexican, or Bohemian, leaves school for the barren monotony of factory work, too tired after to do anything creative, his gift wasted.

The Hull House "Saturday Painters" were a group of committed, aspiring adult artists, some of whom had painted their first pictures under the guidance of Enella Benedict. Tied to low-level jobs during the week, they continued to paint at the Hull House art studio on Saturday afternoons. Sadie Ellis, whom J.A. had helped to win an Art Institute scholarship when she was 16 years old, had had to give up the scholarship to earn wages for her family. (Sadie's friend, Blanche Maggioli, had continued on at the Art Institute and later worked on films in the California studio of her Farragut High School classmate from Chicago, Walt Disney.) As one of the "Saturday Painters," Ellis recalled:

> The cloud of my dull week at the mail order house would disappear the moment I started up the stairs to the studio on Saturday afternoon and smelled that special fragrance of linseed oil mixed with the smell of fresh canvas and rotting fruit — we were too poor to regularly buy fresh fruit for our still lives so we just left it in place week after week — and with the smell came Ivor Winter's great, booming voice filling the air. He was a big man and loved to sing while he painted. It was always the same song — 'I Dreamt I Dwelt in Marble Halls.'

Miss Benedict was tireless — she'd come from teaching at the Art Institute all morning and spend the afternoon with us. After we had worked at our easels for hours and dusk would set in, Nesta Smith and her chamber musicians would play a concert in the studio. Everyone was invited. Still in our paint spattered shirts and smocks we'd listen to Mozart or Schubert with the setting sun casting apricot light over everything. If you told me at that moment I could be anywhere in the world I wanted, I would not have moved from my chair.

Of special pleasure to J.A. was her relationship with the eight Elson children, all of whom were students of the arts at Hull House. The senior Elson had been a rabbi in Russia and spoke five languages. In the new country he was a cigar maker in his nephew's shop. All eight Elson children walked the three-mile round trip from their home to Hull House. Abe and Manny studied art, Sam and Joseph violin (fee for a violin lesson was 25 cents an hour with Wilfred Woolet, a violist with the Chicago Symphony), Ruth and Elizabeth took voice and drama lessons, and Alex and Charles were in the theatre program. In addition, Alex studied the cello.

When Joseph was 18 years old and ready to advance in his violin studies, J.A. wrote a letter of recommendation to the Curtis Institute which admitted Joseph, then expelled him a few months later. His unforgivable act had been to enter the concert hall without a ticket (which he could not afford) to hear a performance by the Philadelphia Symphony Orchestra. J.A sent a carefully phrased letter to Curtis suggesting that a student to whom music meant so much ought to be nurtured, not expelled. Curtis did not relent. Undaunted, Joseph auditioned with the New York Symphony and was promptly hired.

J.A.'s letter of recommendation for Elizabeth helped her win a scholarship to Yale University. Upon completing her studies, she worked with the WPA Theater in San Francisco and soon after became the first woman on the faculty of the Yale School of Drama. Charles matured into a gifted set designer who worked with the Metropolitan Opera and taught at Hunter College. Alex wrote an important book on the juvenile justice system and practiced law in Chicago's Loop until 1999.

Alex had performed "door duty" at Hull House on weekends while going to college, and upon entering the University of Chicago Law School received from J.A. a gift of Carl Sandburg's biography of Lincoln. Thanking J.A. he wrote: "I am sure an expression of appreciation is unnecessary, and fortunately so, for I feel utterly incapable of meeting the task. This much, however, I do want to say. My association with you at H-H has increased my admiration for you and has confirmed my faith in your ideals. . ."

Remembering the joyous public fairs and festivals she had watched in Europe, J.A. promoted similar events in the Hull House neighborhood, believing them to be yet another way for immigrants to keep their music and art alive. In *The Spirit of Youth and the City Streets* she wrote:

> From the gay celebration of the Scandinavians when war was averted and two neighboring nations were united, to the equally gay celebration of the centenary of Garibaldi's birth, from the Chinese dragon cleverly trailing its way through the streets, to the Greek banners flung out in honor of immortal heroes — after all what is the function of art but to preserve in permanent and beautiful form those emotions and solaces which cheer life and make it kindlier, more heroic, and easier to comprehend. . . which lift the mind of the worker from the harshness and loneliness of his task and by connecting him with what has gone before, free him from a sense of isolation and hardship?

Unable in her youth to join in athletics because of her troublesome back, J.A. nonetheless embraced sports as good for the body and soul. Just provide the facilities, the personnel, the place, she challenged city officials, and the people will come. She described a typical scene at a baseball game:

The enormous crowd of cheering men and boys are talkative, good natured, full of the holiday spirit and absolutely released from the grind of life. They are lifted out of their individual affairs and so fused together that a man cannot tell whether it is his own shout or another's that fills his ears. . . [He] does not call the stranger who sits next to him his 'brother' but he unconsciously embraces him in an overwhelming outburst of kindly feeling when the favorite player makes a home run. Does not this contain a suggestion of the undoubted power of public recreation to bring together all classes of a community into the modern city unhappily so full of devices for keeping men apart?

The Hull House playground had been open for only a short time when J.A. proposed to city officials that they, not a settlement struggling for funds, should run it. The city declined. But the Board of Education had been coaxed into an awareness of the need for recreational facilities by the Chicago Federation of Settlements in which J.A. was an active member. By 1892, the Board had created the position of Supervisor of Physical Education and financed the first gym ever built in an American public school. With public support for recreation growing, the city, after some years, agreed to take over the Polk Street playground. Hull House continued to use it for nursery classes and assigned a full-time kindergarten teacher to oversee the youngest children. In 1898, Mayor Carter Harrison sought to promote the formation of parks by creating a Park Commission. The Commission proved so effective that by 1910 Chicagoans had spent or committed over a million dollars for the creation of city parks. Architects Daniel Burnham and Frederick Law Olmsted were enthusiastic about designing and landscaping the new parks with the result that Chicago became, and still is, the proud possessor of one of the great park systems in the world.

J.A.'s participation in the lives of neighborhood children made her a natural ally of Lucy Flower, initiator of the movement to establish a Juvenile Court in Chicago. To this day J.A. is often wrongly credited with founding the Juvenile Court, an achievement many other women have also claimed. She commented with amusement on the phenomenon of all these "Juvenile Court Founders":

> One evening upon my return from the committee arranging for celebration of the 25th anniversary of the Juvenile Court, when we had been solemnly assured by one woman after another that she herself had been really instrumental in securing the court, I said to Julia Lathrop that as chairman of the committee I had the honor officially to inform her that every woman in Cook County except Mrs. Flower and herself had been personally responsible for the existence of the court. To this Julia Lathrop replied that in a sense it was true, that the court could not have been secured without the backing of thousands of women, and, with a suspicious twinkle, added that if each of these women felt personally responsible for it, the demonstration was complete that the court was well entrenched in the mother heart of Cook County.

Lucy Flower, former schoolteacher and wife of a prominent attorney, had long been outraged by officialdom's sloughing off its legal responsibility to find homes for abandoned children. When her efforts on behalf of these children were consistently ignored by the chairman of the Board of County Commissioners, Flower decided on a dramatic tactic — she bundled up one of the homeless babies, laid it with a supply of diapers and milk on the astonished commissioner's desk, and left. Numerous diapers later the county accepted its responsibility for abandoned children.

Flower then turned her attention to the treatment of young children who were often jailed for trivial misdemeanors, a cause with which J.A. strongly identified. She had listened to distraught mothers pleading to get their young sons out of jail — "a good boy who had never before done anything bad." In *The Spirit of Youth and the City Streets*, J.A. wrote about youths "overborne by their own undirected and misguided energies," who, "in a mere temperamental outbreak in a brief period of obstreperousness" commit an act which "condemns a growing lad to a criminal career." She cited a dozen court records in which boys were charged with "stealing a bathing suit, staying away from home to sleep in barns, stealing a horse blanket to use at night when sleeping on the wharf, breaking a seal on a freight car to steal grain for chickens, stealing candy from a peddler's wagon 'to be full up just for once.' " Living with hardened criminals often influenced these boys to commit more serious acts when they were freed, dooming them to lives of lawlessness.

The unrelenting efforts of Flower, strongly supported by Julia Lathrop, Louise Bowen and J.A., were finally rewarded in 1899 with the enactment of a law establishing the first Juvenile Court in the country. The new law authorized a judge to make young offenders wards of the state and either put them on probation or assign them to a correction institution instead of carting them off to adult prisons.

Alzina Stevens, a Hull House resident, was the ideal person for the job of probation officer. Due to J.A.'s efforts, Stevens already had provisional charge of every young person arrested for a trivial offense in the Hull House neighborhood. She was, in effect, already performing the duties of a probation officer. In a dismal show of civic unconcern, however, the new law had provided no funds to pay a probation officer's salary.

Flower promptly offered to provide the salary if the court would appoint Stevens. Her offer was accepted and the newly formed Court Committee raised the money. Under the stewardship of Julia Lathrop, followed by Louise Bowen, the committee raised funds for the salaries (meager as they were — $60 a month) of over a dozen probation officers. So valuable was the probation work acknowledged to be — in three years the number of children sent to the County Jail dropped from 1,705 to 60 — that the county decided to assume the salary responsibility.

To help rehabilitate troubled juvenile offenders, J.A. and her sister reformers founded the Juvenile Psychopathic Institute and made the happy choice of hiring Dr. William Healy to direct it. In addition to counseling severely troubled youths, Healy conducted thorough and careful studies on child behavior which ultimately formed the basis for his pioneering book, *The Individual Delinquent*. Healy validated what J.A. had concluded from her own experience — environment rather than heredity was the major cause of delinquency.

In time Healy developed the Juvenile Psychopathic Institute into a much needed research center. The problems J.A. and her co-workers confronted in their efforts to stem the tide of juvenile crime, poverty, broken families, drugs, gangs, and illiteracy were escalating dangerously. The urgency to find ways to keep children as young as 11 and 12 from taking drugs was brought home to J.A. when a mother, "frightened over the state of her youngest boy of 13 who was hideously emaciated and his mind reduced to vacancy," came to plead for help. "I remember the poor woman as she sat. . . holding the unconscious boy in her arms, rocking herself back and forth in her fright and despair, saying: 'I have seen them go with the drink and eat the hideous opium, but I never knew anything like this.' "

An investigation by Hull House revealed that a drug dealer working out of a local pharmacy had systematically fed a group of eight boys samples of cocaine, and that after three months the boys were hopelessly addicted. They worked at odd jobs and managed to produce eight dollars a night which gave them each four doses — "share and share alike," they said proudly.

When apprehended, the boys consented to treatment provided they could stay together. J.A. argued against those who wanted to separate the boys; keeping them together would help their collective gang spirit overcome the overwhelming desire for the drug. Her opinion prevailed and the boys were sent to Presbyterian Hospital for four weeks of treatment after which they were bundled off to the country for six more weeks — a typical Hull House therapy. They all did fairly well, but J.A. feared their rescue had come so late that the struggle to stay off the drug would require whatever meager strengths the boys could muster; she was not optimistic about their futures.

In the face of the city's hysterical cry for revenge against the 20-year-old anarchist who in 1901 assasinated President McKinley, J.A.'s vigilant compassion led her to ask:

> Was it not an indictment to all those whose business it is to interpret and solace the wretched, that a boy should have grown up in an American city so uncared for, so untouched by higher issues, his wounds of life so unhealed by religion that the first talk he ever heard dealing with life's wrongs, although anarchistic and violent, should yet appear to point a way of relief?

"We care more for products and economic gain in this country than for our children," she wrote in *The Spirit of Youth*. She exhorted the United States to take care of its young:

> We may either smother the divine fire of youth or we may feed it. We may either stand stupidly staring as it sinks into a murky fire of crime and flares into the intermittent blaze of folly or we may tend it into a lambent flame with power to make clean and bright our dingy city streets.

J.A. would have been saddened to learn that her words were as relevant at the end of the century as they were at its beginning.

Chapter 12

Petticoat Government and the Dunes Apostles

When Florence Kelley was asked whether Hull House could accomplish all it did without people like herself going through the wear and tear of living there, her answer was an unequivocal "no."

> You have to experience the general ugliness, the lack of oxygen in the air you daily breathe, the endless struggle with soot and dust and insufficient water supply, the hanging from a strap of the overcrowded streetcar at the end of a day's work; you must send your children to the nearest wretchedly crowded school and see them suffer the consequences, if you are to speak as one having authority and not as the scribes.

Upon Mary Linn's death, J.A. became the guardian of her sister's three younger children, James, Esther and Stanley. She had grown particularly attached to 11-year-old Stanley while caring for him during Mary's bouts with illness. Certain he would not lack affection in the warmhearted community of Hull House, she brought him to the House to live with her in her apartment. But Stanley, frail from birth, suffered from the noxious odors in the Hull House neighborhood and his doctor cautioned that if he did not leave for cleaner air the consequences could be serious.

J.A. had no alternative but to send Stanley to a boarding school.

One can imagine her feelings as she said good-bye to her young nephew, so newly severed from his mother. Her own sorrow led her to consider the feelings of parents of other sickly children who had no funds to pack them off to healthier places. "I felt ashamed that other delicate children who were torn from their families, not into boarding school, but into eternity, had not long before driven me to effective action."

But what action? The large, wooden garbage boxes fastened to the pavement along the city streets had troubled her from the moment she had first seen them. In addition to the normal refuse of a neighborhood were the fruit and vegetable peddler's rotting discards and the manure illegally trashed by stable owners, sometimes left to decay for weeks before pick-up.

The children of the neighborhood, J.A. observed, played games in and around these huge garbage boxes.

> They were the first objects that a toddling child learned to climb; their bulk afforded a barricade and their contents provided missiles in all the battles of the older boys; and finally they became the seats upon which absorbed lovers held enchanted converse.

Her first step was to set up a series of talks to help immigrant women understand that "sweeping refuse outside a doorway and allowing it to decay innocently in the open air and sunshine may have worked in their native villages, but in a crowded city neighborhood, if the garbage is not properly collected and destroyed, a tenement house mother may see her children sicken and die." She also obtained the expert assistance of city-planner George Hooker, Hull House's first male resident (1890), who set up a plan for a systematic investigation of the city's garbage collection to determine its connection to the 19th ward's notorious death rate.

Three evenings a week volunteer investigators from the Hull House Women's Club, all homemakers and many of them wage-earners, tirelessly walked the alleys in the humid heat of July and

August to check for health violations. In two months they had recorded no fewer than 1,037 violations.

Nothing changed. However much the neighbors improved their habits of cleanliness, the death rate in the ward remained alarmingly high. In spring, when new contracts for garbage removal were awarded, J.A. obtained the backing of two businessmen and submitted a bid from Hull House. The result was hardly one she could have anticipated. The Hull House bid was thrown out on a technicality, but the mayor appointed her the first woman garbage inspector in the City of Chicago. Her territory was the 19th ward.

Journalists seized the opportunity to add a bit of spice to their reporting. One imagined how the "Queen of Garbage" would be clothed:

> A trim uniform of cadet gray, with a jaunty military cap set upon her well-poised head, a stunning tailor-made coat liberally adorned with gilt, a proud star on her breast, a short skirt and — shall we say? — the daintiest of knickerbockers underneath.

As garbage inspector, J.A. received $1,000 a year, the first and only salary of her career. (In her 46 years with Hull House she accepted no recompense.) It was not exactly a soft job. Whatever the weather, frigid or hot, wet or dry, she rose at 5:00 a.m., dressed in her oldest clothes, hurried into the kitchen and drank the cup of coffee that Greek Annie, the Hull House cook, had poured for her, resisting Annie's delectable pastries. (From age 35 on, despite her vigilance in keeping a daily account of her weight, J.A. began to put on pounds which she was never was able to lose.) By 6:00 a.m. she had mounted her seat in the garbage inspection buggy and the driver signaled the horse to begin the familiar route.

People on their way to work paused to watch the ungainly vehicle bearing a regal woman in black make its noisy way. Children would giggle and run after the buggy as they did the ice and milk trucks. At the end of the morning J.A., in the buggy, would follow the collectors in their garbage wagons to the "dreary destinations at the dump, contents dropping intermittently from the loaded wagons."

J.A. was hardly a herald of good tidings to the negligent landlord, building contractor, or stable owner who had "arranged" to have a policeman pick up the dead horse in the stable alley. They might heed J.A.'s warning about the illegality of what they were doing for a week or so and then revert to their old practices. Looking back over that quirky year, J.A. observed that her greatest achievement was the discovery of pavement buried under eighteen inches of densely packed garbage. Hull House workers succeeded in removing several inches of the refuse. J.A. noted that the Italians living on the street "were much interested but displayed little astonishment, perhaps because they were so accustomed to see buried cities exhumed."

After the neighborhood volunteers had removed as much of the debris as their olfactory glands could tolerate, J.A. locked horns with the street commissioner who refused to take responsibility for the remainder of the excavation. Confident of the power of direct experience, J.A. prevailed upon the reluctant mayor to accompany her to the street in question. After observing the excavation site at an aromatically safe distance, the mayor ruled in favor of J.A.

The City Club (created in the wake of the Pullman Strike) held monthly discussions of urban problems which J.A. tried to attend. The Club's elevator operator, a tatter of gloom hanging about him, would routinely ask as they ascended in the black cage, "So, what are you lunching on today, Miss Addams? Tuberculosis or crime?"

"Neither," she responded one day. "Garbage."

Her response was not entirely a joke. How to make the garbage disposal system work so that the nieghborhood had clean air occupied her constantly as she thought of Stanley. On the lighter side were the complaints of neighborhood women who were offended by J.A.'s "messing around in the alleys. It wasn't fit work for a lady." Neither, of course, had been "stuffing" a bird in a taxidermy laboratory. From her Rockford days on, J.A. found herself pushing at the boundaries of what society dictated a woman could or could not do.

After riding the garbage circuit for a year, J.A. arranged for another Hull House stalwart and college graduate, Amanda Johnson, to take on the job. J.A. was physically and mentally spent by her service and, as winter began to take its merciless toll, her poor health was exacerbated by the knowledge that increasing numbers of her neighbors were dying of starvation and disease. "During the many relief visits I paid that winter to tenement houses and miserable lodgings," she wrote, "I was constantly shadowed by a certain sense of shame that I should be comfortable in the midst of such distress."

The reality that Hull House, with its best efforts, could help only a small number of suffering people, fed that shame. J.A.'s sturdy optimism began to falter. Were settlement workers frauds, living among the poor while failing to share the common lot of hard labor, miserable housing, meager food, and the clawing fear of ending in a pauper's grave?

J.A. had long been an admirer of Tolstoy the novelist. When she read *What Shall We Do?*, written in response to the great famine in Moscow, she admired him also as a man of conscience. Tolstoy determined that he could only honor his beliefs if he abandoned his substantial material possessions and "got off the backs of the poor" by providing for his own needs. Giving up his life of comfort, he moved to the country, dressed in peasant garb, worked in the fields and ate the simple food of the peasants. In his free hours he did not write, but fashioned boots.

J.A. had ample time to mull over Tolstoy's ideas and his personal solution when she was struck down with a virulent case of typhoid, probably contracted on her visits to indigent families. Both her doctor and her limited energy compelled her to rest for several months. She looked forward to the healing powers of spring, but when that season did not bring renewed health she accepted Mary

Smith's invitation to join her and her parents on a trip to Europe, hoping the change of scene and activity would help restore her.

Letters of introduction to a myriad of organizations working for the London poor filled her suitcases; one would not think J.A. was going on a rest cure. Once in Russia, she managed to arrange for a disciple of Tolstoy's, Aylmer Maude, to take both herself and Smith to visit Yasnaya Polyana, Tolstoy's home north of Moscow.

Tolstoy had never heard of J.A. or of Hull House and Maude gave him a short introduction. Tolstoy listened carefully, then reached out and took hold of a sleeve of J.A.'s dress. "Isn't there stuff enough on one arm to make a frock for a little girl?" he asked. "And don't you think such a dress a barrier to the people?"

"I was too disconcerted to make a very clear explanation," J.A. recalled. She wished that she had had the presence of mind to tell Tolstoy that monstrous as her sleeves were,

> they did not compete in size with those of the working girls in Chicago and that nothing would more effectively separate me from the people than a cotton blouse, following the lines of the human form; and even if I had wished to imitate him and dress as a peasant, it would have been hard to choose which peasant among the thirty-six nationalities we had recently counted in our ward.

Tolstoy's questioning continued. Though he treated J.A. with kindness, he was clearly unimpressed with her answers. When he learned that she owned a farm and depended upon others to work it, he queried, "So, you are an absentee landlord? Do you think you will help the people more by adding yourself to the crowded city than you would by tilling your own soil?"

During the train ride back to Moscow and the return voyage to the United States, J.A. and Smith talked incessantly about their meeting with Tolstoy. Though she was moved by meeting him, it was Tolstoy's presence more than what he said that J.A. remembered. "One cannot come near the man without feeling his genius," she said. But she continued to feel as she had when she had written to Smith a year before, "I do not believe that Tolstoy's position is tenable. A man cannot be a X-tian [Christian] by himself."

Nonetheless, on her return to the comfort of Hull House, J.A. could not rid herself of guilt when thinking about Tolstoy's words. She decided she would do a modicum of what he asked: she would contribute two hours a day to the "bread labor" of the world by baking bread, a skill John Addams had insisted his daughters acquire by the time they reached 12 years of age.

Greek Annie nearly panicked when J.A. appeared in her domain early one morning and announced that she was going to bake bread. But she need not have worried. J.A.'s foray into bread-baking was short-lived:

> In the face of the half dozen people invariably waiting to see me after breakfast, the piles of letters to be opened and answered, the demand of actual and pressing want — were these all to be pushed aside and asked to wait while I saved my soul by two hours work baking bread?

Taking early retirement from the kitchen, J.A. had satisfied herself, at least for the present, that settlement work was her work, however imperfect it might be. Yet Tolstoy had sensitized her to her role as absentee landlord. She visited the farm that had been a legacy from her father, was mortified by the living conditions of hired hands and their overseer, and decided to dispose of the property. Whatever money she needed she resolved to make by lecturing and writing.

Meanwhile, Amanda Johnson had been conscientiously performing her job as garbage collector for three years when she was summarily fired as a result of Johnny Powers' maneuvering. "Imagine," wrote a leading journalist of the day, "a short stocky man with a flaring gray pompadour, a smooth-shaven face, rather heavy features and a restless eye. . . with one finger aloft to catch the [Chairman's] eye," and you have Powers as he appeared before the Civil Service Commission bristling with outrage as he demanded

Johnson be fired for electioneering on the job! When he lost that round Powers pulled another card out of his starched white sleeve. As Chairman of the City Council Finance Committee, he and his fellow committee members were suddenly confronted with a dire lack of funds and were forced to merge the Bureau of Street and Alley Cleaning with the regular Department of Streets, thereby eliminating Johnson's position and leaving a space open for one of Powers' cronies.

Hull House residents were outraged. Determined to defeat Powers this time they decided to pit their own candidate against him in the 1898 election. (The Hull House candidate had won in 1896, only to be bought off by Powers.) With no alternative but to run a man (women had not yet won the vote), the residents settled on a member of the Men's Club, Simeon Armstrong, a well-liked Democrat who had lived in the ward for over 30 years.

The adrenaline began to flow. Hull House and neighborhood volunteers mounted a campaign that was efficient, vocal and strong. To J.A.'s relief, Armstrong turned out to be an effective speaker. In his first public appearance, he denounced the boodle alderman's heinous practice of giving away millions of dollars worth of franchises to streetcar and gas companies who then overcharged the public. Powers, he said, "does not take money from the rich and give it to the poor, but takes money from the poor and in turn gives it to the rich."

Aroused from complacency by Armstrong's aggressive tactics, Powers began to take a more active role in his campaign. "Hull House," he asserted, "will be driven from the Ward and its leaders will be forced to shut up shop." One of the signs waved by Jesuit cadets to whom Powers had just given a "gift" of $1,000 read, "No petticoat government for us!"

The word "petticoat" brought to mind the image of a delicate woman pouring afternoon tea. But J.A.'s attack on Powers and his cohorts (he once boasted that he had over 2,600 of *his* men working in public departments) had nothing of the tea party about it. She charged that his so-called generous gesture of giving everyone in the neighborhood a turkey on Christmas was designed to obscure the fact that he was doing nothing about filthy streets, unsafe working conditions, hiked-up streetcar fares and the need for a school and decent housing. "I may not be the sort of man the reformers like," Powers replied, not bothering to answer the corruption charges, "but I am what my people like."

Never forgetting that they were up against a formidable foe, the Hull House campaign workers put in long hours.

> I have been dead tired for three days now [Alice Hamilton wrote to her sister]. That campaign literature business was lengthy and dreadful. We began on Thursday in the afternoon as soon as the new registration lists came in. All the first evening it was addressing envelopes. That kept up until Friday night until the last of twelve thousand was done. . . A great many volunteers came in and of course Miss Addams insisted on working though she is still on the sick list. By half past four (on Saturday) we had really finished and were the raggiest, flabbiest bunch of people you ever saw. The poor men even looked more weary than I. Mr. Hill is on the last edge and Mr. Bruce looks like a wreck. . . While we were sitting around in the evening the big Powers parade came by. It was Powers' last supreme effort and it was very imposing indeed. We all ran down to see it as it came down Polk street and turned north on Halsted. Of course we had run out with nothing around us, so the men had to lend us things and we stood all wrapped up on the corner and with our bare heads showed very plainly, I'm afraid, that we were from Hull House.

J.A., not Simeon Armstrong, received most of the hate mail written by Powers' supporters. To much of the public, J.A. *was* Hull House. One letter was notably obnoxious:

> Because Mr. Powers is a man of principal [sic] who loves a woman in a woman's place, not as a female politician, he has been subject to newspaper notoriety by you who has long since forgot the pride and dignity so much in demand in a beautiful woman. When a man prepares to take unto himself a wife will

he go into an alleyway among the rubbish and filth to find a good true virtuous woman? No, a woman with pride and virtue would have to shrink in horror from such a life. . .

J.A. was incensed because she was attacked, not for her ideas, but because she dared enter the sacrosanct world of men's politics. Underlying the most virulent criticism was the sexual implication that by doing so she had "fallen" from virtue.

The election returns brought a crushing defeat to Armstrong and assured Powers of his kingship once again. Florence Kelley refused to surrender. She was geared to continue the fight into the next election, but J.A. thought it a waste of energy to spend more time on Powers. She analyzed in a speech, which she later converted to an article, what Hull House had learned about ward politics in the last several years. Clearly Powers' supporters didn't see him as a nefarious, opportunistic politician, but as a kindly visitor. They brought their troubles to him much as they would to a priest, but no priest they had ever known could produce a job, a loan or an early release from prison. In the face of Powers' concrete favors, J.A. acknowledged that the promises of the reform candidate were pure air. She concluded that to accomplish any reforms in a city like Chicago, the place to go was City Hall, Springfield or Washington. She published her analysis under the title *Ethical Survival in Municipal Corruption*, one of the first serious attempts to understand the methods and motives of a city boss.

"I feel like a funeral," Starr commented, "but let us hope it will count for something in the next fight."

There were in fact to be many more fights for J.A. — more heated and personally hurtful than attempting to defeat a corrupt alderman. So it was with relief as well as gratitude that a long-held dream of hers was realized without a single skirmish — the establishment of a Hull House country camp where city children might escape the steamy Chicago summers.

When Joseph Bowen died, Louise Bowen determined to purchase land in the country and establish a Hull House camp in his honor. Joseph Bowen had devoted many hours to leading outings for Hull House boys and a summer camp seemed to be the perfect memorial.

"We called it a club," Bowen recalled in *Open Windows*, "because we felt it was something the children and Hull House people should feel they owned themselves and this idea carried out, the children paying a small sum, if able, for board." Bowen and J.A. searched for the right campsite with characteristic energy and persistence. They personally checked out 67 possible locations before selecting 72 acres in Waukegan, Illinois, 35 miles north of Chicago. J.A. spoke at the opening ceremony:

> It was by far the most beautiful [site] of all. Sometimes one would like to move the ravine from one place, the gentle slopes from another, the woods of oak and birch from another and put them together in a way Nature herself seldom permits, but in this place all desirable things seem to have been combined without the interference of man, although we are happy that he had long ago been permitted to add a garden, an orchard, a wall surrounded by lilacs and an interesting old house.

The interesting old farmhouse, which became the home of the camp director, was used throughout the year as a weekend retreat for the Hull House Players, the Italian Women's Club, the Gloomdodgers, the Jane Club, and an occasional honeymoon couple who would gratefully retreat into its secluded shelter. When asked what motto should be put over the door of the farmhouse, J.A., after some thought, suggested, "Secure, from the slow stain of the world's contagion." She said, "All of us who live in the midst of the city find ourselves easily stained by the contagion of the world and to have a place secure from it to which we may repair is not only delightful but necessary to the health of our souls."

But what of the mothers of the campers? J.A. asked millionaire Julius Rosenwald to help build a refuge for women who once "gathered oranges in Calabria and olives in Greece, who have gleaned the poppy strewn wheatfields of Europe and dug for peat in the bogs of Ireland. . . They too need to feel the earth beneath their feet, the sight and smell of growing things."

Rosenwald responded by financing the building of a special cottage for mothers and their very young children. The cottage had a spacious screened area so that the women could sit at their ease and talk, sew, nurse their infants or just daydream while their children were safely at play. They were served ample amounts of good food and fresh flowers graced their tables. Added to their pleasure was the happiness of seeing their older children thrive in the country air. One mother was astonished to find that her skinny son had gained 17 pounds in the two weeks he was at the camp.

Most of the girls who came to camp had never had a bed to themselves. At Bowen Country Club (BCC) they each had their own small cot and with it came the responsibility of making their bed and changing its sheets. This and other disciplines (including a daily shower) accorded with J.A.'s vision for BCC — that it be educational as well as recreational, and that the campers be taught decorum and the niceties of living to better equip them in making a place for themselves in the wider society.

The dinner bell summoned campers into a dining room of tables covered with tablecloths, brightened by fresh flowers from the camp garden. (One girl confided that the only flowers she had ever seen were at her grandmother's funeral.) Healthy food in good-sized portions was served on plates with a blue willow design. Children who were used to grabbing dinner from the pot on the kitchen stove learned to sit through an entire meal and use the proper silverware. Napkins were new to them and most had to be shown how to cut meat with a knife. One eight-year-old girl became so enamored of eating on a tablecloth that she continued the practice upon her return home by spreading newspapers on the kitchen table.

The happiness of the children was a balm to J.A.'s disheartened spirit. The children, in turn, showed their graditude in different ways, none more startling than that of the young boy who ran over to J.A.'s table on one of her visits to BCC and presented her with a very large, very wet fish he had caught that morning in the ravine.

In the evening everyone — children, counselors, directors, and the "good ladies," Bowen and Addams, whenever they visited — sat around the campfire and sang favorite songs.

> When you're feelin' kinda blue
> And don't know what to do
> Come right out to Waukegan
> The home of the BCC.

At the end of the session most campers returned to homes where fathers still hadn't found work, where they shared beds with numerous brothers or sisters, and where they went to sleep hungry after a supper of thin soup and half a potato. But they had been introduced to a new world and dreamed of returning the next year.

One of J.A.'s more benign battles worked itself out in an arena more sweet-smelling than that of the 19th ward — the lakeshore in the Indiana Dunes. J.A. and some of her colleagues had become eager participants in the Saturday morning walking trips organized by the National Playground Association. The walks centered on the stretch of lakeshore called the Great Dunes. J.A. became a member of the "Dunes Apostles," a group of devoted nature lovers who successfully worked through the legislative process to set aside the Indiana Dunes, first as a state park and then as a national lakeshore.

To bring public attention to the cause of protecting the Dunes, in 1917 the Apostles decided to stage the Great Dunes Pageant on the floor of a huge dune blowout, several hundred feet across. "Spectators to the pageant had a panoramic view of the lake, beach and stage before them," J. Ronald Engel wrote in his book, *Sacred Sands*, "while one half mile to the east they could see the three dune peaks named by early settlers, The Three Sisters."

By 1919 victory was acheived and a ceremony was held in Lake Front Park, Gary, Indiana, to celebrate the establishment of the dunes lakeshore as a state park. It must have been with uplifted spirits that the Dunes Apostles listened to W. D. Richardson of the Friends of Our Native Landscape give his dedication speech:

> I dedicate this park to the unborn generations of man that they may see this landscape as we have seen it, in full faith that they will have eyes to see nature, understanding to comprehend nature, and a love that will perpetuate the beauties of nature. . .while charging future generations to maintain this dune landscape untouched and undefiled that the unborn races of man may come here from whatever harassments there may be in future civilizations to tread these singing sands. . . and so to be inspired and reanimated with greater capacity for living.

Citing the opening of the Hull House public playground as the first civic action highlighting the human need for open space, Engel wrote, "If, as Plato said, the end of every story is inherent in its beginning, the Dunes movement may be justly considered a creature of the settlement house." Robert Gottlieb, author of *Forcing the Spring*, made a similar point:

> Just a hundred years ago, Addams led an intrepid group of women through the polluted streets and houses of the 19th Ward. . . As activists and researchers, their mission was to document the environmental and occupational hazards of their neighborhood and, by extension, of the highly polluted industrial cities of America. The resulting *Hull-House Maps and Papers* established a benchmark for environmental research at the time. In the process it helped set in motion an urban reform movement that sought to change the most flagrant of the environmental conditions described. . . Jane Addams was, in fact, an early environmentalist.

Like many other groups J.A. helped launch, the environmentalists were destined to be both crucial and controversial.

Chapter 13

Clothed in Brick and Mortar

J.A. was standing on Polk Street observing the progress of the foundation being laid for the new gymnasium when a neighbor walked by.

"Hull House is spreading out," he remarked.

"Perhaps we are spreading out too fast," J.A. replied.

"Oh, no," he rejoined, looking down at his shoes anchored in the mire of the unpaved street. "You can afford to spread out wide; you are so well planted in the mud."

The building housing the Coffee House, theater and gymnasium was constructed in 1893, two years after the first new building to adjoin the Hull mansion, the Butler Art Gallery, was erected. The Children's Building was added in 1896, as well as a third story to the original Hull mansion.

"These first buildings were very precious to us," J.A. recalled, "and it afforded us the greatest pride and pleasure as one building after another was added to the Hull House group. They clothed in brick and mortar and made visible to the world that which we were trying to do; they stated to Chicago that education and recreation ought to be extended to the immigrants." J.A.'s concern with the aesthetic appearance of Hull House extended to its exterior. "As the House enlarged for new needs and mellowed through slow-growing associations," she wrote in *Twenty Years*, "we endeavored to fashion it from without, as it were, as well as from within. A tiny wall fountain modelled in classic pattern, for us penetrates into the world of the past, but for the Italian immigrant it may defy distance and barriers as he dimly responds to that typical beauty in which Italy has ever written its message."

When not traveling, J.A. began her day by attending to the business side of Hull House, which grew steadily more demanding as the Settlement expanded to 13 buildings by 1907. In *Twenty Years* she wrote, "We were often bitterly pressed for money and worried by the prospect of unpaid bills and we gave up one golden scheme after another because we could not afford it; we cooked the meals and kept the books and washed the windows without a thought of hardship if we thereby saved money for the consumation of some ardently desired undertaking." Donations such as furniture, rugs and linen were of course also welcome. One donor surprised Hull House residents with a most lively contribution. J.A. sent a thank you letter:

Dear Mr. Ward:
   The squirrels arrived Saturday morning in excellent condition with the slight exception of the nose of one which was unfortunately barked. The entire settlement was occupied in nursing him on Sunday and they were put into the kindergarten Monday morning quite restored from fatigue and bruises. The children are much delighted with them, as you may well imagine. . .

Undaunted by the wealth or prestige of a potential donor, J.A. became skilled at knowing when to push for funds and when to tread lightly. She drove a hard bargain with contractors and frequently managed to get services donated. Though she confided to family and friends that she often felt like a battered, inept business agent, she succeeded with remarkable finesse in keeping Hull House alive, weathering bad publicity, economic depressions and World

War I.

Administering Hull House business, chairing meetings, lobbying, traveling nationwide and abroad to lecture, J.A. nonetheless jealously guarded time to participate in the daily lives of her Hull House neighbors. The poet Muriel Rukeyser put in words what J.A. had known intuitively — the world is made of stories not atoms. The stories told to J.A., often in English so broken it took an act of the imagination to understand, moved her to what she considered simple acts of neighborliness. And once she knew a family she would remember everything about them for years.

> Good day, Mrs. Pasquesi. How does your husband like his new job? And how is Stella doing in her new school? No, I didn't know Mrs. Karlinski's baby was stillborn. How very sad. I will visit her tomorrow. Ah, Jacob, I saw your painting in the art gallery. I think it's your best work so far. And how is your grandmother?

If a family could not afford a wedding party, J.A. would host a reception for the newlyweds, complete with Greek Annie's pastries, fresh flowers and music. On one such occasion she not only served as hostess, but had to find the missing groom.

> We had a forlorn wedding yesterday. . . [W]e brought the young man in time for the ceremony with the help of his employers, but the little bride sobbed throughout in the most piteous way and would not look at the groom nor the white roses which he tried in vain to give her. . . [I]f it had not been for the memory of poor Tooney's [the deceased father of the bride] desire for a ceremony I could not have gone through it.

A young Russian immigrant, newly come to the city and neighborhood and finding only loneliness and discouragement, followed his brother's advice and sought the refuge of Hull House.

> The first time I approached Hull House the door was open and I walked in. No one was in the reception hall so I sat down near a table, eyeing the books and magazines. Presently Miss

Addams appeared. From the many pictures I recognized her instantly. She greeted me cordially, then said, 'Don't you want to read the Atlantic Monthly just out?' The Atlantic Monthly proved tough reading. After all, I came to see Jane Addams and Hull House, not to read the Atlantic Monthly! Miss Addams passed through several times. Realizing I was lingering rather than reading, she tried conversation: 'Living around here?' she ventured. 'On DeKoven Street.' 'Oh, then we are neighbors. You must come often,' she said warmly. That's what I had hoped for.

In 1895, Dorothea Moore, the wife of one of the residents, described a typical day at the Settlement:

> Now the house is like some creature slowly awakening from sleep. It begins to put out its hands, touching. . . with humility as well as hopefulness and trust the lives of those about it. By nine o'clock the visiting nurse may be seen packing her bag from her supply chest. . . The workers whose province lies outside. . . visit police stations in search of the astray boy or girl. . . By two in the afternoon the kindergarten training class is filling the largest room in the Children's Building, the lively and wide-awake session of the Women's Club is at its climax, the gymnasium is mildly noisy and from far up in the upper story come the sounds of the children's chorus. . . [T]he leisurely last moments of the dinner hour are apt to be invaded by classes, and from now on there is a riot of young people, the studious. . . attend Extension classes, the younger, gayer crowd, dancing and dramatic clubs. . .

In a letter to her sister, Alice Hamilton described a "typical evening" at Hull House:

> Here in the back parlour I am sitting and opposite to me is Miss Johnson, who is the street-cleaning commissioner. She is having a most killing time interviewing an old Irishman who wants a job from the city. He has brought his wife with him and she is scolding him for saying he is sixty. She says he's only forty-five. . . Miss Johnson wants to know when his birthday comes, and his wife says, 'Say the fourth of July, it sounds well.' . . . At the other end of the table sits Miss Brockway, the sweet

little girl who is engaged to Miss Addams' nephew. Miss Kelley is lying off on the sofa. In the front parlor are Mr. Deknatel and Mr. Valerio. Mrs. Valerio speaks Italian. . . and is taking the names of the people who are registering for classes. Miss Addams is on the sofa with a very nice North End man. . . They are looking over plans for an addition to the coffee-house. Miss Watson, Mr. Swope, Mr. Ball, Mr. Hooker, Miss Pitkin, Miss Gayles and all the others are managing classes and clubs in various rooms. In a few minutes a certain Dr. Blount is coming. It is a she-doctor and a socialist. I met her some time ago and she it is whom Miss Addams destined to help me in some scheme for the amelioration of the condition of the Italian neighbors. Then at nine o' clock we are to have a resi-dent's meeting, to divide up the duty of tending the door and showing people over the house. Dr. Blount has just gone. We went up to Miss Addams' room and discussed a scheme which I haven't time to expound to-night.

Writer and one-time Hull House resident Francis Hackett wrote:

The essential fact of Hull House was the presence of Miss Addams. This is strange because while one was living there Miss Addams was away a good deal of the time, and when she was there one did not have a great deal to do with her; yet Hull House, as one clearly felt at the time, was not an institution over which Miss Addams presided, it was Miss Addams, around whom an institution insisted on clustering. . . She had the power to value human beings, to appreciate them, and to feel them. . . I can well remember how often. . . Miss Addams would say, 'Mr. Hooker! You can help us. What do you think?' Her attitude was, 'You can help,' and because she elicited good will in a common cause, that cause preoccupied the resi-dents. . . though there was little prestige or publicity and no pay. The House not only recruited strong characters, it was excited about them.

The small children called Hull House "the kindergarten," or never having seen grass before — "the place where the green is." The Italian neighbors called it "La casa di Dio" (The House of

God), but, added Moore, "to most of its intimate friends and to many at a remote distance it is the place where Jane Addams lives."

Without guidelines to follow (those of Toynbee Hall applied only in a limited way), J.A. created them. She kept no records on the troubled people she helped beyond their names and addresses, nor, as other social work agencies emerged, did she ask to see the records of other caseworkers. She believed in taking men and women as she saw them, not filtered through someone else's judgment. More importantly, she did not want to stigmatize anyone with a record of what were mainly small transgressions — stealing coal in winter, or a dress from a clothesline — which might forever handicap their future chances for employment.

Her position, though perfectly logical to her, was anathema to other agencies. With no records to check, what did she do about those who were given a relief check from one agency and then attempted to get another from Hull House? "I would much rather take the risk of being cheated," J.A. responded, "than endanger someone's chances for getting a job for the rest of their life."

Holding to that principle meant that J.A. sacrificed contributions from donor agencies (notably, the Chicago Community Trust) which required records of clients seen and helped. J.A. also rejected the opportunity to join a federal fund drive, fearing that if she did so, the independence of Hull House might be compromised.

In 1907 Graham Taylor, director of The Commons, a settlement on Chicago's South Side, judging it time to require formalized training for social workers, established a school of social work which would award licenses to its graduates. He enlisted Julia Lathrop to head the school and Lathrop selected as her assistant a bright young lawyer and Hull House resident, Sophonisba Breckinridge. When Lathrop left the school to head a child welfare agency, the fledgling institution became affiliated with the University of Chicago as the School of Social Work Administration. Grace Abbott, another Hull House resident, served as its first dean.

J.A. regarded the opening of the school with mixed feelings.

While recognizing the desirability of formal training, she worried that it might do more to encourage conformity than sensitivity. The school's training focused on the psychology of the individual and great importance was placed on gathering data and utilizing a growing number of psychological tests. The school sought to make social work a science; J.A. believed it to be an art.

The point was illustrated by a later incident involving Sadie Ellis. An overworked staff member of United Charities asked if J.A. could loan the agency one of her social workers. Anyone who had apprenticed under J.A. — University of Chicago Professor Robert Merriam called her a "professor without a chair" — was considered by some agencies to be a qualified social worker. J.A. sent Ellis who, in addition to teaching the children's art classes, had worked closely with her in counseling sessions and was now handling casework of her own.

Ellis did well at United Charities. In need of funds, however, when the opportunity arose, she moved on to the Chicago Public Relief Agency, which was able to pay a higher salary. Soon she was in line for promotion to supervisor, but the promotion was denied when it was learned that Ellis had not taken the required courses at the School of Social Work Administration. Her background, the agency contended, had been more in art than in social work.

To support Ellis' qualifications, J.A. wrote a letter asserting that teaching art, especially in a settlement, was excellent preparation for social work. As an example of her resident's special talents, she recounted how Ellis had successfully handled a challenging situation. The police, having difficulty breaking up fights between Italian and Mexican gangs, peremptorily installed the Italians in Ellis' art class, hoping to separate the Italian and Mexican boys, if only temporarily, and avoid detention. With no experience teaching these sullen, unruly gang members, Ellis did the first thing that came to her mind — she chose the two boys who seemed to be the leaders and directed them and two regular class members to tape large sheets of newsprint paper on the wall. She then told each of the four boys to choose a team of three painters and, with the consent of their teams, to decide on a subject for a mural.

The stratagem worked. Giving the gang leaders positions of authority had surprised and flattered them; each had wanted his team's mural to be the best and worked hard, if not always harmoniously, with his team members. Ellis' experiment proved so successful that group painting became a basic part of her art classes. (Group painting was only the first of many Ellis experiments using art as therapy. Forty years later Ellis would be internationally acknowledged as the "Mother of Art Therapy.")

J.A.'s letter did nothing to change the Relief Agency's decision. Upon Ellis' dismissal, J.A. promptly hired her as a full-time paid social worker for Hull House. She was glad to have "one of her own" back in the fold, and confided her frustration with some of the licensed social workers to Ellis:

> Our new social worker visited a young single mother living in a tenement with five children under the age of 12. She turned up at the woman's apartment unannounced at 9 o'clock in the morning. The harassed mother was trying to get the children dressed and fed. Two of them had to be readied to go to school. The social worker is observing closely, accumulating facts. After completing her visit she sends me the recommendation that the relief payments to this woman be discontinued because she is a poor housekeeper!

J.A. soon came to regard the obsessive collecting of facts by the new professionals as a disease which she named "Factophilia." She acknowledged that minimal records would have to be kept on clients as the number of social service agencies grew, but believed that workers should be encouraged and trained to rely on direct experience with a client instead of on a sheaf of records. A side effect of Factophilia, she said, was the accumulation of ominous amounts of paperwork which she presciently observed would someday smother the social worker.

The plight of the aged poor was one of the pressing problems J.A. had long criticized government for ignoring, but to no avail. The aged were voiceless, and their powerlessness doomed them in a city where the politics of greed and power ruled. J.A. was perpetually distressed by the numbers of old people who had nowhere to go but to the dreaded Cook County Poorhouse. She had known many of the women when they had felt "bustling important." But in the Poorhouse, stripped of all they knew, they sat in their barren rooms consumed by loneliness and idleness. "To take away from an old woman whose life has been spent in household cares all the. . . little belongings to which her affections cling," J.A. wrote, "and to which her very fingers have become accustomed, is to take away her last incentive to activity, almost to life itself."

To bring some interest and human connection into the lives of these lonely old people, if only for a short time, J.A. would invite five or six of them on "two week vacations." She arranged lodging for a dollar a week in an acquaintance's home and provided two good meals a day in the Hull House Coffee House where the "vacationer could count on numerous cups of tea among old friends to whom they would airily state that they had come out for a little change." But this effort touched only a few lives and was difficult to sustain. In her last appearance before Congress, a short time before she died, J.A was still arguing passionately for an old age pension.

Another J.A. innovation was more successful. Many who came for help to the "place where Jane Addams lives" were immigrant parents disturbed by growing estrangement from their teenage children. Quick to learn the ways and language of the new land, the young looked down on parents who knew little English and clung to their old country ways. Girls were ashamed of mothers in shapeless dresses, with kerchiefs around their heads. One boy, afraid of ostracism from his group, threw stones at an Italian peddler, concealing the fact that the man was his father. How could Hull House, originally envisioned by J.A. and Starr as a bridge builder between people of different economic levels, help bridge the gulf between immigrant parents and their Americanized children?

J.A. was walking down Polk Street one spring afternoon when she paused to observe an Italian woman on the steps of her tenement spinning yarn. The woman was using the stick method common to Eastern Europe and her hands moved with amazing dexterity. As J.A. paused to watch, a thought came into her mind. Would a young textile worker be interested in seeing how yarn had been woven long before machines were invented? Might not that young worker gain respect for a mother or father with the skill to spin yarn with such a simple tool?

At that week's residents meeting, J.A. proposed to set aside a room at Hull House for an exhibit of the different spinning methods used by people of various ethnic backgrounds. So enthused were some of the residents that they began a treasure hunt for old equipment, and ferreted out four different kinds of spinning wheels. The project soon expanded from exhibiting spinning wheels to inviting local spinners to demonstrate their spinning styles. As the idea of a "live" museum began to evolve, the crafts of basketmaking, pottery, metalworking, woodworking and embroidery were added. Soon the room was brightened with illustrations of the various crafts mounted on the walls.

Saturday night was set aside for artisans to congregate in the dining room and demonstrate their skills. Starr made arrangements for classes to be given in pottery, metalwork, enamel and wood carving, including special classes for children and the blind.

Thus the Labor Museum was born, the first such endeavor in the United States to recognize the value of the arts and crafts of immigrant artisans. J.A. hoped that museum visitors would feel some kinship with ethnically different neighbors when they saw that industry developed in similar ways among workers of many nations. One hardy Irishman paid the museum his highest compliment. Willingly — and no one seemed more surprised than he — he gave up Saturday night at his favorite saloon to watch five women, Syrian, Greek, Italian, Russian and Irish, spin at their wheels.

A visitor to the Labor Museum described what she saw in 1904 when the Museum was four years old and had expanded to fill several rooms:

> We opened the door of the humming activity of the wood and metal shops; for a shop this room is in appearance, much more than a museum. The big beam overhead, the swinging rack for lumber, the tool cases lining one wall, the heavy benches and work tables, the vises, the mallets, the enameling and glazing furnace, the battered table with a blowpipe at one end spitting blue and yellow flames: all make up an interior not lacking in a certain grim picturesqueness. . . Here in the alcove of the wood and metal working rooms is a big vat of clay, a couple of potter's wheels and a case of admirably modeled, glazed and decorated pottery. Standing at the table is a clean old German kneading clay, his squat bowed legs far apart, his long and powerful arms beating upon the clay like piston rods. . .

During the 1890s, while serving on an ad hoc committee to study school problems, J.A. had abandoned the educational system designed by her former mentors Ruskin and Carlyle to prepare men for a life outside of industrialism. She had come to believe with Dewey that education must be integrated with life. For the immigrant child life was lived in an industrial society, a fact she charged public schools with ignoring by failing to "connect [the child] to the industrial culture in which he would most certainly participate. . . [O]nce at work the child used his hands for unknown ends and head not at all." J.A. directed the first curator of the Labor Museum, Jesse Luther, to only offer classes that related directly to the experiences of the students.

During the three years J.A. had served on Chicago's Board of Education she had been unable to effect any changes, a great frustration to someone who believed well-working public schools were of prime importance in a social democracy. But life is filled with small astonishments. The old Italian woman spinning on her stoop had opened up a way for J.A. to bring progressive education, in small measure, to the immigrant young and old. How fine it was when the joyless lives of immigrants were lightened by the pleasures of learning new skills and teaching their own skills to others, perhaps — it was possible! — to their own or to their neighbor's children.

Jesse Luther had many occasions to explain J.A.'s vision to perplexed visitors who did not understand what made the fledgling institution, which looked like a group of manual training shops, a museum.

> The word museum was purposely used in preference to the word school, both because the latter is distasteful to grown-up people from its association with childish tasks and because the word museum still retains some fascination of the show. It may be easily observed that the spot which attracts most people at any exhibition, or fair, is the one where something is being done. So trivial a thing as a girl cutting gloves or a man polishing metal will almost inevitably attract a crowd. . .[I]t is believed. . . that when the materials of daily life and contact remind the student of the subject of his lesson and its connections it would hold his interest and feed his thought as abstract and unconnected study utterly fails to do.

A gift shop was opened when it became evident that tourists visiting Hull House (in numbers that increased impressively each year) were eager to purchase the many handcrafted products. The shop became so popular that weavers and potters had trouble keeping up with the demand for their work. Making and selling a handmade scarf or earthen bowl helped to boost the morale of both women and men; in addition in one evening's sales one could earn a week's factory wages. And though it did not happen nearly as often as J.A. had hoped, there were children who gained respect for a father who was admired by "American strangers" for his skill as a master metalworker, or for a mother who was admired as a skilled weaver of baskets. J.A. recalled

> a certain Italian girl who came every Saturday evening to a cooking class in the same building in which her mother spun

in the Labor Museum exhibit; and yet Angeline always left her mother at the front door while she herself went around to a side door because she did not wish to be too closely identified in the eyes of the cooking class with an Italian woman who wore a kerchief over her head, boots and short petticoats. One evening, however, Angeline saw her mother surrounded by a group of visitors from the School of Education who much admired the spinning and she concluded from their conversation that her mother was the 'best stick-spindle spinner in America.' [A]fter that she openly came into the Labor Museum by the same door as her mother. . .

Julius Rosenwald, president of Sears, Roebuck and Company, friend and financial supporter of Hull House, had for sometime considered the building of a museum devoted to the history and current technology of the world's industries. Visiting the Labor Museum one evening, he saw in modest miniature an implementation of part of that project by people with no money to spend. Spurred to action, and with the aid of vast wealth, he built the Rosenwald Museum, known today to Americans and visitors throughout the world as the Museum of Science and Industry.

"Make no small plans" was the motto Daniel Burnham threw out like a bright banner over the city of Chicago as he set out to build a great park system. J.A. had a genius for beginning with a small plan that would, by dint of imagination, cooperation and faith, blossom into the realization of a large vision.

The Bowen Country Club garden.

Bowen Country Club

Dining room on the left; Good Fellow Hall, the activity center, on the right.

Free time at BCC on a sunny afternoon.

Art class in garden at BCC.

Art class in Hull House alley.

Boys Club – from city streets to a day in the country.

Members of Mignonette Club at BCC. By the 1930s, the Mignonettes had been meeting for 17 years.

Mothers and young children at lunch on the Commons piazza at BCC.

With the Best Light You Have

*I*n the preface to *Twenty Years at Hull-House*, J.A. wrote that she embarked on the difficult task of writing the book "because Settlements have multiplied so easily in the United States I hoped that a simple statement of an earlier effort, including the stress and storm, might be of some value in their interpretation and possibly clear them of a certain charge of superficiality." The second, "less worthy" motive was to "extinguish" the writing of two planned biographies, one of which made life in a settlement "all too smooth and charming."

These remarks would lead a reader to expect a history of Hull House, not the autobiography of its founder. In his introduction to the 1990 edition of *Twenty Years*, James Hurt contends that it is both; J.A. and Hull House share center stage. "There would have been no Hull-House without the personality and experiences of the person who created it, but equally, perhaps, there would have been no Jane Addams if she had not created Hull-House in an extraordinary act of, among other things, self-making." J.A. herself says that "no effort was made. . . to separate my own history from that of Hull House during the years when I was launched deep into the stormy intercourse of human life."

The duality of *Twenty Years* helps explain puzzling omissions in the book. Hardly a single sentence is devoted to Mary, the young Jenny's loving surrogate mother, and none to the other siblings, feisty Alice, beautiful Martha or dreamy John Weber. Though profoundly important in her personal life, J.A.'s sisters and brother never became part of her Hull House life, and were therefore not included in *Twenty Years*. J.A. had little interest in writing anything about herself that did not relate in some way to Hull House. George was accorded a few sentences because J.A.'s memories of their childhood games led ultimately to the establishment of a Hull House playground and summer camp.

It was deeply troubling to J.A. that as she moved her pen across the page to write about the young "Knight of the Green Plume," the adult George was living in unrelenting depression. He secluded himself in his room at the Homestead where he read, listened to music and played against himself in chess. Ocassionally he would break his solitude for a game with Mary Fry whom he had taught to play. Fry described him as a person "of large physique and brilliant intellectual capacity before his depression so deteriorated him," and affectionately described him as the kindest man she knew.

The writing of *Twenty Years* was completed on November 14, 1909 just as George, 49 years old, suffered a fatal stroke. The funeral at the Homestead was not held until November 17 so that Alice, who had been traveling, could attend. Because of the delay, Fry placed large cakes of ice around the bed on which George had been laid.

Upon her arrival at the Homestead, J.A. asked Fry, whom she had always liked and respected, to accompany her to the large upstairs bedroom where George lay. Once in the familiar room, J.A. pulled a chair close to the bed and sat quietly for a long time. Then she put her hand on George's. "We did have good times, old boy, didn't we?" she said.

The year 1909 was also the hundredth anniversary of Abraham Lincoln's birth. A petition circulated nationwide called for concrete efforts to be made to improve the status of Americans set free by the Civil War. Ida B. Wells, the black civil rights activist, and J.A. were among the signers. They represented Chicago in a conference convened to determine how far the country had lived up to its obligations to assure each citizen, irrespective of color, equal opportunity before the law.

Only a small number of blacks lived in the Hull House neighborhood before the 1920s, but when opportunity presented itself, J.A. supported black rights. She invited the members of the National Association of Colored Women to lunch at Hull House, though a few of the residents were worried that the presence of black people might keep some of the neighbors away. She was a cofounder of the National Association for the Advancement of Colored People and, citing J.A. as "one of the few we can lean upon," the membership of the Association elected her to its executive committee. As a member of the Chicago Urban League, J.A. called upon all women to speak out against those misguided souls who claimed that lynching was committed in the name of chivalry:

> To those who say that most of these hideous and terrorizing acts have been committed in the name of chivalry, in order to make the lives and honor of women safe, perhaps it is women themselves who can best reply. . .[T]he honor of women is only secure in those nations and those localities where law and order and justice prevail. . . [The] woman who is protected by violence allows herself to be protected as the woman of the savage is, and she must still be regarded as the possession of man. As her lord and master is strong or weak, so is the protection which she receives; that if she takes brute force as her protection she must also accept the status she held when brute force alone prevailed.

Some years later when the stockyard strike broke out, most of the hired strikebreakers were black. Author Ernest Poole in his book, *Giants Gone*, wrote about the role J.A. played in those difficult times:

> [M]en and their families starved and grew so bitter against the

colored strikebreakers. . . that a plan was laid to drown scores of them in the river called Bubbly Creek. . . Learning of that, on a hot Sunday in August I came to Hull House and told Jane Addams of the plan. . . All that stifling Sunday she went about begging from rich friends, and she brought me $5,000 that night. 'Tell them I'll get more if I can, and ask Mike Donnelley [the strike leader] from me to use every power he has to keep his men from anything so fatally stupid as murder.' And so the strikebreakers were not drowned.

In full gallop on the campaign trail to win another term as president in 1912, Theodore Roosevelt was anxious for J.A.'s support. He realized he was too much the vigilant militarist for many liberal-minded Americans, but a J.A. endorsement might bring some of those undecided voters into his camp.

When Roosevelt came to Chicago, J.A. accompanied him to the Second Regiment Armory where he was to speak at a meeting sponsored by the Union League Club. Immigrants were to be his audience who, having just earned their citizenship papers, were now able to vote. But only, of course, if they were men, J.A. reminded him. Women were still deprived of the vote (and would be in federal elections until 1920).

As related by Weber Linn during their ride to the meeting in the Union League Club's open car, Roosevelt and J.A. had a lively conversation about the right of women to vote. The discussion ended with this exchange:

"How long," Roosevelt asked, "have you been a suffragist?"

"All my life," J.A. replied.

"Well," Roosevelt said, "I haven't fully made up my mind. I used to be opposed to it. . . But there are some mighty good arguments in favor of it. . . [You] are one of the best arguments yourself."

In his address that evening, Roosevelt concluded with a passionate plea in support of woman's suffrage. J.A. was delighted at the sudden conversion. No one in the audience would have suspected that Roosevelt had been an advocate of woman's suffrage for less than an hour.

After the meeting, as J.A. and Roosevelt were being driven back in the Club's car, a gust of wind blew J.A.'s hat into the muddy street. Roosevelt promptly removed his own hat to relieve J.A.'s embarrassment at being the only bareheaded person. (The following day J.A. received a $50 check from the Union League Club to replace her lost hat. She returned the check with the explanation that the hat had cost only $10 and she had already worn it for two years.) The story of the blustering Colonel removing his hat to save "Gentle Jane" embarrassment immediately became worldwide news.

Roosevelt continued his advocacy of woman's suffrage, if only to secure J.A.'s backing. But many of J.A.'s colleagues and supporters were becoming increasingly disillusioned with his escalating militarism. He supported a large navy, fortification of the Panama Canal, and opposed Philippine independence. How, her associates asked J.A., could she ally herself with the "Roaring Moose of Oyster Bay"? (The Progressive Party had adopted the bull moose as its symbol, and the meetings at which Progressives developed their party platform were held at Roosevelt's summer home in Oyster Bay, New York.)

It was not Roosevelt she was supporting, J.A. painstakingly explained, but the Progressive Party's stance on woman's suffrage and effective labor legislation. Such legislation would help prevent industrial accidents, occupational diseases, overwork and involuntary unemployment. By endorsing the very reforms that the National Association of Social Workers had recommended, Roosevelt, she asserted, had given social work a dignity and place in the national life which it had never enjoyed before.

But when Roosevelt refused to seat black delegates from Florida and Mississippi at the Progressive Party Convention, J.A. exhausted her skills of persuasion in an effort to make him reverse his decision. The letters she received only increased her anguish: "Oh, woman of the warm heart and golden tongue, who has done so much for humanity. . . do not identify yourself with those who have joined hands to crush the poor African. . ." A black leader sent a telegram from Boston: "Colored Massachusetts appreciates your opposition excluding colored delegates but beseeches you consistently not be false to colored race and betray cause equal rights by seconding nomination of Roosevelt. . . Women's suffrage will be stained with Negro blood unless women refuse alliance with Roosevelt."

J.A. asked herself whether her Abolitionist father would have remained in any political convention in which colored men had been treated slightly. He had always espoused one standard of judgment: not to complicate moral situations, already sufficiently difficult, by trying to work out another's point of view, but to look a situation fairly in the face with the best light one had.

She decided to suppress her misgivings for the sake of the social good. Once the Progressives were in power, she told herself, she would work for a system of federal arbitration in interracial difficulties, much like the Hague court in international affairs. J.A.'s announcement was widely reported. One newspaper related melodramatically, "Jane Addams' friends stood outside her door at the Congress Hotel and wept in the night hours."

The days leading up to the convention were filled with exhilaration, hope and late-night meetings. "By night and day," J.A. said, "through much enthusiastic discussion, the platform seemed to be coming nearer to our hearts' desire. . ."

On the first day of the convention every state delegation entered the hall in marching order. It was a boisterous, happy, sometimes rude crowd. The delegates, convinced that the Progressive Party was going to right all wrongs, developed a missionary zeal so contagious that Oscar Solomon Straus, former Secretary of Commerce and Labor and an influential leader in Jewish affairs, joined the New York delegation in singing "Onward Christian Soldiers," the convention's theme song.

When J.A. rose to second the nomination of Roosevelt,

applause, cheers and foot-stamping rang through the Coliseum. In contrast to the taller, heftier men in black, J.A. seemed particularly feminine in her long white dress. Her voice, which had become more resonant with age, reached the hundreds of people in the last rows of the huge hall. Deliberately she focused her remarks on the party platform, not on the candidate: "A great party," she proclaimed, "has pledged itself to the protection of children, to the care of the aged, to the relief of overworked girls, to the safe-guarding of burdened men. . ."

As she left the podium, a group of women holding a "Votes for Women" banner marched behind her, initiating an enthusiastic demonstration that lasted ten minutes. To many Americans, J.A.'s participation in the convention, a male stronghold, symbolized women's coming of age in the United States and signaled the impending triumph of the movement for social reform.

"What a grand new service you have rendered the human race," rhapsodized a Wellesley College professor. "Thousands of women are blessing you this day because your leadership brings us perceptively closer to the Kingdom of Heaven." In an article entitled "The Lamb Tags on to the Lion," a somewhat different view was expressed by a New York newspaperman:

> No matter how resolutely the fighting man had determined to fright the souls of fearful reform adversaries, he found it a difficult, if not impossible, task to hand it to them raw and straight as he had intended, once Jane had got through with him. She could always. . . manage to leave the impression that it was very bad manners to make a noise, and the fire-eater usually found himself roaring as gently as any sucking dove. . . Jane had a curious little way of her own of clipping claws and extracting fangs. . . and she and all her associates detested noise of all sorts, especially political, to all appearances, more than anything else in the world. And now she has hooked up with the Biggest Noise of them all, and actually nominated him for the Presidency. . . Perhaps the only explanation is that after all the Socialists couldn't roar loud enough and she has been waiting all these years for Theodore the Thunderer to take the cen-

ter of the stage.

Following the convention, J.A. hit the campaign trail with the vigor of a woman half her age. She spoke in North and South Dakota, Iowa, Nebraska, Oklahoma, Colorado, Kansas and Missouri, addressing miners and factory workers, trade unions and women's clubs. The exhaustion of such a tour was more than made up for by the comradeship of like-minded people, combined, she wrote, "with the heartiness of western good will [that] kept my spirits at high tide in spite of the fatigue of incessant speaking."

But the "Kingdom of Heaven" was destined to remain far distant. J.A.'s heady but short period of hope ended abruptly with the electoral results. Roosevelt and Republican William Howard Taft were defeated by Democrat Woodrow Wilson. News writers estimated that J.A. had brought in a million votes, but the estimate, she said, like the report of Mark Twain's death, was greatly exaggerated.

After the defeat by Johnny Powers, J.A. and Starr had comforted themselves with the hope that what they had done would count for something in the next electoral battle. In like spirit, J.A. hoped the education the Progressive Party had given the country on the need for social reform would influence the new president.

Disappointing to J.A. in some respects, Woodrow Wilson's administration gave her hope in others. When the time was ripe, she assured herself, he would help preserve peace in a world increasingly threatened by war. World peace had now become the overriding cause that put this 54-year-old woman of fragile health once again on the campaign trail, this time a trail that would cross the Atlantic and take her to many of the great capitals of the world.

Chapter 15

The Demons of Solitude

*W*hen did J.A. take her first public stand for peace? She smiled ruefully upon recalling the occasion. It was spring 1897 on Halsted Street. Young boys, happily shedding winter jackets, were marching in formation with sticks serving as wooden guns propped on their shoulders. With much earnest talk J.A. had persuaded them to carry shovels instead of guns so that after their drill they could help clean up the streets. And so the boys had marched with shovels, but only — J.A. quickly saw — while she was present. As soon as she moved out of sight the shovels were dumped and the boys resumed marching with their "guns."

In 1898 the Spanish-American War broke out. J.A.'s first reaction, wrote Allen F. Davis, "was not so much shock and horror, as it would later be with the outbreak of World War I, but rather a realization that a far-off event was changing the life in the Hull House neighborhood." J.A. addressed the Academy of Political and Social Sciences in December of that year and spoke about the harmful effects of war on children:

> The predatory spirit is so near the surface in human nature that there has been an increase in murders in the neighborhood since the war. . . Children were 'playing' war in the streets. In no instance. . . were they 'freeing Cubans,' but with the vio-

lence characteristic of their age, they were 'slaying Spaniards.'

As the Spanish-American War claimed its toll of lives, J.A. wrote to Mary Smith, "I can do nothing but feel a lump in my throat at the whole thing. I have really been quite blue, not play blue but real depths [blue] and will have to be more of a Tolstoyan or less of one right off." Speaking on a program devoted to the ideas of Tolstoy, she and psychologist William James, while decrying war, were both uncomfortable with Tolstoyan nonresistance. Each was painfully and methodically searching for a "moral equivalent to war."

A longtime friend observed that there were no surprises in J.A. — she did precisely what those who knew her expected her to do. "There was a logic in her life. . . a rare consistency that made her career a perfect round."

It was J.A.'s implacable logic that led her to pacifism. How could it have been otherwise when the very foundation of Hull House rested on the principle that mutual understanding among people could change the world? Only through such understanding could society move toward freeing mankind from poverty, disease and ignorance. "War fatally reversed the process of cooperating good-will, which, if it had a chance, would eventually include the human family itself," she wrote in *Peace and Bread in Time of War*. War was an obsolete way of dealing with tensions between people and nations. The enlightened way, she contended, was to reject the bloody battlefield for the mediation table.

And there was reason to hope that the world was moving, albeit slowly, toward mediation and away from war. Andrew Carnegie, the United States industrialist and peace advocate, had just demonstrat-ed his faith in the World Court by building a magnificent Peace Palace in The Hague to house it. Following its founding in 1899, the Court had successfully mediated a number of international dis-agreements.

By the time war broke out in Europe in 1914, J.A.'s pacifism was inviolate. She immediately joined with a group of colleagues in the social justice movement to explore ways to deal with the hostilities. They had devoted many years to the goal of reducing poverty and promoting understanding between different national, religious and racial groups. Nothing of human value, they were convinced, could be achieved through war; what was required in the present circumstances was the cooperation of all civilized nations.

The meetings gathered more and more adherents and by the end of the year J.A. signed a letter with Carrie Chapman Catt, an American suffrage leader, calling numerous women's groups to a conference to be held in Washington on January 10, 1915. But, J.A. admitted to Catt, "I am undertaking all this with a certain sinking of the heart, knowing how difficult it is to take any wise action among many people who do not know each other well."

On the appointed day some 3,000 women assembled in a Washington hotel. J.A. presided and gave the keynote address, striking a theme she would repeat over and over. Women, who bring life into the world, were the natural preservers of peace, she said. Their instincts direct them to preserve life; therefore they must speak out to counteract the more violent nature of man which had so often catapulted the world into war before peaceful means had been given a chance to work. J.A. compared war to human sacrifice. In the ancient past, refusing to send their sons into battle, women had said, "No, we will not sacrifice our children upon the altars of tribal gods." Today's women must also take a stand; history shows us, J.A. contended, that men would not do it.

After an intense, day-long meeting, a Peace Platform was adopted. Its preamble stated:

> We, women of the United States, assembled in behalf of World Peace, grateful for the security of our own country, but sorrowing for the misery of all involved in the present struggle among warring nations, do hereby band ourselves together to demand that war be abolished. . . We demand that women be given a share in deciding between war and peace in all the courts of high debate — within the home, the school, the church, the industrial order and the state. . . [So] demanding,

we hereby form ourselves into a national organization to be called the Woman's Peace Party.

The platform's eleven planks included the demand for "continuous mediation" to be provided by neutral nations. The press, which had given worldwide coverage to Theodore Roosevelt's gentlemanly removal of his hat, all but ignored the creation of the new peace party and its choice of J.A. as its chairperson.

A few months later, J.A. received a cablegram from a prominent Dutch suffragette, Aletta Jacobs, inviting the Woman's Peace Party to send delegates to an international congress of women to be held at The Hague from April 28 to May 1, 1915. Just at this time J.A.'s last surviving sister, Alice, died after a lingering illness. J.A. had little heart for a European conference as well as doubts about the enterprise. Yet as chair of the Woman's Peace Party she could hardly decline. Feeling the need for the support of a good friend, she asked Alice Hamilton to accompany her. Hamilton believed the whole endeavor hopelessly idealistic. Nonetheless, she consented, desiring to give what comfort she could to her grieving friend while keeping a medical eye upon her.

J.A. accompanied Alice's body to Cedarville; then she and Hamilton joined the delegates who set sail on April 16 in the Dutch ship, Noordam. The European women on board were well aware that they ran the risk of being condemned as traitors if apprehended. That risk and the very real danger from German submarines made the 12 days spent on board ship a harrowing journey.

"This is a most unusual trip," Hamilton wrote to Mary Smith.

It's like a perpetual meeting of the Woman's City Club or the Federation of Settlements. . . It is interesting to see the party evolve from a chaotic lot of half-informed people, and muddled enthusiasts, and sentimentalists, with a few really informed ones, into a docile, teachable, coherent body, only too glad to be led by those few. We have long passed the stage of poems and impassioned appeals. . . now we are discussing whether it is more dangerous to insist on democratic control of diplomacy than it is to insist on neutralization of the seas. There are still some five or six whom we regard with a little mistrust and who may possibly disgrace us at the last moment but most of us are very quiet and tractable. . . J.A. is really having a good time. She has made every woman on board feel that she is an intimate friend and they all adore her.

When the Congress opened at The Hague, J.A., who had been asked to serve as chair, looked down from the podium and welcomed 1,136 women from 12 different countries. Stating their belief that the right of women to vote went hand in hand with the success of the peace movement, the Congress drew up a set of resolutions that called for the representation of women in both national and international political life, a permanent international court, liberal peace terms, permanent disarmament, freedom of the seas and the right of each country to rule itself. The most dramatic resolution called for a conference of neutral nations which would promptly offer the warring countries a chance for continuous mediation as a way to end the war. The women resolved to send representatives to all the belligerent and neutral nations of Europe as well as to the President of the United States to inform them of the Congress' resolutions.

Theodore Roosevelt called the peace platform "silly and base," and the women's peace movement "both foolish and noxious. . . which if successful would only do harm." He ridiculed J.A., on whom he had lavished such high praise when she had supported his presidential candidacy, calling her, "poor bleeding Jane."

Roosevelt's condemnation received wide publicity, but J.A. had little time to mull over the former president's attack. She had been one of the two women (Aletta Jacobs was the other) selected to visit the heads of the warring countries with the Congress' message. Another delegation was selected to visit the neutral countries. J.A. feared these visits would be an exercise in futility, but, as she talked to the European women whose countries were at war, she realized that to them the proposed visits were both dignified and vital. With her "confidante in white linen," as Hamilton dubbed herself, J.A. together with Jacobs set off for Great Britain, Germany, Austria, Hungary, Italy, France, Switzerland and Belgium.

On the first leg of the journey, Hamilton wrote to Louise Bowen:

> I am sitting in the headquarters of the Woman's Peace Party waiting while Miss Addams goes over minutes and reports with a very meticulous English lady. Downstairs a taxi is ticking away and the thought of it gives me indigestion, but Miss Addams keeps saying she is coming.

The women crossed and recrossed international boundaries. All around them were the brutal signs of war — barricaded cities, bombed-out buildings, wounded and crippled soldiers. The delegation was greeted with respect, sometimes even cordiality, by the heads of state, but none of the interviews gave J.A. any reason to be hopeful. She found it difficult to talk peace to people who had lost sons in the war, for there was no way to avoid implying that the cause to which the sons had given their lives was not worth the sacrifice. "Your tongue cleaves to your mouth," she admitted.

The separate delegation visiting the neutral nations did receive some encouragement from the Swedish prime minister. He would take the initiative in calling a neutral conference if he were assured that the warring nations would find that acceptable. But the response of Germany and England — that they would not be unfriendly to such a conference but were doubtful that anything could come of it — failed to give the prime minister the degree of assurance he needed. Weary and disheartened, and having concluded that only the White House could bring about mediation, J.A. decided to sail directly for home and skipped a planned meeting of the two delegations in Amsterdam.

A committee of nearly 50, waving white ribbons reading "Welcome Home, Jane Addams," greeted her ship as it pulled into New York harbor on July 5th. Many more gathered four days later in Carnegie Hall to hear J.A. speak on her experiences. After facing such genuine emotion and high patriotism in Europe, she said that she had no desire to "loose any more emotion upon the world." She noted that each warring nation she visited solemnly assured her it was fighting in self-defense. Foreign offices were unanimous in saying that a willingness to negotiate would be seen as a sign of weakness. It was clear that if a conference were to be convened, it would have to be by the United States.

Drawing to the end of her speech, J.A. said that many young men she had spoken with did not believe in war and needed stimulants to enable them to engage in the utter brutality of bayonet fighting. The next morning a newspaper headline screamed, "Troops Drunk-Crazed, says Miss Addams." Reporting little else, the comment from the "radical Miss Addams" about stimulants dominated the newspaper coverage of the Carnegie Hall speech. J.A. had trespassed on the sacred. She had dared to suggest that some soldiers were not brave men fighting to the end for their country, but cowards who needed a stiff drink before going into battle. War correspondent Richard Harding Davis claimed that Miss Addams denied the soldier the credit of his sacrifice. The message she sends to the soldier's children, he said, was that he did not die for France or England, or for them, but because he was drunk.

"Journalistic attack continued for week after week in every sort of newspaper and in a certain number of them in England and France," J.A. said. "It also brought me an enormous number of letters, most of them abusive." Only once, after a speech delivered in Chautauqua, New York, did she try to make clear to an Associated Press reporter what she had actually said about the bayonet charges, but his published article was so hopelessly garbled that she gave up in despair.

According to Allen F. Davis, the effect of the newspaper maelstrom that summer of 1915 toppled J.A. from her pedestal as "one of the most admired, indeed worshipped American women." It was at this time that J.A. redefined "freedom of the press" as the "freedom to misinterpret any statement they [the press] does not like and to suppress any statement they do not understand."

Later that year the press pounced on yet another opportunity to attack J.A. Henry Ford, a new convert to pacifism, volunteered to finance an unofficial conference separate from the White House. Against J.A.'s strong advice he chartered a ship, Oscar II, to transport the delegates to Stockholm, the selected conference site. Ford flamboyantly promised to get the boys out of the trenches by Christmas and set December 4, 1915, as the departure date of the "Peace Ship."

Repelled by the silly, frivolous publicity about Oscar II, many seasoned delegates, John Dewey among them, withdrew from the enterprise. Hoping that she might lend the project some stability, J.A. chose not to withdraw, contrary to the counsel of Louise Bowen and Mary Smith. However, when the Oscar II sailed from New York harbor, J.A. was in the hospital suffering from a severely worsened kidney ailment.

Tension and squabbling between Ford and the other members of the peace project led Ford to abandon his own ship on Christmas Eve. Although the remaining delegates reorganized themselves in Stockholm, and some constructive work was done, the project soon foundered and sank. A number of reporters hovering around the newsworthy Miss Addams plunged in for the kill, flatly accusing her of faking illness to wriggle out of the embarrassing venture.

Distressed as she was by the continuing journalistic assaults, J.A. was far more distressed by the relentless passage of days, each one filled with the devastation of cities and the waste of lives. She was determined to see the President; she had to persuade him to take the lead in calling a conference of neutral nations. After the cancellation of several appointments, J.A. at last had her meeting. Wilson listened politely but was firmly noncommittal about the United States in the role of neutral convener.

In the ensuing weeks and months, J.A. and other peace activists persisted in their efforts to move Wilson to take the lead for peace. J.A. talked with Wilson's top aide, Colonel Edward House, and Secretary of State Robert Lansing. She had another interview with the President in January 1916 at which he said that the Woman's Peace Party platform was the best formulation which had been presented to him. Indeed, for a brief period, it seemed as if all the hopes the peace liberals had placed in Wilson were to be justified. In December 1916 Wilson asked the belligerents to state their peace terms. And in January 1917 he spoke of an international organization to guarantee world peace and of ending the war before one side had achieved victory.

But the time of hope was short-lived. The Germans resumed submarine warfare, the U.S. broke diplomatic relations over the issue, and Wilson delivered his war message in April 1917. The entry of the United States into the war presented the greatest challenge to J.A.'s pacifist ideals that she had yet encountered. Friends and colleagues urged her to support the war. Even John Dewey began to speak of the "social possibilities of war," and Louise Bowen, deeply upset by J.A.'s passionate pacifism, predicted that if she adhered to her peace-at-all-costs stance she would be committing intellectual suicide. The two friends spoke little to each other during this fraught time, and several years passed before their friendship was restored to its former intimacy.

J.A. was also the maverick among the residents at Hull House, most of whom supported the war. Eight young male residents volunteered for active service and six of them were immediately sent overseas. A contingent of the Boy's Band, with their bandmaster, went to the front. George Hooker, Hull House's first male resident, was head of the Draft Board in the Hull House district with a corps of volunteers from the Hull House residential force of men and women. J.A. did not seek to interfere with any of these activities — they were the will of the majority.

Nor did J.A. and her sister pacificist remove themselves from the fray. Instead they sought to help their warring country in ways

congenial to their beliefs. Alice Hamilton inspected munitions factories to monitor the release of poisonous gases, and Rachel Yarros
traveled the country talking on what was discreetly called social
hygiene. Soldiers from the district were given their last meal at Hull
House before they left for France, "with their families and sweet-
hearts outside the door until the meal should be finished and they
could give their last farewells in the Hull-House courtyard."

The Settlement's "unshakeable tolerance," and "the fundamen-
tal respect its members have for one another's firm beliefs," a local
newspaper said, "explains how Hull-House has been able to hold so
long its great company of valiant souls, slacking neither their valor
nor their comradeship. . . They differ violently but with great fellowship, like knights who battle in the tourney but drink to one
another's prowess before and after."

J.A.'s health was deteriorating. In the fall of 1915 she suffered a
reoccurrence of a kidney and bladder ailment which continued to
plague her, reducing her to what she characterized as "three years of
semi-invalidism." She spent some time with Louise Bowen in Bar
Harbor, hoping that the tranquility of her friend's home and the
beauty of the woods and water would be restorative. She returned
to Chicago somewhat rested, but her usual resiliency faltered in the
face of the burgeoning opposition and ridicule heaped upon her.
She wrote in *Peace and Bread in Time of War*:

> During weeks of feverish discomfort I experienced a bald
> sense of social opprobrium and widespread misunderstanding
> which brought me very near to self-pity, perhaps the lowest pit
> into which human nature can sink. Indeed the pacifist in war
> time, with his precious cause in the keeping of those who con-
> trol the sources of publicity and consider it a patriotic duty to
> make all types of peace propaganda obnoxious, constantly
> faces two dangers. Strangely enough he finds it possible to
> travel from the mire of self pity straight to the barren hills of
> self-righteousness and to hate himself equally in both places. . .
> From the beginning of the great war, as the members of our
> group gradually became defined from the rest of the commu-
> nity, each one felt increasingly the sense of isolation which rap-

idly developed after the United States entered the war into that destroying effect of 'aloneness'. . . We never ceased to miss the unquestioning comradeship experienced by our fellow citizens during the war nor to feel curiously outside the enchantment given to any human emotion when it is shared by millions of others. . . and long desperately for reconciliation with friends and fellow citizens. . . Solitude has always had its demons, harder to withstand than the snares of the world.

In these periods of "faint-heartedness," J.A. repeatedly asked herself who was she to differ with men of exquisite conscience, like John Dewey. Although they abhorred war as much as she, they were convinced that this war for the preservation of democracy would make all future wars impossible. Again and again she had to answer from the depths of her own conscience that war in the interest of democracy was a contradiction in terms.

> What, after all, has maintained the human race on this old globe, despite all the calamities of nature and all the tragic failings of mankind, if not faith in new possibilities and courage to advocate them. Doubtless many times these new possibilities were declared by a man who, quite unconscious of courage, bore the 'sense of being an exile, a condemned criminal, a fugitive from mankind.' Did everyone so feel who, in order to travel on his own proper path, had been obliged to leave the traditional highway?

J.A. cut back on her public speaking. It was clear that she would not get a fair hearing in the press. Rotten fruit and vegetables were thrown at the doors of Hull House. Hate letters piled up on her desk under the brooding eyes of Tolstoy.

Chapter 16

A New Force in the World

*C*hildren the world over had been going to bed hungry since the beginning of the Great War. Early in 1918 Herbert Hoover asked J.A. to help deliver an urgent message to their fellow Americans — if everyone conserved food, the United States could feed its own people and still have enough to send to the hungry in Europe.

J.A. welcomed the assignment; it would give her an opportunity to speak of the need for international cooperation to prevent worldwide starvation. Once again she hit the campaign trail. In some cities she was still regarded with suspicion, even contempt. In others, she was cheered by mainly female audiences stirred by her message — what they did in the kitchen could help their country and the world. Her conservation efforts moved some of her milder critics to overlook her pacifist "foolishness." The antagonism against her began to die off at the edges, but the center remained grimly hostile.

On March 16, 1918, J.A.'s brother Weber died at Elgin State Hospital, ending his long struggle with mental illness; he had been stricken with septic poisoning that led to a fatal dysentery. The official letter informing Weber's wife, Laura, of his illness did not reach her until after his death.

J.A. had received the telegram advising her of Weber's death in New Orleans where she had gone with Mary Smith to recover her strength after a hard winter. She arrived two days before the funeral and stayed with Anna Addams at the Homestead. Since George's death, mutual grief had lessened the tension between the two women though they were still not at ease with each other. J.A. wrote to Marcet about the funeral:

> The service was held in his [Weber's] own house which had been heated for two days and was very comfortable. It was filled with people all anxious to do him honor and I think the service brought much comfort to Laura. We were all grief-stricken that we had not known of his acute illness in time to go to the hospital. We had always hoped he might die at home.

Mary Fry also wrote to Marcet:

> As I looked at Aunt Jane standing by the open grave I realized how she must feel to be the last member of her family. It must be a relief to her and Aunt Laura to know that the suffering is ended but it will be agony for some time to come to think of Mr. Addams dying there alone. . . He was conscious at the end and might have longed to see his family.

The November 11, 1918, newspapers carried the long-awaited banner headlines — the Great War was over. Mingled with the joy was the sorrow of families who had lost sons and husbands. J.A. had suffered her own great loss. Three weeks before the Armistice her sister Mary's oldest son, Captain John Linn, had been killed by shell fire in the Argonne as he walked among the tents distributing chocolate to war-weary soldiers. J.A. and John Linn had always had a particularly affectionate relationship, and he had been sending her weekly letters from the front. In his last letter he had predicted that he would die.

The Armistice brought a peace troubled by hysteria and persecution. The Russian Revolution, occurring at the same time as the Great War, led many Americans to link the two and condemn anyone critical of the United States as a "Commie lover." Pacifists were automatically labeled "Reds."

> It took me some time to discover why pacifism should so often connote Bolshevism [J.A. wrote], until it was gradually made clear that some people believed that the pacifist advocated reducing the armed forces of the country so that when the Bolshevists arrived in America, they should find no resistance. We were slow to understand this elaborate charge and it would have been hard to anticipate an interpretation so complicated and remote.

A War Department official produced a list of 62 persons who had been under surveillance as possible enemies to the United States. Jane Addams was first on the list. Her dossier showed that she had opposed drafting men into the army and advocated that conscientious objectors be offered an alternative to military duty. Even more significant, Hull House had always given radicals a place to speak, and bred the "Hull House Variety of Parlor Bolshevists." "Was it not true," a reporter asked, "that practically all the radicalism among women in the United States centered about Hull House in Chicago and the Children's Bureau in Washington [headed by Julia Lathrop] with a dynasty of Hull House graduates in charge of it since its creation?" To many Americans, Hull House had become a nest of radicals and J.A. the master builder.

On occasion the wild hysteria of the Red Scare was absurd enough to provide welcome hilarity for Hull House dinner table conversation. J.A. reported that an excited man ran into the House yelling that the "Romanians north of Madison Street were hatching a plot against the government." "I reminded him that the Romanians were on the side of the Allies. 'I never can get those Balkan countries straightened out' was his apology, and I was in no position to remind him that it was not his geography that was at fault but his state of mind."

On another occasion J.A. was called on by a very young Secret Service agent who informed her that Bulgarian Communists were holding a meeting in Bowen Hall and that he was under orders to arrest the leaders. "The dangerous alien enemies were merely attending an afternoon concert," J.A. told him, but he ignored her, only to return an hour later to report dolefully that he had not been able to ferret out a single communist leader — everyone had just sat in the hall listening to music. What, he asked J.A., would she do in his place. "Resign," J.A. answered.

"I never heard of his fate," J.A. wrote in *Second Twenty Years at Hull-House*, "but I was thankful we got through the entire period of the war and post-war without a single arrest, if only because it gave a certain refuge to those who were surrounded by the suspicions and animosities inevitably engendered by the war toward all aliens."

Turning her back on the hatemongers, J.A., as president of the Woman's Peace Party, threw her still considerable energies into setting up an international peace conference in Zurich to take place at the same time as the Versailles peace treaty negotiations. Though dubious about the conference, Alice Hamilton and Florence Kelley agreed to accompany J.A. to Switzerland, but only, Kelley insisted, to "black J.A.'s boots and lug her suitcase."

Before leaving for Zurich, J.A. stopped in Cedarville to see her ailing stepmother, but the old woman was unconscious and J.A. had to depart without speaking with her. Anna Addams died several weeks later. In J.A.'s absence, Mary Smith attended the funeral and reported that Mrs. Addams had been laid out in her casket with her head resting on a small pillow that had been J.A.'s last gift to her.

Only through dogged persistence was J.A. able to persuade the Red Cross to escort her and Alice Hamilton on a pre-conference tour of towns devastated by the war. She hoped, among other things, to find the grave of her nephew, John Linn. During their five-day journey the two friends traveled in cold rain, slogging through mud from one tragic village to another. "The humble stone houses," wrote Hamilton to her sister, "weren't the sort of thing that artillery ought to attack. It is like killing kittens with machine guns; they are so small and helpless."

In spite of the weather, J. A. asked their driver to take them to the Argonne where she and Hamilton walked through the cemetery in ankle-deep mud looking for John Linn's grave. On the second day, shortly before the graveyard was enveloped in darkness, they found it — a mound of earth marked with a cross. The rows of graves seemed to the grieving aunt to go on forever.

The Zurich conference was attended by over 1,500 delegates from 16 countries. By the second day Kelley had become a convert. She wrote to Smith: "As you doubtless know, my going was an act of faith, not conviction. . . but next time I would go on my knees. It was unbelievably wonderful. . . The will toward peace and international neighborliness so often trampled under during the war became alive again in that hall."

J.A. presided at the conference and, according to Hamilton, seemed revitalized by the proceedings. The women voted to send a resolution to the peace negotiators urging an end to the food blockade which was prolonging a terrible famine in Europe. Upon receiving the resolution, Wilson responded with a telegram to J.A. agreeing with the sentiments expressed but advising that lifting the blockade was impractical at that time.

The Zurich conferees received an advance copy of the peace treaty drawn up at Versailles and were deeply concerned about its implications. The Versailles measures were so harsh that the Zurich reviewing committee feared the treaty would ultimately lead to more war and bloodshed. Though they approved the proposed formation of the League of Nations, they objected to provisions that would weaken the League's ability to keep world peace. Finally, they called for the inclusion of a Women's Charter that would grant women full rights, including suffrage. The conferees then formed themselves into a permanent body, The Women's International League for Peace and Freedom (WILPF), with J.A. as its first president. J.A. addressed the assembled women in the final speech of the conference: "We shall have to believe in spiritual power. . . We shall have to learn to use moral energy to put a new sort of force into the world and believe that it is a vital thing — the only thing in this moment of sorrow and death and destruction, that will heal the world."

"The Congress is over," Hamilton wrote, "and was a success in every way. J.A. got in bed last night at some time after midnight and couldn't sleep for over an hour, partly from excitement, partly from tiredness. She. . . carried through a very difficult piece of work — handling a meeting of women from eighteen different countries and at least three different languages."

J.A. had expected to return to Chicago after the conference but changed her plans when she and Hamilton were invited by the Quakers to distribute food in Germany.

> [In] Leipzig we visited a large playground in which 625 children from six to twelve years of age spend the day and are given a midday dinner. It consists of one pint of thin meal soup, to which had been added a little dried vegetable. Out of 190 children who were seated at one time in the dining room all except one were thin and anemic, . . .with pallid gray faces, swollen bellies, matchstick legs, and shoulder-blades like wings.

J.A. believed that if help were not given to the children "quickly and abundantly," much of the present generation in Germany would be doomed to an early death or a handicapped life.

Upon her return in the fall of 1919 and on into the next year, J.A. spoke to as many audiences as she could reach about the urgency of sending food to Germany. She also managed to raise some money for that purpose, but at great cost to her energy and morale. Military organizations continued to attack her because of her stance on disarmament. According to an ROTC publication, "For 20 years Jane Addams directed her efforts to international and subversive channels until today she stands out as the most dangerous woman in America." The Daughters of the American Revolution withdrew the honorary membership they had given her in 1900, deriding her for aiding the Communists in their attempts to start a civil war in America. J.A. dryly observed that she had thought she was in the DAR for life, not for good behavior.

Although J.A. tried to minimize the effect upon her of the flood of anger and insult, Hamiliton and Smith could both see that she was deeply upset. "You know," J.A. said, "I am really getting old. I find it not as easy to love my enemies as it used to be." She turned what energy she could muster to the hunger and joblessness in her own neighborhood. She was besieged with cries of help — a homeless woman who was to have a baby, where should she go? A man who had lost his leg, what job could he get? Louise Bowen wrote in *Open Windows*:

> There were times at Hull House when Miss Addams and I did not know what to do with the crowds of unemployed, particularly after the first World War. . . Hull House tried then as it has always tried, to give help to all these people. . . We called on the members of the Hull House Woman's Club, and using the little kitchen at Bowen Hall, very early Sunday mornings they made quantities of coffee in large coffee urns and really thousands of sandwiches. . . The men and women could take as much coffee and as many sandwiches as they wanted. Miss Addams and I made speeches to them about what we had accomplished the past week in finding jobs for some of the men.

J.A. tried to create as many jobs within Hull House as she could. The job she "found" for the circus trapeze performer as official Hull House window-washer gave her particular satisfaction and some welcome amusement.

> It was a pleasure to see him run along the sills and open and shut the windows on the third and fourth floors, and he never had an accident. He took great pride in being able to do this and was always watched when at work by crowds of children who told everybody to come and see the circus performer washing the windows.

"One day a rough looking man came to Hull House to see me,"

Bowen wrote,

> and said that he represented the men out of employment
> who had come Sunday afternoons to Bowen Hall. He told
> of the many men who wanted to commit suicide but who
> had told him they had heard Miss Addams and me talk
> about not becoming discouraged and had made up their
> minds to give up the idea. He said that they had all gathered
> together some of their pennies for a present for us. He pre-
> sented me with a little dirty brown package of dates. He said
> he hoped we would enjoy them.

From the capitals of the war-scarred world and countless podi-
ums across the land, J.A. would return to Hull House to confront
problems that were as intractable as those she had encountered
abroad. But a small boy's gift of a fish, the jobless men's package of
dates, the publication of sonnets by a young Greek poet she had
helped — these were the realities of J.A.'s life as well as failed peace
plans, corrupt politicians, FBI surveillance, blacklists and heckling
audiences. During her afternoons at Hull House children would
gather around her chair to hear a story. One might hope that the
hatred and indignities heaped upon her were forgotten, if only for
the brief interlude of the Children's Hour.

Chapter 17

A Hard Mistress to Serve

Though J.A. was treated with respect at the meetings of the National Federation of Settlements, the new generation of social workers considered J.A.'s brand of social work old-fashioned. It was clear that J.A. had been reduced to the role of emeritus, a demotion she did not take to kindly.

> If my ideas are a wreck, as some people say [she remarked], I can still feel the rudder in my hand and I think I can still steer. I have been asked if I have the courage to begin my work over again. I can only say that it takes more courage to abandon one's principles and habits of life than to keep on with them.

But when she was not elected president of the Federation, in spite of Graham Taylor's active campaigning on her behalf, she knew, like it or not, that she was no longer considered relevant by her young colleagues.

According to Weber Linn, J.A. fought her status both as traitor and emeritus leader with a defensive armor of laughter. "No one who was much in her company can forget the flow of stories in those years," he said. After receiving a particularly nasty hate letter, J.A. reminded Linn of Mrs. Noah Webster's exclamation upon encountering her husband kissing the cook, "Mr. Webster, I am surprised!" and of Webster's response, "My dear, it is we who are surprised; *you* are astonished." "But we pacifists," J.A. added, "are not even astonished."

J.A. decided to spend more time traveling, leaving Hull House in Bowen's competent hands. "It's not that I'm adventurous," she said to Linn, "but I do like to get about." Her trips were hardly relaxed. She made most of them as a delegate: in 1913 to the annual meeting of the International Suffrage Alliance in Budapest; in 1915 to The Hague; in 1919 to Zurich; in 1921 to Vienna; in 1922 to The Hague again; in 1926 to Dublin; in 1928 to Honolulu; and in 1929 to Prague. In January 1923, following the second Hague convention, she startled everyone, including her doctor, by embarking on a trip around the world with Mary Smith. To reassure the anxious physician that she would be all right, J.A. told him that Robert Louis Stevenson had observed that most of the important things in the world were done by people who weren't feeling very well.

J.A.'s letters made it clear that one of the reasons she chose to travel was that she no longer felt her own country to be a hospitable place. "To some," she said, "it almost seems as if an internationally minded person should be defined as a friend of every country but his own." Her enthusiastic reception abroad was a balm to her assaulted spirit. She visited India, the Philippine islands, Manchuria, Korea and China. She was particularly interested in the women of Japan and India. Limited by repressive, iron-clad convention, they took on the responsibility of the terribly poor with a determination that shamed her when she remembered the freedom she had had as a young person, and "how slowly I had realized what that freedom was for."

Thousands squeezed into the largest public hall in Osaka, Japan, when she spoke on "Women and Peace." Later while attending a dinner given in her honor by the governor of the province, she became ill and had to be driven to a Tokyo hospital. A tumor was discovered in her breast and it was strongly advised that she have a mastectomy. Hamilton put everything aside and traveled to Tokyo where she remained with her friend for three weeks of convalescence. When J.A. was well enough to move on, she and Smith went to Honolulu for further rest.

On her return to Chicago from her international odyssey, J.A. was greeted with requests from women worldwide to deliver a Christmas message. It was one of J.A.'s more somber speeches:

> We know the world is not at peace nor is there enough active good will in it to accomplish the healing of nations. . . The divided nations of Europe are in a panic of fear and apprehension. . . The United States of America, caught in a traditional dislike of foreign entanglements abandons the solemn covenants made in her name, restricts her immigration, increases her tariffs and refuses to consider her war losses as part of the international responsibility she assumed in 1917.
>
> May China and Japan. . . realize that that nation is already perishing by the sword, when military authority dominates civil life. . . when the fear of warlike neighbors is deliberately utilized to postpone the day of disarmament.
>
> In Africa, in India, in the Philippines. . . may the millions. . . renew their resolution to continue the policies of a great teacher who more than any other is steadfastly committed to the typical Christian adventure, as yet un-tried, of nonresistance. May at least one nation of Oriental peoples actually fulfill that essential doctrine preached by Him who was born on Christmas Day on Eastern soil.

It was a bleak time for those who still dared call themselves Liberals. "I do not know that we can correctly say that liberty is dead, but there is a heavy hand of intolerance resting on the world," University of Chicago Professor Robert Merriam observed. Journalist William Allen White painted an even grimmer picture, characterizing Americans as living in a cramped and ill-conditioned world, rattling their little tin bank in one hand and their steel sword in the other. The WILPF had been prescient in its prediction that under the Treaty of Versailles, Europe would continue to suffer chaos. Internationalism, J.A. feared, indeed spirituality, was at its lowest ebb.

To rally the forces of liberalism and social progress, a dinner was planned in Chicago in January of 1927. Unknown to J.A., a committee decided that the event should be held in her honor. The Furniture Mart, with the largest floor space in the city, was rented for the occasion. Louise Bowen was to be the toastmistress, but illness kept her at home and Julia Lathrop took her place. J.A. had requested quite firmly that she not be mentioned and that the remarks made at the dinner be "philosophic." Needless to say, the request was ignored.

One of the letters read that evening was from William Kent, the reluctant donor of the land for the first public playground:

> Her [J.A.'s] idea of mutual benefit from democratic association took a long time to percolate through my mind. But my admiration of her made me think diligently and so in the end I blundered into the basis of her theory and practice. . . She holds the leadership of the whole world, of those who are intelligently striving for practical idealism.

The tributes rolled on. Judge Hugo Pam said:

> I am the only speaker tonight whose father and mother were immigrants. . . I was born within two blocks of Hull House. . . but little did I think as I trudged past that corner in the seventies on my way to school that it was to become the Mecca of every spiritual pilgrim in this great city, the laboratory testing life, out of which was to come the certainty that to devote oneself to the welfare of others is the surest way of achieving one's own welfare.

Finally, J.A. rose to respond.

> I suggested that we try to keep this dinner impersonal, make it a discussion of the Liberal in the present situation. . . and I realize that I have merely been the hook upon which to hang all the fine things that have been said. I am very grateful for the affection and interest you have brought here this evening; yet in a way humiliated by what you say I am, for I know myself to be a very simple person, not at all sure I am right and most

of the time not right, though wanting to be, which I am sure we all know of ourselves. I can only hope that we may go on together, working as we go for the betterment of things, and with thorough enjoyment and participation in those things which are making for righteousness.

Although more than 1,500 people gathered at the Furniture Mart to honor J.A. as one of the great leaders and humanitarians of the time, the honoree stood before them and claimed to be a simple woman who was often not sure of what she was doing. Why? Jill Ker Conway, in *When Memory Speaks*, theorizes that J.A. was quite deliberately continuing a 40-year stratagem to gain support for her controversial reforms by assuming the role of a woman who was more fitted to run a home than an organization, who was a passive player in her own history and who, should she achieve something of significance in the wide world, would not claim credit for it.

The realities of J.A.'s life suggest a different interpretation. For the last several years J.A. had been fighting exhaustion of body and spirit. In her eyes many of her most important accomplishments weren't holding. Yes, she had pioneered the field of social work, but it had been taken out of her hands and professionalized in a way that was antithetical to her own strong beliefs. Yes, she had seconded the nomination of Theodore Roosevelt, but his militaristic instincts had prevailed over his openness to social reform. Her hopes for a quick end to the Great War had never been realized; Woodrow Wilson had profoundly disappointed her by his unwillingness to convene a conference of neutral nations. And Versailles had made a shambles of the post-war opportunity to forge a real peace.

At home, Hull House had lost many of its staunch supporters and no one was stepping forward to take their places. Money was desperately needed for a new furnace and badly leaking roofs, but where could it be found? J.A.'s personal life had been dimmed by the recent deaths of beloved friends and she felt deeply the pain of being the last surviving member of her immediate family. She knew, having tended her ill brother and sisters, that each of them had died disappointed in their lives, as had George, his brilliance laid waste by chronic depression.

Addressing the mass of faces looking up at her, J.A. was feeling neither powerful nor successful. She did not, for the sake of the occasion, fake satisfaction. Rather, she gave voice to her genuine feelings. Some good things had happened, many had not. Do not salute me, but rather do in your own lives what I have not managed to do or to finish in mine.

One old-timer at the dinner observed that never had there been such a gathering since Mark Twain had praised General Grant at the Army of Cumberland reunion in 1879. J.A. would not have felt flattered by the comparison.

In her peace work abroad, J.A. had been a guest at the palace of one of the most famous of the members of the WILPF — Marie, Queen of Romania. One afternoon while going through the day's mail with Sadie Ellis, J.A. received a letter informing her that the queen would be traveling to the United States and would like to visit. "Queen Marie received me at her palace," J.A. said, "and I'll be happy to receive her at mine."

The queen traveled with a party of 17 and an entire railway car of luggage; her "American trousseau," as it was called, filled more than 50 trunks. The Royal Romanian, the train that carried Her Highness and her party on their tour of the United States, was described by the *New York Times* as one of the most beautiful and elaborate trains ever placed on rails.

The American public proved to be insatiable on the subject of the beautiful, charismatic queen, devouring stories about her as soon as they appeared in print. For her meeting with the debonaire mayor of New York City, Jimmy Walker, Queen Marie was dressed in a burgundy velvet sable-trimmed coat and gold turban. Her 20-car entourage, preceded by a platoon of mounted police, brought her to New York City Hall where she was to be presented with the gold medal of the City of New York. Never before had the Mayor presented the medal to a woman, and as he addressed Queen Marie he became flustered and hesitated before pinning it to her bodice.

"Proceed, Your Honor," the Queen said smiling. "The risk is mine."

"And such a beautiful risk it is, Your Majesty," the Mayor responded.

No wonder then that the Hull House neighbors expected J.A. to honor her guest with High Tea, perhaps even inviting them to attend as she had done before on occasions of import. Men and women did the unprecedented — took time out from work and formed a gapers row three deep along Halsted Street. Upon seeing the excited, jostling crowd, J.A. had to raise her voice to make herself heard as she stood in the Hull House doorway.

"I'm very sorry, ladies and gentlemen. When guests visit Hull House on a weekday afternoon, they take tea in the Coffee House just as I do. Please go back to work."

J.A. had asked Sadie Ellis to "tote" the Queen, the word residents had coined for escorting a visitor through the many Hull House buildings. "I showed the Queen around the House," Ellis told the few residents lingering at the dinner table that evening.

> She asked many questions and was interested in everything. . . At the end of the tour Miss Addams met us at the Coffee House. We each picked up a damp tray, Queen Marie following our lead, and helped ourselves to a cup of tea and the usual cake, cookies and crackers, some a bit stale, that had been left over from lunch. We sat at one of the scratched black tables and talked quite easily. When the visit was over Queen Marie assured us that she had had the best time of her trip. Would we please tell her what those wonderful square white pastries were? Salerno crackers, I told her, and she said she must buy a quantity to take back to Romania.

The evening following Queen Marie's visit, J.A. insisted that a carpenter working late on the job join her and the other residents in the dining room for dinner. The embarrassed man apologized — he was in his working clothes and couldn't possibly stay. J.A. insisted, and once in the dining room graciously directed him to take the seat to her left. "That's just the way it was," Ellis said. "If a queen visits in the afternoon Miss Addams invites her to tea in the Coffee House. If a carpenter is still working at dinnertime, he is invited to dinner in the dining room." Ellis recalled dinner that evening:

> When the lettuce salad was served Miss Addams did not pick up fork or knife. She discreetly waited to see what the carpenter would do, and when he picked up the lettuce and ate it from his hand, without hesitation Miss Addams picked up her lettuce and did the same.

J.A.'s first attack of angina occurred in 1926 in Dublin. From that time on, she suffered from a weakened heart that made it impossible for her to continue to live in her high, second-story rooms at Hull House. She moved into a first floor room of Mary Smith's home, but persisted, against the explicit directions of her doctor, in climbing the Hull House stairs to the second floor. "Miss Addams never was one to rust away," he said dryly.

J.A. had given Ellis the responsibility of planning all the festivities for the Settlement, trusting her artist's eye in the printing of invitations and the decoration of the House for festive events. But J.A. took one reception completely out of her assistant's hands — the wedding reception celebrating the March 1927 marriage of Sadie Ellis and Leon Garland.

Garland, a shy, dark-eyed Russian immigrant, both a painter and metalworker, had been invited to join the Saturday Painters by Morris Topchevsky, who was later to study with Diego Rivera. "You pay nothing for the use of the Hull House studio," Topchevsky had told the artist. "It's the best bargain in Chicago."

Sadie and Leon had first met at a session of the Saturday Painters and in their two-year courtship, centered most of their social life around Hull House. Leon taught metalworking and batik at the Settlement, and was an active member of the Dill Pickle, an intellectual Socialist organization that met at Hull House. Like J.A., however, Leon preferred to do his battling indoors rather than in the streets, and painted dramatic posters espousing liberal causes.

After the wedding, the young couple moved into one of the artists' lofts that had been built when the open-air nursery for tubercular children was remodeled. Sadie recalled that she and Leon had been in their loft for a few days when early one morning they heard a soft knock on the door.

> We had been given no furniture yet so we were sleeping on two cots pushed together in the middle of the room. When the caller identified herself as Miss Addams, Leon leaped out of bed and ran into the bathroom. Miss Addams had come to see what furniture we needed. Looking around the bare loft, she concluded we needed everything. She took my hand and led me out of the room. 'We will see what we can do,' she said, and knocking on the doors of some of our neighbors she told them that the Garlands needed furniture and was there anything they could contribute? She would point out a small end table or chair and say, 'You might be able to spare that for the Garlands, don't you think?'
>
> I was terribly embarrassed but I couldn't stop her. She arranged to have Frank Keyser move the looted furniture to our apartment and then walked back with me to see if she had missed anything. Leon, hearing our footsteps, had run back into the bathroom.
>
> 'Is there anything lacking in your bathroom?' Miss Addams asked as she moved toward the closed door. I put my hand out to stop her. 'Miss Addams, there's a man in there.'
>
> She smiled. 'Give him my regards,' she said and left us to ourselves.

With the Garlands nested in their honeymoon loft, J.A. insisted that the stubbornly independent Enella Benedict, who had serious health problems, move out of her isolated apartment into the loft adjoining the young couple. With the Garlands' permission, J.A. had a door installed between the two apartments. Benedict had only to open it or knock on the wall if she needed help.

J.A. was in the Garland loft talking to Sadie and Leon one evening when three loud thumps interrupted their conversation. Sadie thumped back to indicate she was home. The next moment Benedict poked her head through the open door, her wrinkled patrician face expressing girlish glee. "I'm so happy!" she said. "My doctor just died! Now I can eat nuts!"

After five months in their "honeymoon cottage" the Garlands informed J.A. that they had saved enough money to go to Paris and Germany to study art for two years. "When you return you'll tell us all about what you learned," J.A. said, and promised that she would rent their apartment on a temporary basis only so it would be theirs again when they returned.

The young couple cut their trip short by six months. Leon had fainted in the bathroom of the Berlin Opera House, raising concerns about his health. They had also been the brunt of frightening anti-Semitism. Landlords had slammed doors in the Garlands' faces upon learning that they were Jews, and Leon had been manhandled by a Nazi policeman who had correctly assumed that because of his beard he was Jewish.

Soon after the Garlands' return, J.A. attended a national meeting of the WILPF. She looked forward to seeing a young peace worker, Lillian Cantor, whom she had grown to know when Cantor had arranged a speaking tour for her in Pennsylvania. Cantor aspired to be a social worker and J.A. had always been her model. At a White House reception given by Eleanor Roosevelt for the WILPF, J.A. had introduced Cantor to the first lady as "our baby pacifist."

Cantor had just returned from a trip to Europe and was deeply disturbed by the escalating power of Hitler and the Nazi party. She feared that the looting of the shops of Jewish merchants and the wrecking of a Jewish newspaper office was a foretaste of terrible times to come. During the WILPF meeting, she proposed a resolution condemning "what Hitler and his philosophy were doing to the human race." Cantor recalled:

> When I finished making the proposal Miss Addams rose from her seat. I saw tears in her eyes. 'I cannot vote for that resolution, Lillian,' she said, 'because it is an aggressive act and as such promotes war.' The resolution was defeated. Three hundred women walked out of the meeting in protest. I did not have the privilege of seeing Miss Addams after that. I wrote to her once or twice but she never answered. I think as things went on it was just too much for that gentle soul to bear.

To J.A.'s enormous distress, many of the protesting women canceled their WILPF membership because of the rejection of the Cantor resolution. It was a source of the deepest pain to be the cause of divisiveness in the organization which, next to Hull House, was the closest to her heart. Peace continued to be a hard mistress to serve.

Welcome by Japanese children.

Jane Addams being introduced to audience in Japan.

Mary McDowell and Jane Addams

Jane Addams at Chautauqua, NY.

JANE ADDAMS AND THE CONFERENCE

It is impossible to convey in any adequate way the contribution of Jane Addams to the Conference. No attempt will be made to do anything but make available a list of her official appearances and of her membership on divisions and commissions.

PAPERS READ BY JANE ADDAMS BEFORE THE NATIONAL CONFERENCE OF SOCIAL WORK

Place	Year	Title of Paper	President	Division	Page in *Proceedings*
Toronto........	1897	Social Settlements	Alexander Johnson	Social Settlements	338
Atlanta........	1903	Child Labor and Pauperism	Robert W. de Forest	Destitute Children	114
Portland, Me...	1904	Neighborhood Improvement*	Jeffrey R. Brackett	General Session	456
Richmond, Va...	1908	Child Labor and Education	Thomas M. Mulry	Children	364
Buffalo........	1909	Immigrants†	Ernest P. Brecknell	General Session	213
St. Louis.......	1910	Charity and Social Justice	Jane Addams	President's Address	1
Boston.........	1911	Standards of Education for Industrial Life	Homer Folks	Standards of Living and Labor	162
Boston.........	1911	The Call of the Social Field	Homer Folks	Securing and Training Social Workers	370
Cleveland......	1912	The Child at the Point of Greatest Pressure	Julian W. Mann	Children	26
Cleveland......	1912	Participated in Symposium on "The Treatment of Women Offenders"‡	Julian W. Mann	Courts and Prisons	559
Kansas City, Mo.	1918	The World's Food and World-Politics	Robert A. Woods	Social Problems of the War and Reconstruction	650
New Orleans...	1920	The Spirit of Social Service	Owen R. Lovejoy	General Session	41
New Orleans....	1920	The Immigrant and Social Unrest	Owen R. Lovejoy	General Session	59
Toronto........	1924	International Co-operation for Social Welfare	Grace Abbott	General Session	107
Cleveland......	1926	How Much Social Work Can a Community Afford? From the Ethical Point of View	Gertrude Vaile	General Session	108
Des Moines....	1927	Social Consequences of the Immigration Law	John A. Lapp	General Session	102
Boston.........	1930	Social Workers and the Other Professions	Miriam Van Waters	General Session	50
Detroit........	1933	Problems for Contemporary Youth‡	Frank J. Bruno	Children and the Immigrant	P. 24 of Program

* Report of Chairman of Committee.
† Report of Chairman of Committee.
‡ Not published in *Proceedings*.

Page from program book of the National Conference of Social Work, 1934.

HULL-HOUSE
800 SOUTH HALSTED STREET
CHICAGO

April 4th, 1930.

My dear Mrs. Garland:

Your letter came only
two days ago and we are all delighted that
you will be back next October. The little
roof house will be ready for you with one or
two improvements which I hope you will like.

We have missed you both
very much and I hope you will feel that
returning to Hull-House is like a homecoming.

I am getting this off
at once and mean to write a longer letter
very soon.

Faithfully yours,

Jane Addams

Letter to the Garlands in Europe.

Sadie Ellis Garland working at Jane
Addams' desk after return from Europe.

HIS was the last appeal Miss Addams wrote before she died. We are sending it out with her signature hoping everyone will remember her great concern for the Hull-House children.

HULL-HOUSE
800 SOUTH HALSTED STREET
CHICAGO

1935
Second Letter

May we again remind you that without your generous cooperation it will be impossible to send our full quota of fifteen hundred children and many of their mothers to the country this summer.

The Northwestern R. R. is giving them free transportation, the vegetables for their use are growing in the club garden and we await only a word from you to carry out the full plan.

With sincere appreciation of your kindness in the past, I am

Faithfully yours,

Jane Addams

Jane Addams' funeral in Hull House Courtyard, 1935.

Chapter 18

All the Bells Were Tolling

*W*eber Linn had this story to tell: J.A. was diagnosed with a stomach tumor that had to be removed but severe bronchitis forced a delay. He visited her at Mary Smith's home as she was convalescing. "I have something I want you to read," J.A. said, "but it must be kept confidential." She directed him to the telegram in the top dresser drawer.

Linn read: The Norwegian Minister in Washington advises Miss Jane Addams that she and Dr. Nicholas Murray Butler are the co-recipients of the Nobel Peace Prize. The presentation ceremony will be made on December 10th, 1931 in Oslo. Would she please keep the information "entirely personal."

"I regard you as entirely personal," J.A. told Linn when he congratulated her.

To many of J.A.'s colleagues and friends the award was anticlimactic. Proposed for the Nobel Prize several times in the 1920s, J.A. had been disappointed on each occasion. The prize, she felt, would bolster the flagging reputation of Hull House as well as give the greatest credence possible to the foundering cause of peace.

On December 10, when the Nobel Prize was awarded, J.A. was not in attendance; she was in Johns Hopkins Hospital in Baltimore undergoing the delayed tumor operation. The American ambassador in Norway received the gold medals for both J.A. and Butler. In the award presentation J.A. was called "the foremost woman of her nation, not far from being its greatest citizen [who had] clung to her idealism in the difficult period when other demands and interests overshadowed peace. . ."

Congratulatory letters, cables and telegrams from over 20 different countries poured into Johns Hopkins Hospital. J.A. donated the $16,480 prize money to the WILPF. Friends wished that she had kept some of it for her escalating medical bills. The inheritance from her father was long since spent, much of it, of course, on Hull House. But it was for her work with the WILPF that J.A. felt she had been awarded the prize, and the League therefore should be given the money.

The Red-baiting, isolationist mood of the country had shifted somewhat by the 1930s, and the attacks on J.A. had diminished. Universities that had studiously ignored her were now almost comically eager to award her an honorary doctorate degree, among them Northwestern University, Swarthmore College, the University of California, Mt. Holyoke College, and a grossly laggard University of Chicago. To her amusement, she was included in assorted lists of the greatest women in America. When *Good Housekeeping* magazine named her the first of America's Greatest Women, she remarked, "One of the committee formerly regarded me as a traitor. I'm quite sure that two of the others had never heard of me before the contest."

J.A. was equally unimpressed by her inclusion in a list of the 24 living persons "certain to be remembered in a hundred years," but was gratified by the vote of 1,000 San Quentin Penitentiary inmates who decided that, among the 12 greatest men of the century, Jane Addams had to be listed — along with Clarence Darrow, Thomas Edison, Henry Ford, Abraham Lincoln, the Wright Brothers and Henry Wadsworth Longfellow. When newspapers began to report her speeches with unaccustomed geniality she commented, "Perhaps they think I am too old to make much trouble for anyone anymore."

J.A. distributed the $10,000 dollars she had accumulated from other awards to her unemployed neighbors, hoping to alleviate their suffering for a short time at least. "I have watched fear grip the people in our neighborhood around Hull House," she said, "men and women who have seen their small margin of savings disappear, heads of families who see and anticipate hunger for their children before it occurs. The clutch of fear. . . is certainly one of the most wretched things to endure."

She continued to believe that much of this misery could be alleviated with proper legislation. Though disappointed in Hoover's handling of the Great Depression, she supported him for re-election in 1932, hoping that he would follow through on promised reform proposals. After Franklin Roosevelt's victory, J.A. was appointed to the advisory committee of the Housing Division of the Public Works Administration. She was enormously cheered when Chicago began three slum clearance projects in preparation for the building of its first public housing very close to Hull House (named The Jane Addams Houses after her death).

J.A. joined committee after committee, assuming among other positions the vice-presidency of the American Association of Social Security. In 1934 she wrote a friend, "It is really a wonderful time in which to live in spite of much suffering due to unemployment. . ." It was difficult to believe that her health was as poor as it was.

Though troubled by the Japanese invasion of Manchuria and the growing strength of Nazism in Germany, J.A. resolutely held to her view that peace could be preserved through international cooperation. "A great Kingdom of Peace lies close at hand," she said, "ready to come into being if we would but turn toward it." She looked to literature for the support and guidance she could no longer expect from colleagues. In Emerson, a literary mentor from her Rockford days, she found comfort and wisdom.

> The manhood that has been in war must be transferred to the cause of peace before war can lose its charm and peace be venerable to men.

It is really a thought that built the portentous war establishment, and a thought shall melt it away.

J.A. was also seriously concerned about the effects of the Great Depression on young people.

> To leave school or college full of high hopes and to find that there is no place in the world where one may be put to honest work is profoundly discouraging. . . [E]ven actual hunger is not as grave a problem as that arising out of the spiritual demoralization of those who in the eagerness of youth seek work and cannot find it anywhere. They will become morally scarred veterans of a conflict as devastating as war.

Though gratified by the numbers of young people who participated in Hull House activities, J.A. was distressed that so many of them were caught up in self-improvement without interest in projects to help others. Most disturbing was their conformity, and their reluctance to do anything that "rocked the boat." Those who chose smooth sailing in life accomplished little, J.A. knew, as she searched in vain for a fledgling Florence Kelley, Julia Lathrop or Alice Hamilton. Perhaps, she speculated, her generation had been too exclusively concerned about the welfare of those at the bottom of society. Did the pendulum have to swing back and forth endlessly between self-interest and social concern?

In 1932 J.A. suffered the loss of two of her dearest friends, Julia Lathrop and Florence Kelley. She found it harder to sustain her besieged hope for industrial reform without their empowering spirits and healing laughter. Two years later, J.A. herself was struck down by a severe heart attack. She had been convalescing at Mary Smith's home for several months, too ill to leave her bed, when Smith contracted virulent pneumonia. J.A. was unaware of how ill Smith really was. Within a few days Smith lapsed into a coma from which she never recovered. After a loving friendship of 45 years, the two women, in rooms just 20 feet apart, had been unable to bid each other good-bye.

The funeral service for Smith was held in the Smith home. J.A. could do no more than lie in bed in her second floor room, facing the door and straining to hear the Hull House children singing and the words spoken by grieving friends. To her nephew she confided that she could will her "funny old heart" to stop beating for she longed to relax deeply and forever, but the thought of what Smith had meant to her for nearly half her lifetime restrained her from being cowardly.

"It is before breakfast the day after Mary's death," wrote Hamilton to her sister:

> Here is J.A. ordered to bed for four more weeks at the least. . . [She] is so endlessly pitiful, it breaks my heart so that I can hardly think of my own grief. . . Grief is different when one is old. All the time the feeling is with me that it is none of it for very long, and that I have had it, had something rich and beautiful for so many years. I cannot really lose Mary, she is part of my memory. . . I think Miss Addams knows that it cannot be very long for her. She seems very quiet, very dear, very remote.

Following the prescribed bedrest, J.A. was shepherded away by Bowen to spend part of the winter in Arizona. There she began work on a biography of Julia Lathrop, a writing endeavor which was "much like writing my own autobiography over again from another point of view." But J.A. could only work on the book for short periods at a time. "I am too near her," she told Linn. "And I miss her too much."

Though still easily fatigued, J.A. insisted on visiting a sick friend before leaving Arizona. She was about to climb the long stairway to the elderly woman's bedroom when her friend appeared and forbade her to climb so many stairs. In character, J.A. suggested a compromise — they should meet halfway. And so the two old friends sat on the middle stair and chatted as if comfortably seated in a tea room.

Upon her return from Arizona, J.A. moved into Bowen's home.

She insisted that she was perfectly fine — that "her funny old heart was behaving splendidly." But, she said to Weber Linn who had told her that he intended to write the story of her life, "if you really are going to write my biography, you had better get to work." The next day she and her nephew went over to Hull House and J.A. showed him all her files.

"What you're going to do with them I can't imagine," she said.

"I shall give them to the Jane Addams School of Social Work at the University of Chicago," Linn answered, "when they call it that."

"You shall have them on your hands for a long while," J.A. responded. "Some day they will call it the Abbott School, after my two good 'abits' " (referring to Edith and Grace Abbott).

J.A. again gave her doctor cause to sigh resignedly when she announced that she was going to attend the 20th anniversary of the WILPF in the spring of 1935. (She was unaware that the event was to be held in her honor.) The ballroom of Washington's Willard Hotel was filled to the rafters the evening of the celebration, with a crowd milling around outside unable to get in. J.A. pushed the many laudatory personal tributes aside, saying that "she did not know any such person as described here tonight."

"With humor and drive," Paul Kellogg, editor of *Survey* wrote, "Jane Addams threw the occasion forward. It was a matchless play of her gift for taking the mystery out of greatness and achievement so that every listener could grasp what impelled her and how they themselves might take hold."

Longtime peace advocates spoke — Eleanor Roosevelt among them — as well as leaders in their fields who as young people had been drawn into the orbit of Hull House. One of them, Sidney Hillman, president of the Amalgamated Clothing Workers of America, credited J.A. with making possible an agreement between employers and employees that had laid the foundation for industrial peace for over 100,000 workers.

Voices were piped into the ballroom from Japan, England, France and Russia, in what was described as "the most widespread appeal for international peace in world history." J.A. responded:

> The Women's International League joins the long proces-
> sion of those who have endeavored for hundreds of years to
> substitute law for war, political processes for brute force; and
> we are grateful to our friends from various parts of the world
> who recognize at least our sincerity in this effort. . .
>   We don't expect to change human nature, we people of
> peace, but we do expect to change human behavior. . . I per-
> ceive a rising tide of revolt against war as an institution, against
> war as such. Yet we are suffering still in many ways from a war
> psychology; the armies have been demobilized, the psycholo-
> gy has not. The worst thing about war is not the poison gas
> which wipes out lives and destroys cities, but the poison it
> spreads in the minds of men. . . In case of any more unfortu-
> nate accidents, we must be ready not only with political insti-
> tutions, the League of Nations and the World Court, but with
> an educated public opinion which shall fight this poison's
> spread.

The anniversary celebration was like a tonic; it rejuvenated J.A.
and she exulted in the feeling that she was "still in the front line
trenches." To Weber Linn she said, "Probably no one ever gets over
that feeling though I have always wondered when I should understand I am an old lady."

Attempting to cope with her own losses, J.A. was particularly
sensitive to the anguish of Sadie Garland; Leon, 36 years old, had
been stricken with a massive heart attack. One morning while Sadie
was at the reception desk, J.A using a cane walked into the room.

"Sadie, why aren't you at the hospital with Leon?" she asked.

"It's my time at the desk," Sadie replied. "There's no one to
relieve me."

"And don't you think I can handle the desk?" J.A. hurried Sadie
from the desk to the door, and slipped a bill into her hand to pay
cab fare to the hospital.

J.A. had decided to host a ceremony to dedicate the Mary Rozet
Smith Cottage at Bowen Country Club. With Leon convalescing in

the loft apartment, she and Sadie were in the office addressing invitations to the dedication, scheduled for May 26, 1935, when a resident entered the office and asked J.A. if two visitors might see her for a moment.

> The two women were escorted into the office [Ellis related], and one of them presented J.A. with a strikingly beautiful orchid. 'An elegant flower for an elegant lady,' she said. When the women left I was startled to see that Miss Addams' eyes were filled with tears. I had known her for twenty years and had never seen her cry before. 'Sadie, I don't feel like an elegant lady,' she said. 'I feel like a pauper, always begging for money.'

Soon after the invitation work was resumed J.A. put down her pen. She was not feeling well, she said. Sadie called a resident to drive her to Bowen's home.

Bowen, writing to J.A.'s nephew, Stanley (by then a married man with children), described what happened next:

> She was taken ill in the night on Tuesday and did not call for help, although there was a bell right at the head of her bed. When I reproached her in the morning. . . she said, 'I thought that bell was just in case I had a pain in my heart, and this one was down on one side.' I had Dr. Britton up in a few minutes and as he did not know what it was — the pain was in the groin on the left side — called Dr. Herrick. . . Dr. Herrick telephoned back to get a surgeon and they got Dr. Curtis, head of the Passavant Hospital, on Friday night. . . [T]here was a mass of some kind that would have to be removed at once. We did not tell her that night, but the next morning Dr. Britton came about 7:30 and told her she must go to the hospital. She took it very philosophically and was wrapped up in a blanket awaiting the ambulance. I went in there at once and she looked, I think, pretty mournful. She was reading a book and just glanced up at me and said, laughingly, 'I ought to be giving you last messages I suppose, but I do want to finish this book. . .' 'Don't look so solemn, dear.'

Three hours later J.A. underwent surgery that confirmed the

worst fears — advanced stomach cancer. If J.A. survived the operation she would at the most have nine months to live and the pain would be agonizing.

With Hamilton keeping constant vigil by her side, J.A. passed in and out of consciousness. When she rallied slightly Hamilton leaned over to catch her weakened voice. "I knew a doctor," J.A. whispered, "who used to say the hardest thing in the world to kill was an old woman."

Sadie Garland visited J.A. on the morning of May 20.

> Miss Addams was very pale against the white sheets. I couldn't speak. I lifted her hand and kissed it. With great effort she brought my hand to her lips and did the same. That was the last time I saw her. She died the next day.

J.A. lay at rest in Bowen Hall from Wednesday afternoon, May 22nd, until 11 o'clock the next morning. Hamilton remained in the hall the entire time, catching a catnap as she sat in a chair. Sadie joined her and the two women watched silently as the seemingly unending line of mourners filed past the casket — children carrying flowers, mothers with infants, workmen with lunch boxes, city officials, union leaders, friends from abroad, colleagues from settlements throughout the country. The line would thin, then build again. Some two thousand people an hour paid their respects.

A torrent of telegrams expressed sorrow — from the President of the United States, the President of Czechoslovakia, the Premiers of England and Canada, the Ladies' Garment Workers Union, the City Club, the Boy's Reading Club, the Saturday Painters, the local Boy Scout troop.

Services were to be held Thursday afternoon in the Hull House courtyard. Sadie knew that J.A. had loved lilacs — they reminded her of spring in Cedarville. Gathering as many as she could from the Bowen and Smith gardens, she set lilac branches in containers so that blossoms cascaded from windows and down the high fire-escapes. Against the ruddy brick terrace she set bowls made by Hull

House potters filled with every shade of tulip. An observor wrote:

> Up Halsted and Polk little Greek business places and restau-
> rants were draped in purple. Since the day before the throngs
> had filed through Bowen Hall. Dr. Hamilton, who had been
> with her to the last, greeted old neighbors just as Miss Addams
> would have done. The sun shone down — as it had not done
> in weeks — on the Hull House Court which was filled an hour
> before the service. . . Suddenly everything became perfectly
> quiet and music began from some inner room, string music by
> the Hull House orchestra.

Bowen described the funeral in a special issue of *Survey* devoted to J.A.

> The funeral was at 2:30 in the afternoon. . . J.A. lay in a
> casket with a loose, light blue robe around her, her hair pushed
> back from her forehead as she always wore it. On either side
> of the casket were brightly colored tulips, so that it looked as
> though she were lying on a bed of flowers.
> Dr. Gilkey of the University of Chicago officiated, the
> benediction being pronounced by Dr. Graham Taylor, her life-
> long friend. . . Dr. Gilkey, in his opening sentence spoke of the
> epitaph to the great architect, Sir Christopher Wren in St.
> Paul's cathedral — 'If thou seekest a monument, look about
> thee,' adding that if you would see Jane Addams' monuments
> you had only to look about you. . . the men she had made
> decent and self-respecting, the women whose burdens she had
> lifted, the young she had guided to useful adulthood and the
> little children to whom she had given the opportunity for play.

Paul Kellogg, editor of *Survey*, wrote:

> At the hour when Hull House was hushed for the funeral of
> its great mistress, memorial services to Miss Addams were held
> in Philadelphia and other cities. On a green slope in
> Westchester County, where members of the United
> Neighborhood Houses of New York assembled for their
> spring meeting, John Dewey, whose association goes back to
> the early days on Halsted Street, spoke of her 'way of living' at

Hull House as a 'companionship which has extended from the neighborhood to the world.'

The mourners in the courtyard lingered until dark; they could not bear to leave. The next morning J.A. was taken to Cedarville. As the hearse slowly rolled through the town all the bells were tolling. Weber Linn described the final services:

> At Cedarville the coffin was placed for an hour in the room of her old home in which she had been born, then in splendid sunlight taken to the hillside cemetery across the road, below the cliffs on which her father had planted, ninety years before, the Norway pine-cones which he had brought with him on his journey from Pennsylvania. She was carried. . . up the narrow winding road to the 'Addams Lot' on the highest point; and there, while the oldest friends of her childhood, and their children and their grandchildren, and even their great grandchildren waited, she was committed to the earth.

J.A.'s tombstone, a simple marble oblong, was inscribed according to her wishes: "Jane Addams, Hull-House and Women's International League for Peace and Freedom. 1860 - 1935."

Today, on the road from Freeport to Cedarville, an historical marker reads:

> **Cedarville** Birthplace of Jane Addams 1860 - 1935, Humanitarian, Feminist, Social Worker, Reformer, Educator, Author, Publicist. Founder of Hull House, Pioneer Settlement Center, 1889, President Women's International League for Peace and Freedom, Nobel Peace Prize, 1931.

"She had compassion without condescension. She had pity without retreat into vulgarity. She had infinite sympathy for common things without forgetfulness of those that are uncommon.

That, I think, is why those who have known her say that she was not only good, but great. For this blend of sympathy with distinction, of common humanity with a noble style is recognizable by those who have eyes to see it as the occasional but authentic issue of the mystic promise of the American democracy. It is the quality which reached its highest expression in Lincoln, when, out of the rudeness of his background and amidst the turmoil of his times, he spoke in accents so pure that his words ring true enduringly. This is the ultimate vindication of the democratic faith, not that men can be brought to a common level, but that without pomp or pride or power or privilege, every man might and some men will achieve again and again the highest possibilities of the human spirit."

Walter Lippmann, 1935

Afterword

It was one of those rare days in May treasured by Chicagoans hungry for spring. The sky was a cloudless blue and the pink and white crab apple trees in Grant Park were in full bloom. I was driving with my 89-year-old Aunt Sadie to the Jane Addams Hull House Museum. From the time I had begun to tape my aunt's memories of Jane Addams and Hull House, I had tried to persuade her to make this trip. There were things I was sure she would take pleasure in seeing, among them a large brass bowl etched by her first husband, Leon Garland, and photographs of many old friends, now deceased. But she had been so devastated by the demolition of the Settlement in 1963 that she had adamantly refused to go near "the scene of the crime."

Finally she had relented, and so on this lovely day we drove to the museum housed in the two buildings that had been spared the wrecker's ball. My aunt had said nothing during the drive; she stared straight ahead, one restless hand drumming her knee. Her apprehension was palpable.

The Hull mansion looked handsome, but restored to its original facade it was not the building my aunt remembered. Once in the sunny reception room she stared in one direction, then the other. She was having trouble orienting herself. The front doorway was not where she remembered it. Her face was tense.

Had I made a terrible mistake?

Then she recognized the fireplace and the portrait of the beloved nursery school teacher, Jenny Dow, that hung above it. She also recognized a table that held postcards and material about Hull House.

"I used to work at that table," she murmured. She looked around the room again, trying to get her bearings by fastening on things she remembered. "It's much too orderly," she said. Startled by the loudness of her voice in the empty room, she whispered, "Every corner of this room was filled with bags of children's clothes, toys, boots. Neighbors brought what they couldn't use anymore and looked for things they could use. And I don't see any magazines or books. They were always around for people to borrow and read."

"Well," I said inanely. "It's a museum now."

"Too quiet." She turned toward the stairway going to the second floor. "I would like to see Miss Addams' desk."

"Are you sure you want to climb that stairway?"

She answered by tightening her grip on my arm.

It was a slow ascent. She had to stop several times to regain her breath. Finally we reached the second floor. As we entered Jane Addams' office, she released my arm and walked around the room slowly, pausing in front of a portrait of Tolstoy in peasant dress. She looked at the large oak desk as if to absorb its every detail, then sat down behind it with great deliberation. She was absolutely still. Minutes passed before she laid her fingers on the desk's polished surface. She spoke, but her voice was barely audible.

"I feel her presence." Her voice gained strength. "Yes, I feel her presence. She is still with us."

Sadie Garland Dreikurs and
Barbara Garland Polikoff

Following the death of Jane Addams, Sadie Garland continued to work at Hull House under Jane Addams' successor, Charlotte Carr. Sadie's husband, Leon, suffered a massive heart attack and died in 1941 at the age of 46. Before Leon's death, the Garlands had become friends with Rudolph Dreikurs, a Viennese psychiatrist and proponent of Adlerian psychology. Dreikurs had been employed by Carr to consult with Hull House social workers, particularly in their work with troubled youth. After working together at Hull House for two years, Dreikurs and Sadie were married in 1944.

The couple took up residence in an apartment overlooking Lincoln Park. Sadie traveled with Dreikurs on his lecture tours in the United States and abroad and typed his lengthy book manuscripts, acquiring in the process a knowledge of Adlerian psychology which, combined with her skills as an artist, enabled her to develop a pioneer art therapy program at St. Joseph's Hospital, Chicago. She then joined Dreikurs on his lecture tours as a professional, training psychologists and social workers in her art therapy methods. After Dreikurs' death in 1974, in spite of a serious heart ailment, she continued her work alone. She made 17 teaching trips to Israel, as well as several to China, Holland, Sweden and Germany. At home in Chicago she taught art therapy to graduate students at the Adler Institute founded by Dreikurs. She was awarded a number of honorary degrees, and became widely known as the "Mother of Art Therapy," continuing to teach well into her eighties. In 1987 the Adler Institute renamed its counseling center, The Sadie and Rudolph Dreikurs Counseling Center.

Sadie bequeathed an oil painting by Leon Garland to the Jane Addams Hull House Museum. It depicts the Hull House courtyard which, as a girl of eleven, she had walked through to enter for the first time "the place where Jane Addams lives."

Barbara Garland Polikoff has written award-winning adult and young people's fiction. She and her husband divide their time between their Highland Park, Illinois, and Palmyra, Wisconsin homes. They have three grown children and three slightly grown grandchildren.

Selected Bibliography

Adams, Rosemary K. ed. *A Wild Kind of Boldness*. Grand Rapids and Cambridge, UK, William B. Eerdmens, jointly with Chicago Historial Society, 1998.

Bryan, Mary Lynn and Allen F. Davis. *100 Years at Hull-House*. Bloomington: Indiana University Press, 1990.

Bowen, Louise. *Open Windows*. Chicago: Ralph Seymour, 1936.

Carson, Mina. *Settlement Folk: Social Thought and the American Settlement Movement, 1885-1930*. Chicago: University of Chicago Press, 1990.

Chafe, William H. *The American Woman: Her Changing Social, Economic and Political Roles, 1920-1970*. New York: Oxford University Press, 1972.

Conway, Jill Kerr. *When Memory Speaks*. New York: Alfred Knopf, 1998.

Davis, Allen F. *Spearheads for Reform: The Social Settlements and the Progressive Movement*. Oxford: Oxford University Press, 1967.

Davis, Allen F. *American Heroine: The Life and Legend of Jane Addams*. New York: Oxford University Press, 1973.

Farrell, John C. *Beloved Lady*. Baltimore: Johns Hopkins University Press, 1967.

Hamilton, Alice. *Exploring the Dangerous Trades*. Boston: Little Brown and Co., 1943.

Heilbrun, Carolyn. *Reinventing Womanhood*. New York, London: W. W. Norton, 1979.

Heilbrun, Carolyn. *Writing A Woman's Life*. New York: Ballantine Books, 1988.

Kelley, Florence. *Autobiography of Florence Kelley*. Chicago: Charles H. Kerr Publishing Company, 1986.

Lissak, Rivka. *Pluralism and Progressives: Hull House and the New Immigrants*. Chicago: University Of Chicago Press, 1989.

Linn, James Weber. *Jane Addams: A Biography*. New York: D. Appleton Century, 1935.

Muncy, Robyn. *Creating an American Dominion in American Reform*. New York: Oxford University Press, 1991.

Platt, Anthony M. *The Child Savers: The Invention of Delinquency*. Chicago: University of Chicago Press, 1977.

Sicherman, Barbara ed. *Alice Hamilton: A Life in Letters*. Cambridge: Harvard University Press, 1984.

Scott, Anne Firor. *Natural Allies: Women's Associations in America*. Urbana: University of Illinois Press, 1991.

Steber, Eleanor. *Hull House Women*. New York: New York University Press, 1998.

Trolander, Judith A. *Professionalism and Social Change: From the Settlement House Movement to Neighborhood Centers, 1886 to the Present*. New York: Columbia University Press, 1987.

Books by Jane Addams

Democracy and Social Ethics. Cambridge: Harvard University Press, 1964.

Twenty Years at Hull-House. Urbana and Chicago: University of Illinois Press, 1990.

A New Conscience and an Ancient Evil. New York: Macmillan, 1912.

Newer Ideals of Peace. New York: Macmillan, 1907.

The Long Road of Woman's Memory. New York: Macmillan, 1916.

Peace and Bread in Time of War. Boston: G. K. Hall & Co., 1960.

The Spirit of Youth and the City Streets. New York: Macmillan, 1911.

The Second Twenty Years at Hull-House. New York: Macmillan, 1930.

The Excellent Becomes the Permanent. New York: Macmillan, 1932.

My Friend Julia Lathrop. New York: Macmillan, 1935.

Women at the Hague. New York: Garland Publishing, 1972 (with Emily G. Balch and Alice Hamilton).

Notes

Entries without ascribed source are from the Jane Addams Memorial Collection, Jane Addams Papers, Microfilm Edition, University of Illinois at Chicago. Abbreviations are: EGS — Ellen Gates Starr; JA — Jane Addams; Starr MSS — Ellen Gates Starr Papers, Sophia Smith Collection, Smith College; SGD — Sadie Garland Dreikurs; SCPC — Swarthmore College Peace Collection.

Chapter 1
4.   "Myself and Wife left Kreidersville. . .": James Weber Linn, *Jane Addams*, 6.
     "city commenced ten years ago. . .": Ibid., 7-8.
5.   "be missed. . .": Ibid., 22-23.
6.   "[With the] sincere tribute. . .": Jane Addams, *Twenty Years At Hull-House*, 8.
7.   "all that careful imitation. . .": Ibid., 7.
     "would vote according. . .": Ibid., 20.
8.   "There were at least two pictures. . .": Ibid.
     "With a playful touch. . .": Ibid., 7.
     "gorgeous beyond anything. . .": Ibid., 9.
9.   "I complied. . .": Ibid.
     "night after night. . .": Ibid., 5.
     "standing in the doorway. . .": Ibid.
10. "why people lived. . .": Ibid.
     "It is good skating. . .": JA to Alice, December 1869.

Chapter 2
12. "[We] carried on games. . .": *Twenty Years*, 10-11.
15. "I don't feel. . .": Paul E. Fry, *Generous Spirit, The Life of Mary Fry*, 38, n.p., n.d.
     "I cannot number. . .": JA to Vallie Beck, March 21, 1877.
     "that slender, sunny-haired. . .": Marcet Haldeman-Julius, *Jane*

Addams As I Knew Her, The Reviewers Library, 1936, 1. One of several booklets published by Marcet Haldeman-Julius and her husband.

16. "is simply a piece. . .": JA to Vallie Beck, March 30, 1877.
    "accomplished little. . .": Ibid., August 3, 1879.
17. "I left the lamp-lit. . .": *Twenty Years*, 12.
    "And while he was much too wise. . .": Ibid., 13.
18. "wrapt me. . .": Ibid., 14.

Chapter 3

19. "She had very pretty, light brown hair. . .": Linn, 40-41.
20. "You will gain. . .": JA to EGS, August 11, 1879.
21. "I know that there is very little. . .": Ibid.
22. "develop moral and religious. . .": Linn, 44.
23. "it did not matter. . .": *Twenty Years*, 9.
    "Miss Sill does everything. . .": JA Notebooks, Box 42, SCPC.
    "I wish you were here. . .": JA to EGS, January, 29, 1880.
    "I have been trying. . .": Ibid., August 11, 1879.
    "You long for a beautiful. . .": Ibid.
24. "I find myself . . .": Ibid.
    "I do not think. . .": Allen F. Davis, *American Heroine: The Life and Legend of Jane Addams*, 22.
    "to an outward symbol. . .": JA to EGS, June 1884.
25. "grow accurate and intelligible. . .": *Twenty Years*, 37.
    "Jane insisted on giving. . .": Linn, 48.
26. "So much of our time. . .": *Twenty Years*, 28.
    "We took large themes. . .": Ibid., 29.
27. "social evils can only be. . .": Ibid.
    "Probably no man. . .": Linn, 56.
28. "Must we crowd education. . .": *American Heroine*, 26.
    "had passed from accomplishments. . .": Linn, 62.
    "and the impervious will. . .": *American Heroine*, 19.
29. "I see her as plainly. . .": Linn, 47.
30. "Our class appointments. . .": JA to John Addams, May 8, 1881.
    "Always do what . . .": Linn, 62.

"Nora, when we speak. . .": Ibid., 63.

"But the brave warriors. . .": Essays of Class of 1881, 36-9.

31. "an accurate perception. . .": Ibid.

"Let her not sit. . .": Ibid.

"We have expressed. . .": Ibid.

Chapter 4

33. "upon Canada's shore. . .": Linn, 7.

"If the Spring puts forth. . .": JA Notebooks, 1877-8, SCPC.

35. "I will not write. . .": JA to EGS, September 3, 1881.

"In the long vacations. . .": *Twenty Years*, 38.

36. "Get out of bed. . .": Emmest Ernest, *S. Weir Mitchell*, as noted in *American Heroine*, 28.

"When her health. . .": *The Subjective Necessity for Social Settlements*, an essay originally published as *A New Impulse to an Old Gospel*, in the *Forum*, November 1892, reprinted in part in *Twenty Years*, 115-127.

37. "My dear friend. . .": JA to EGS, January 1883.

38. "What thou hast promised. . .": Linn, 69.

"pounded and rubbed. . .": Ibid., 70.

"I want Harry to know. . .": JA to Alice, January 1883.

39. "My dear friend, I was. . .": JA to EGS, April 1883.

"I received your sweet letter. . .": EGS to JA, April 25, 1883, Starr MSS.

40. "I found your paper. . .": EGS to JA, April 28, 1883, Starr MSS.

"Failure through ill health. . .": JA to EGS, May 1883.

"We have been in the midst of. . .": JA to EGS, March 1883.

"would lose all hold. . .": JA to EGS, April 24, 1883.

41. "spending two years. . .": *Twenty Years*, Introduction, Henry Steele Commager, 1990 edition.

"People complain. . .": JA to EGS, August 12, 1883.

"We are off. . .": JA to Alice, August 22, 1883.

Chapter 5

43. "A small party. . .": *Twenty Years*, 41.

"Owner said to have. . .": Linn, 71.

"a black valley. . .": Ibid.

"We spent last Sunday. . .": JA to Alice, 1883.

44. "crossing and recrossing. . .": *Twenty Years*, 45-6.

"There is every temptation. . .": JA to George, May 1884.

45. "May I congratulate you. . .": JA to George, June 9, 1884.

"[The] assumption [is]. . .": *Twenty Years*, 42.

"not have lost. . .": Ibid.

46. "They take little. . .": JA to Alice, February 28, 1886.

"Stanley suddenly transferred. . .": JA to Alice, January 7, 1886.

"Mary and I read aloud some. . .": JA to EGS, January 7, 1886.

47. "I am afraid . . .": JA to Anna Haldeman Addams, October 16, 1886.

"That must be my. . .": Linn, 33.

48. "I seem to reach. . .": *Twenty Years*, 47.

"I had hoped. . .": JA to Alice, December 6, 1887.

"quite impressed. . .": Linn, 85.

49. "We have had two days. . .": JA to John (Weber) Addams, January 1888.

"cathedral of humanity. . .": *Twenty Years*, 50.

50. "The time I was abroad. . .": JA to Alice, February 16, 1888.

"he was so torn. . .": *Jane Addams As I Knew Her*, 5.

"I am dreadfully sorry. . .": JA to Alice, July 5, 1888.

51. "Your kind letter. . .": JA to Weber, March 1, 1888.

"In the second act. . .": JA to Laura, April 1888.

52. "The natural and inevitable. . .": *Twenty Years*, 42.

"gradually reached the conviction. . .": Ibid., 44.

"Nothing less than the moral reaction. . .": Ibid., 52.

"It is hard to tell. . .": Ibid., 51.

53. "I had made up my mind. . .": Ibid., 52.

"quite learned about. . .": JA to Alice, n.d. 1888.

Chapter 6

55. "The most interesting. . .": JA to Alice, June 14, 1888.

56. "I was quite sure. . .": JA to EGS, January, 24, 1889, Starr MSS.

"It is difficult. . .": *The College Woman and the Family Claim*, Commons III, September 1898, 3-7.

58. "My Dear Mary. . .": JA to Mary, February 12, 1889.

59. "I was almost immediately requested. . .": JA Notebooks, February 19, 1889, etc., SCPC.

60. "mere foothold of a house. . .": *Twenty Years*, 55.

61. "I remember very well. . .": Anne Firor Scott, "What Jane Addams Has Done for Chicago," *Delineator*, October 1907, 493. "This paper is the result. . .": *Twenty Years*, 58.

62. "She either hides. . .": Ibid. "Jane thirsts very much. . .": EGS to Mary Blaisdell, February, 1889, Starr MSS. "On Sunday afternoon. . .": JA to Mary, February 18, 1889. "The scheme is progressing. . .": JA to Mary, April 1, 1889.

63. "a fine old house. . .": *Twenty Years*, 56. "Halsted Street is. . .": Ibid., 58.

64. "Now comes the great. . .": EGS to Mary Blaisdell, May 18, 1890, Starr MSS.

65. "The fine old house. . .": *Twenty Years*, 57. "Bien. We take a house. . .": EGS to Mary Blaisdell, September 20, 1889, Starr MSS. "The silver and the quilt. . .": JA to Mary, April 1889, as noted in *Twenty Years*, 57. "The establishment of the settlement. . .": *Twenty Years*, 66. "A social settlement. . .": Jane Addams, *The Objective Value of a Social Settlement*, reprinted by The Jane Addams' Hull-House Museum, 1990, 7.

66. "fell into the hands. . .": *Twenty Years*, 214.

67. "There's power in me. . .": JA to Mary, April 1889. "People have been so good. . .": JA to Anna Haldeman Addams, May 9, 1889.

Chapter 7

69. "There are at least. . .": EGS to Mary Blaisdell, May 1889, Starr MSS.

70. "The Italian women. . .": *Twenty Years*, 61. "in the rage by which. . .": Ibid., 62. "We thus found the type. . .": Ibid., 68.

71. "Miss Trowbridge comes. . .": JA to Mary, October 1889.

72. "We would walk into Hull House. . .": Linn, 111.
"I positively feel. . .": JA to EGS, May 31, 1889, Starr MSS.
"It is as if she simply diffused something. . .": EGS to Mary Allen, September 15, 1889, Starr MSS.

74. "I remember the red brick house. . .": Peter d'A. Jones and Melvin G. Holli, *Ethnic Chicago*, Urbana: University of Illinois Press, 1981, 115.
"horrid state of intoxication. . .": *Twenty Years*, 61.
"See, I have brought. . .": Ibid., 62.
"If you would give. . .": Ibid., 103.

75. "As she straightened. . .": Ibid.
"With all the efforts. . .": Ibid.

76. "The room was packed. . .": Ibid., 20.
"Doing things that. . .": *My Friend Julia Lathrop*, 53.

77. "In the crisis of many lives. . .": Francis Hackett, "Hull House - A Souvenir," *Survey*, June 1, 1925, as noted in Mary Lynn Bryan and Allen F. Davis, *100 Years at Hull-House*, 71.

78. "One day while I was working. . .": Mary Kenney, *100 Years*, 21.
"By my manner. . .": Ibid., 73.

80. "Either you conduct. . .": SGD interview, September 1988, Chicago.
"One needs good bracing. . .": Barbara Sicherman, ed., *Alice Hamilton: A Life in Letters*, 120.
"Miss Benedict. . .": *100 Years*, 72.

81. "First an uncomfortable dinner. . .": Beatrice Webb, *100 Years*, 62.

82. "Ladies and gentlemen. . .": SDG interview, April 1986.
"I don't rule. . .": Ibid., June 1988.
"My eyes are blue. . .": Ibid.
"Diversified in belief. . .": *Twenty Years*, 256.

83. "I have always hoped. . .": JA to George Haldeman, June, 1890.
"Miss Starr's mother is visiting. . .": JA to Anna Haldeman Addams, June 3, 1890.
"In spite of poignant experiences. . .": *Twenty Years*, 88.

84. "One snowy morning. . .": Florence Kelley, "I Go To Work," *Survey,* June 1927, later published in *The Autobiography of Florence Kelley,* 77-78.

Chapter 8

85. "Children pick up words. . .": *My Friend Julia Lathrop,* 57.
   "The parrot lived. . .": Ibid.
86. "The discussions ranged. . .": Ibid., 50-51.
87. "It was a solid pressing crowd. . .": Ibid., 68.
88. "I saw these two women do. . .": Ibid., 118.
   "One likes to think. . .": Ibid., 83-84.
89. "There was Miss Vida Scudder. . .": Ibid., 54.
90. "They are not formally. . .": *The Objective Value of a Social Settlement,* 7.
   "sang a great deal in the tender minor. . .": Ibid., also in *Twenty Years,* 137.
   "Perhaps the greatest. . .": Ibid.
91. "It is unfair. . .": Ibid.
   "feel a fatal want. . .": *The Subjective Necessity for Social Settlements,* reprinted by the Jane Addams' Hull-House Musuem, 1990, 9-10.
   "We conscientiously followed. . .": Ibid.
92. "naturally very proud. . .": *My Friend Julia Lathrop,* 55.
   "urged that the idea. . .": Ibid., 56.
   "Don't cave in. . .": Ibid.
93. "I find I am considered. . .": *American Heroine,* 94.
   "Every day I stayed there. . .": John Dewey to JA, January 27, 1897.
94. "What is on your mind. . .": JA to Alice, September 23, 1900.
   "I do wish you would write. . .": Ibid.

Chapter 9

96. "the finest rough and tumble . . .": Linn, 138.
   "the duty of his generation. . .": *The Autobiography of Florence Kelley,* 25.
   "I was the third. . .": Ibid., 30.

97. "starting at the ceiling. . .": Ibid., 96.
"Entering college. . .": Ibid., 45.
"blended knowledge of facts. . .": *100 Years,* 23.
"kind, generous and a born . . .": SGD interview, March 1987.
98. "Do you know what. . .": Linn, 139.
99. "The roaring of wheels. . .": Yiddish song translated into English and sung by the Hull House choir, Eleanor Smith, Chicago: *Hull House Songs,* 1915.
"Sisters of the whirling wheel. . .": Harriet Monroe, *100 Years,* 119.
101. "You bring me this evidence. . .": *The Autobiography of Florence Kelley,* 86.
102. "The public mind. . .": *Twenty Years,* 225.
"Everyone agreed that it was praiseworthy. . .": Muriel Beadle, *The Fortnightly of Chicago,* Henry Regenery Company, Chicago, 103 104.
103. "If the settlement is. . .": Jane Addams, *Hull-House Maps and Papers,* in *Jane Addams: A Centennial Reader,* New York: Macmillan, 1960, 202.
"I am much more. . .": *Jane Addams As I Knew Her,* 29.
"It is so easy for the good. . .": JA, "A Modern Lear," *Survey,* November 2, 1912.
105. "I am quite ashamed. . .": JA to William Demarest Lloyd, June, 1910.

Chapter 10
109. "I have been having another. . .": Mary Rozet Smith to JA, n.d. 1899.
"tender tonic of criticism. . .": *Jane Addams As I Knew Her,* 6.
"in watching. . .": *Open Windows,* 163.
110. "They decided. . .": Ibid., 164.
"The friendship of Mary Smith. . .": Linn, 147.
"I had heard Jane Addams. . .": Louise Bowen, *Growing Up With a City,* New York: Macmillan, 1926, 81-82.
111. "I was made to practice. . .": *Open Windows,* 111.
"I'll accept only under one condition. . .": Ibid., 214.

112. "I can see the crowded room now. . .": Ibid., 212.
    "the women wanted. . .": Ibid.
    "Not even in church. . .": Ibid.
113. "In 1918 Mrs. Joseph T. Bowen. . .": *The Fortnightly of Chicago*, 141.
    "I was speaking one evening. . .": *Open Windows*, 213.
    "We had many causes. . .": Ibid., 206.
    "We were sometimes heckled. . .": Ibid., 214.
114. "in an attempt. . .": Ibid., 114.
    "Talk about making. . .": *Alice Hamilton*, 115.
115. "Mrs. Kelley I find approachable. . .": Ibid.
    "Miss Addams seemed so genuinely distressed. . .": Ibid., 134.
    "We leave. . .": Ibid.
117. "To acquire the joy of work. . .": Ibid., 135.
118. "I am leading the unorganized, unplanned life. . .": Ibid., 118.
    "May I explain. . .": Ibid.
119. "I see by the way. . .": Ibid.
120. "As an American citizen. . .": Eleanor Grace Clark, *100 Years*, 117.
    "If the devil himself. . .": *American Heroine*, 115.
121. "Mr. Deknatel confided to me. . .": *Alice Hamilton*, 119.
    "It's become a national sport. . .": SGD interview, August 1990.

Chapter 11
125. "looked upon the trip. . .": Edith Abbott and Sophonisba Breckinridge, *The Tenements of Chicago, 1908-1935*, Chicago: University of Chicago Press, 1931.
    "The mere consistent enforcement. . .": *Twenty Years*, 171.
    "The modern city. . .": *The Spirit of Youth and the City Streets*, 4.
126. "The classical city promoted. . .": Ibid.
    "This cheap show. . .": Ibid., 93.
    "They made their headquarters. . .": Ibid.
127. "At the very outset. . .": Ibid.
    "Here the arts. . .": Address to the National Federation of Settlements on its Fortieth Anniversary, University of Minnesota, 1893.

128. "Because this fresh imaginative. . .": Ibid., 109.
"Taught to compose. . .": *Twenty Years*, 217.
"All goes merrily. . .": Ibid.

129. "It is only through. . .": Ibid.
"destructive isolation. . .": Ibid., 220.

130. "The belief so dear to American life. . .": *Alice Hamilton*, 112.
"The cloud of my dull week. . .": SGD interview, April 1988.

131. "I am sure. . .": Alex Elson to JA, June 4, 1928, privately
owned.

132. "From the gay celebration. . .": *The Spirit of Youth*, 101.
"The enormous crowd. . .": Ibid., 112.

134. "One evening upon my return. . .": *My Friend Julia Lathrop*, 143.
"overborne by their own. . .": *The Spirit of Youth*, 64.

135. "frightened over the state. . .": Ibid.

137. "We care more for products. . .": Ibid., 5.
"We may either smother. . .": Ibid., 162.

Chapter 12

138. "You have to experience. . .": *The Autobiography of Florence Kelley*,
Introduction.

139. "I felt ashamed. . .": *Twenty Years*, 165.
"played their games. . .": Ibid., 164.
"sweeping refuse. . .": Ibid., 165.

140. "a trim uniform of cadet gray. . .": *Chicago Evening Post*, July 23,
1895.
"dreary destinations. . .": *Twenty Years*, 166.

141. "were much interested. . .": Ibid., 167.

143. "So what are you lunching. . .": *Open Windows*, 237.
"During the many relief visits. . .": *Twenty Years*, 15.
"Isn't there stuff enough. . .": Ibid., 156.
"I was too disconcerted to make. . .": Ibid.
"One cannot come near the man. . .": JA to Mary Smith,
September 4, 1885.

144. "In the face of a half dozen people. . .": *Twenty Years,* 161.
"Imagine a short stocky man. . .": Ray Stannard Baker, *100
Years*, 54.

145. "Hull House will be driven. . .": *American Heroine*, 124.
146. "I may not be. . .": Ibid.
    "I have been. . .": Alice Hamilton to Agnes, April 3, 1898.
    "That campaign literature business. . .": Ibid.
    "Because Mr. Powers. . .": *Chicago Tribune*, January 24, 1889.
147. "We called it a club. . .": *Growing Up With a City*, 91.
148. "It was by far. . .": JA Dedication Speech, Bowen Country
    Club, 1912, SGD Collection.
    "Secure, from the slow stain. . .": Ibid.
149. "gathered oranges in Calabria. . .": Ibid.
150. "Spectators to the pageant. . .": J. Ronald Engel, *Sacred Sands*,
    Middletown, Conneticut, Wesleyan University Press, 1983, 13.
151. "I dedicate this park. . .": Ibid., 129.
    "Just a hundred years ago. . .": Robert Gottlieb, *Chicago
    Tribune,* October, 29, 1993.

Chapter 13
152. "Perhaps we are spreading. . .":*Twenty Years*, 90.
    "These first buildings. . .": Ibid., 89.
    "As the house enlarged. . .": Ibid.
153. "We were often bitterly pressed. . .": Ibid.
    "Good day. . .": SGD interview, April 1989.
    "The squirrels arrived. . .": JA to Henry Augustus Ward,
    February 26, 1896.
156. "Now the house is like some creature. . .": Dorothea Moore,
    100 Years, 47-8.
    "Here in the back parlor. . .": *Alice Hamilton*, October
    19, 1897.
    "The essential fact. . .": Francis Hackett, *100 years*, 71.
157. "The first time I approached. . .": Ibid., 129.
159. "would much rather. . .": SDG interview, 1930.
    "Our new social worker. . .": Ibid.
160. "To take away. . .": *Twenty Years*, p. 123.
162. "We opened the door. . .": Marion Foster Washburne, *100
    Years*, 76.
163. "We used the word museum. . .": Ibid., 77.

"a certain Italian girl. . .": *Twenty Years*, 142.

Chapter 14

165. "of large physique. . .": *Generous Spirit*, 36.
166. "We did have good. . .": Ibid., 73.
167. "To those who say. . .": *Twenty Years*, 121.
168. "How long," Roosevelt asked. . .": Linn, 273.
      "Oh, woman of the warm heart. . .": *American Heroine*, 189.
171. "A great party has pledged itself. . .": Ibid.
      "What a grand new service. . .": Ibid., 191.
      "No matter how resolutely. . .": Ibid.
172. "with the heartiness. . .": Ibid.

Chapter 15

173. "was not so much shock. . .": *American Heroine*, 140.
      "the predatory spirit. . .": Ibid.
174. "I can do nothing but feel a lump. . .": JA to Mary Smith,
      October 6, 1898.
      "There was a logic . . .": John Haynes Holmes, *Jane Addams:
      A Centennial Reader*, 250.
      "War fatally reversed the process. . .": *Peace and Bread in Time
      of War*, 150.
175. "I am undertaking all this. . .": JA to Carrie Chapman Catt,
      December 21, 1914.
      "We, women of the United States. . .": Closing speech at
      Hague Conference, Report of Zurich Conference as cited in
      American Heroine, 259.
      "It's like a perpetual meeting of the Women's City Club. . .":
      Alice Hamilton, 186.
178. "I'm sitting in the headquarters. . .": Ibid., 191.
      "soldiers from. . .": *The Second Twenty Years at Hull-House*, 142.
      "unshakeable tolerance. . .": Ibid., 143.
179. "Journalistic attack continued. . .": *The Second Twenty Years*,
      133.
      "It was at this time. . .": Ibid.
182. "During weeks of feverish. . .": *Peace and Bread in Time of War*,
      139-140.

183. "What after all. . .": Ibid., 149.

Chapter 16

185. "The service was held. . .": *Jane Addams As I Knew Her*, 9.
"As I looked at Aunt Jane. . .": *Generous Spirit*, 20.

186. "It took me some time. . .": *Alice Hamilton*, 262.
"Was it not true?. . .": *The Second Twenty Years*, 151.
"I reminded him. . .": Ibid.
"Romanians north. . .": Ibid.

187. "The dangerous. . .": Ibid.
"I never learned. . .": Ibid.
"The humble stone. . .": *Alice Hamilton*, 226.

188. "As you doubtless know. . .": Florence Kelley to Mary Smith, May 22, 1919.

189. "We shall have to believe. . .": Report to International Congress of Women, May 22, 1919.
"The Congress is over. . .": *Alice Hamilton*, 189.
"In Leipzig we visited. . .": Ibid.

190. "There were times at Hull House. . .": *Open Windows*, 235.
"It was a pleasure to see him run. . .": Ibid., 237.
"and said that he represented. . .": Ibid., 236.

Chapter 17

192. "No one who was much. . .": Linn, 334.

193. "Mr. Webster. . .": Ibid., 349.
"It's not that I am adventurous. . .": Ibid., 355.
"To some it almost seems. . .": Ibid., 356.

194. "We know the world . . .": Jane Addams, Speech given in Osaka, Japan as reported in Linn, 358.
"I do not know. . .": Ibid., 369.

195. "Her idea of mutual benefit. . .": Ibid., 371.
"I am the only speaker tonight. . .": Ibid., 372.
"I suggested . . .": Ibid.

197. "Queen Marie. . .": SGD interview, 1989.

198. "I showed the Queen around. . ." : Ibid.

199. "When the lettuce. . .": Ibid.

200. "We had been given. . .": Ibid., 1986.

"The two women. . .": Ibid.

202. "When I finished making the proposal. . .": Interview with Lillian Cantor Dawson, Sacramento, California, 1985.

Chapter 18

203. "I have something. . .": Linn, 389.

204. "The foremost woman. . .": Ibid., 390.
"One of the committee. . .": *American Heroine*, 283.
"I have watched fear grip. . .": Ibid., 287.
"It is really a wonderful time. . .": JA to Mrs. Barnett, February 10, 1935.

205. "A great Kingdom of Peace. . .": James Farrell, *Beloved Lady*, 211-13.

206. "To leave school or college. . .": Linn, 381.

207. "It is before breakfast. . .": *Alice Hamilton*, 346-7.
"I am too near her. . .": Linn, 410.

208. "if you are really. . .": Ibid., 408.
"What you're going. . .": Ibid., 409.
"With humor. . .": Paul Kellog, *Survey*, July, 1935.

209. "The Women's International. . .": Linn, 416.
"still in the front. . .": Ibid., 418.
"Sadie, why. . .": SGD interview, November 1986.
"The two women. . .": Ibid.
"She was taken ill. . .": Louise Bowen to Stanley Linn, May 27, 1935.

212. "Up Halsted Street . . .": *Survey*, May 27, 1935.
"The funeral was at 2:30. . .": Louise Bowen, *Survey,* May 17, 1935.
"At the hour when Hull House. . .": Paul Kellogg, *Survey*, May 27, 1935.

213. "At Cedarville the coffin. . .": Linn, 424.

Index

Abbott, Edith, 125, 208

Abbott, Grace, 157, 208

Addams, Alice (Haldeman), 4, 10, 14-15, 37-38, 49, 55, 94, 166, 176

Addams, Anna (Haldeman), 11-14, 18, 32, 34, 39, 41, 45-48, 56-57, 83, 94, 187

Addams, James Weber, 4, 40-42, 184-85

Addams, Jane: appearance, 7-8, 15-16, 19; attacks on, 179-83; bayonet story, 179; birth, 3-5; and blacks, 7, 96, 167-70; and bullfight, 51-52; death, 211; death of mother, 5-6; first European trip, 41-52, 134-37; second European trip, 48-54; relationship with father, 2, 6-10, 16-20, 34-35, 57-64; work with food administration, 184-85, 189; funeral, 211-213; as garbage inspector, 173-83; preparations for opening Hull House, 2, 57-64; speaks against lynching, 167; and peace movement, 173-83; Red Scare, 186-87; views on recreation, 123-33; rural childhood, 3-4, 6-8, 12-13; on sexuality in youth, 139-42; and problems of

youth, 41-52, 134-37

Addams, Mary (Linn), 4-6, 11-13, 16, 46, 62, 106-7, 138

Addams, Sarah, 3-6, 11, 14, 16

All Sorts and Conditions of Men, 53

Altgeld, John Peter, 88, 101

Anderson, Sarah, 24, 48, 51

Armour Mission, 58-59

Barnett, Henrietta, 55

Barnett, Samuel A., 53-54, 65

Bear, Polly, 5-6, 16-17

Benedict, Enella, 1-2, 80, 130-31, 200-201

Besant, Walter, 53

Bowen Country Club, 149-50, 209

Bowen, Louise DeKoven, 8, 65, 84, 90, 107, 109-14, 135, 147-48, 178, 180, 190-91, 193, 195, 207-8, 210, 212

Bowen Hall, 110, 211

Breckinridge, Sophonisba, 157

Bullfight, 51-52

Cantor, Lillian, 201-2

Catt, Carrie Chapman, 175

Cedarville, Illinois, 3-4, 6, 10, 12, 14, 19, 25, 33-34, 37-38, 45-47, 56, 94, 123, 128, 176, 187, 211, 213

Chautauqua, New York, 179